THE SPAGHETTI WESTERN DIGEST

Editor/contributor/Interior Design: Michael Hauss
Contributors: Tom Betts, Dennis Capicik, Van Roberts, Steve Fenton, Eugenio Ercolani
Cover Design: Tim Paxton

*Thanks to Eric Mache for providing numerous photos, including the cover photo. Thanks to all who purchased this first issue of The Spaghetti Western Digest. Special thanks to Eugenio Ercolani, Javier Ramos and Chuck Cirino.

**Dedicated to two of the greatest Amigos ever: Tom Betts and Robert Woods!

The Spaghetti Western Digest

The Spaghetti Western Digest includes photos, posters, lobby cards, screenshots, and other items, including drawings and illustrations for the purpose of criticism and documentation. All copyrights held by production companies, artists, authors, and/or any copyright holders.

Nothing within The Spaghetti Western Digest can be copied, transmitted, or shared. Only small quotes from this work can be reproduced in critical reviews. For permission requests, please contact the editor.

ISBN: 9781674380452

Contents

The Making of and the Influence of WAI!

-Tom Betts

I joined Tim Ferrante as co-editor of *Westerns...All'Italiana!*, a fanzine dedicated to European westerns, in the early 1980s. Tim had already produced three issues on his own and was ready to move on to new ventures. I convinced him to continue onward mainly for my benefit as I was a western soundtrack collector, and I had just discovered his fanzine. I wanted to find out more about this genre and its participants. Little did I know how many films were made as I'd only seen a handful in the theater and on television.

I wanted to know more about them. Finally, we worked out a plan to produce a monthly fanzine with him working on it for one month and me the next; that way, each of us only had to create 6 issues a year.

Little did I know what I was getting myself into. We both used the same Brother word processors to keep the style the same. That way, we could exchange information on discs and copy it- This was long before computers, so all research had to be done at libraries, book stores, magazine racks, etc. Book stores became weekly visits. The material was then copied onto the Brother discs and printed out.

The articles were cut up laid out, and photos, ad mats, or other content inserted appropriately into each section. We then correlated the articles and made copies for the number of subscribers we had, which wasn't many. We assembled and stapled each issue, put them in envelopes, addressed them, and took them to the post office for mailing.

A lot of work went into each issue. By word of mouth, we started to gain readership and believe it or not; it went worldwide — first, Canada, then England, then Germany, Japan, and Spain. Our readers, like me, we're grateful for the information that was gathered on this long-neglected genre. They responded by mailing us newspaper and magazine articles, pictures, posters, and anything else related to Spaghetti westerns. Rich Landwehr in New Orleans made a logo for our cover- This wasn't just Tim and my fanzine this became OUR fanzine with all the readers helping spread the word and adding to its content.

Two of our biggest supporters were Eric Mache and Ally Lamaj, who would go on to establish Wild East Productions, today a leader in Euro-western DVDs. Another was Bill Connolly, who after submitting articles on "**The Great Silence**" and "**Django**," two films he saw while growing up on a military base in Japan. Bill was encouraged to continue and started his fanzine "*Spaghetti Cinema*," which covered all sorts of Peplum, Spaghetti westerns, and European Spy films. Then "*MAMA*" (Martial Arts Movie Associates), which included, as the title suggests, Martial Arts Films. As our base continued to grow and the offshoots sprung up, we got interviews with some of the American actors who were part of the Italian movie scene in the 1960s! Actors such as Richard Harrison, Walter Barnes, Neil Summers, Kelo Henderson, Dominic Barto, Robert Woods, Tony Anthony, Gene Quintano, and Lloyd Battista. Eric Mache a graphic artist not only contributed covers but interviewed, Tomas Milian, Franco Nero, Gianni Garko, Eli Wallach and Hunt Powers (Jack Betts). Glenn Saxon was interviewed and mailed into us from Holland. The subscriber's list went from around 25 to over 300 at one time. Requests for back orders started increasing, and I was so overwhelmed by European readership I brought on Phil Dovaston in England to handle the European readership to ease payment in Euros instead of having to go to a bank and buy dollars.

Issue #75
Summer 2009
Pistol Packin'
Preacher
Nora Orlandi Interview
Charles Stalnaker
Interview (Part 1)
Latest DVD Reviews

As our readership grew, we noticed public interest in the genre started up again. Books on the subject were now appearing from authors like Sir Christopher Frayling, Laurence Staig, and Tony Williams and the much-maligned Thomas Weisser. Films began to show up in video catalogs; soundtracks by BEAT and other labels became more prevalent, with Japan becoming a hotbed for Spaghetti westerns on CD.

Ulrich Bruckner, one of our readers, convinced KOCH Media, where he worked, to let him produce some Spaghetti westerns and release them on DVD. I'm not saying this was because of WAI!, but we had a hand in preserving and renewing interest in these films and those who participated in them.

The Fanzine ran for 30 years until I retired from my full-time job. The last dozen or so issues were done electronically and sent out via email.

Westerns…All'Italiana! is now a daily blog and a once a week Facebook page. We've helped produce the First Los Angeles Spaghetti Western Festival in 2011 with the participation of Robert Woods, Mark Damon, Richard Harrison, Brett Halsey, Hunt Powers, Edd Byrnes, Michael Forest, and Dan van Husen.

Fanzines aren't produced to make money. Anyone who's made one knows that. It's made for the love of the subject matter, and the things you learn from that subject matter, the people who take the time to read and enjoy your work and the friends and acquaintances you make along the way. If successful it's a trip of a lifetime!

JAVIER RAMOS INTERVIEW

M.H. First off thank you for submitting to another interview. I was so impressed with your first interview in Volume Two of Spaghetti Westerns! I knew I had to have you back. Your book (written along with Angel Caldito Castellano) Cine del Oeste en la Comunidad de Madrid released this past summer is one of the most important books ever written on the Italian western genre. Your book covers the Madrid area in regard to the westerns filmed there and the various people and companies involved there. What was the first western filmed in and around Madrid?

J.R. The first complete western, filmed in Madrid, was the movie Oro vil. The film was directed by Eduardo García Maroto in 1941, that is, shortly after the end of the Spanish Civil War. The filming locations were the CEA film studios, for the interiors and La pedriza, for the exteriors. Unfortunately, there is no copy of this production left, so I cannot give more details of the film. As a curiosity, note that, within the cast appears a young Corrado San Martin, an actor who would become one of the emblematic of the spaghetti-western.

Above: A Scene from **Oro vil** (1941). Courtesy Javier Ramos

M.H. Paint for us a picture of Madrid before the advent of the Italian western gold rush?

J.R. When the boom of the Italian Westerns exploded, Spain was in a phase of frank recovery with respect to the terrible effects of the Spanish Civil War. At the beginning of the 60s, the economy had grown quite a lot, thanks mainly to the progressive opening of Franco's government abroad. This opening facilitated that the film industry in other countries with a long tradition in cinema, such as the United States or Italy, were interested in filming in Spain, which, in turn, favored the development of the Spanish film industry. As a result, when the Euro-westerns arrived in Spain, Madrid already had numerous competent professionals and excellent facilities.

M.H. Tells us a little about how the local merchants and indigenous peoples of the area became involved in the Italian western genre.

J.R. When Italian westerns arrived in Madrid, the population was already accustomed to film shoots, thanks, above all, to the great productions of Samuel Bronston. In fact, several of these films were shot in the same locations where, later, Italian westerns would be filmed. That is, in places like La Pedriza (King of Kings**), Hoyo de Manzanares (**Pride and Passion**), or Colmenar Viejo (**Spartacus**). Of course, this film boom, both in the Bronston era and lately, with the Italian westerns, favored the economy of many small towns and their inhabitants. Thus, for example, a single day of filming as an extra, a countryman earned the same as what he made in his work for a month.**

M.H. What was the first studio in Madrid?

J.R. The first studio was Atlantica Cinematográfica, created in 1919. But the first studio where an Italian western was filmed were the Cea Studios, created in 1932. As I said, the interiors of the western Oro Vil **(Eduardo G. Maroto, 1941) were shot there.**

M.H. To me the most famous filming location in my mind in and around Madrid would be the fabled Golden City, can you tell us about its origins up until its demise?

J.R. As I tell in my book El cine de Oeste en la Comunidad de Madrid, the town of Golden City emerged in 1962, following the filming of the Spanish-Italian co-production Terrible Sheriff **(Alberto de Martino, 1962). At first, the idea was to build a temporary town and then destroy it. But, finally, seeing the possibilities that the western had, they decided to build a stable set. The town was built by decorators José Luis Galicia and Jaime Pérez Cubero and was used until the mid-1970s. Unfortunately, with the end of the Italian western, the town stopped being used and deteriorated until it disappeared completely.**

WALTER CHIARI · RAIMONDO VIANELLO

DUE CONTRO TUTTI

AROLDO TIERI · LICIA CALDERON · MARIA SILVA
E CON MAC RONAY
UN FILM DI ALBERTO DE MARTINO · ANTONIO MOMPLET
EASTMANCOLOR · PRODOTTO DA EMO BISTOLFI · SCHERMO PANORAMICO

> *"As I tell in my book El cine de Oeste en la Comunidad de Madrid, the town of Golden City emerged in 1962, following the filming of the Spanish-Italian co-production* Terrible Sheriff *(Alberto de Martino, 1962). At first, the idea was to build a temporary town and then destroy it. But, finally, seeing the possibilities that the western had, they decided to build a stable set. The town was built by decorators José Luis Galicia and Jaime Pérez Cubero and was used until the mid-1970s."*
>
> *-Javier Ramos*

M.H. To me, you can't speak of Golden City, without mentioning Eduardo Manzanos, please tell our writers a bit about the man! A man I might add who is as important as any name in the history of the Italian westerns.

J.R. Undoubtedly, Eduardo Manzanos is one of the key people in the success of the genre. His passion for culture and his entrepreneurial spirit led him to be one of the main drivers of the development of our beloved European westerns. He was one of the first producers who noticed the potential of the genre. That was the main reason that led him to embark on the world of cinema, creating several production companies such as Copercines or Cooperativa Fénix Films, with which he would produce and direct (usually in collaboration with Italian producers) in Madrid, dozens of spaghetti-westerns. Although some of them were not of high quality, it must be recognized that some great films were made such as El Coyote, Two Crosses in Danger Pass, *or* Light the Fuse… Sartana is Coming. Unfortunately*, today, his name has been a bit obscured over time. I hope that with my book, he gets some recognition.*

M.H. Being from Madrid yourself, does it bother you that the films are called Italian westerns or even "Spaghetti Westerns." Both titles not referencing the vital part the Spanish cast, crews and artisans played in the formation and continued success of the genre.

J.R. Yes, I would like there was more recognition about the contribution of the Spaniards in the development of spaghetti-westerns. Although the original idea and the primary impulse were indeed Italian, it is fair to recognize that the genre would not have succeeded without the Spanish landscapes, artists, and technicians. In spite of everything, I like the name "spaghetti-western" because it is a term associated with the genre for years. I do not wish to use other variants of the name, such as chorizo-western or paella-western, used with Hispanic westerns. I prefer to call them all spaghetti-westerns.

M.H. What year was the pinnacle of the Italian westerns reached in respect to the Madrid area?

J.R. Think you could say that since 1962, until it was filmed- The Good, The Bad and The Ugly, *in 1965, Madrid was the center of the spaghetti-western phenomenon. In fact, that was the year in which more films of this genre were shot in Madrid; in total, 31 productions were made. From that film, the shootings would gradually move to Almeria, thanks to the tremendous beauty of the desert landscapes of Tabernas. Even so, it would still take a few years for this region to become a symbolic place within the genre.*

M.H. Most people, when they think of Spanish filming locations, automatically think of Almeria, Spain. Tells us how you think, the legacies of Madrid and Almeria add up.

J.R. This is something completely logical, because, although it is true that more westerns were filmed in Madrid than in Almeria and that Madrid has a great variety of landscapes, many of great beauty; Almeria has something that no other region of Europe has: a desert. The desert landscapes of Tabernas have a magnetism that made them the ideal place to locate these cowboy stories. For me, the iconic image of the genre is that of a cowboy riding through the drylands of Almeria. Even myself, I am a great lover of Almeria, and I try to visit it from time to time.

M.H. What western films in your mind are the most important lensed in and around Madrid?

J.R. Undoubtedly, in Madrid, we are proud that scenes of the three emblematic films of the genre have been shot, such as the three in the Sergio Leone Dollar Trilogy. That is to say: For a Fistful of Dollars, For a Few Dollars More *and* The Good, The Bad and The Ugly. *Other great films filmed in Madrid would be* Django, The Big Gundown, Fury of the Magnificent Seven *and* Villa Rides.

M.H. When did the filming around Madrid start to slow down, and why?

J.R. The decline in the filming of Italian Westerns in Madrid could be said to have begun in 1971. From that year, productions made in the Madrid area plummeted, as happened in other regions, as a consequence of the decline of the genre. This decline was due to the overexploitation of the western theme. There had been so many movies filmed that everything was already very repetitive, and the public began to get tired. In Europe, there was a small resurgence after the success of They Call Him Trinity *that caused the rise of the faglioli western, a style characterized by giving a comic tone to the western, which seems less interesting to me.*

M.H. Tells us about the end of Madrid as an Italian western filming location.

J.R.. I believe that the phenomenon of spaghetti-western in Madrid ended in 1975. Although later attempts would still be made to rescue it with interesting productions such as Apache Kid *or* Scalps, *these were isolated efforts to recover something that had already ended.*

Thank you again! Cine del Oeste en la Comunidad de Madrid is available the Amazon world over!

Check out *Spaghetti Westerns!: Volume Two* for the first thrilling, informative interview with Javier Ramos! Also available on Amazon!

Many classic westerns were filmed around Madrid, including these three: **A Fistful of Dollars**, **The Big Gundown** and **The Good, The Bad and The Ugly**

11

Sixguns in the Eclipse
****

Requiem For A Gringo

-Van Roberts

Preface

The best American westerns are distinguished by their adherence to the rituals of the genre as well as the filmmakers' license to reimagine those rituals. Theatrical western films dwindled during the 1950s after television appropriated and overpopulated prime time with them. Eventually, no matter how far theatrical westerns went with either controversial, message-laden plots or heightened violence to differentiate them from those claustrophobic television cowboys, this overabundance eventually sowed discontent among moviegoers and television viewers. Ultimately, the genre cast a long shadow. Happily, neither European filmmakers nor audiences shared this discontent. They revived the genre for future generations who had not yet endured the consequences of prime-time television's excesses. Similarly, the best European oaters were notable as much by what they inherited from Hollywood westerns as well as how they reimagined the content, too. Meanwhile, the Italians—often working in co-productions with the Germans, the French, and the Spanish—succeeded in taking the western to its cinematic apogee. Sergio Leone, Sergio Corbucci, Sergio Sollima, Tonino Valerii, Enzo Barboni, Enzo G. Castellari, and Damiano Damiani established new standards for the saddle-sore genre and rejuvenated the western for another decade.

Nowadays, like the noble buffalo, great westerns are few and far between. The new breed of filmmakers rarely overshadows their venerable forerunners, though some exceptions exist. Thanks to the advances in home video and the various ways audiences watch films and television, westerns have been preserved for posterity. Now, obscure titles are available for scrutiny by new generations. Technological innovations have paved the way for widescreen versions of films with enhanced sound so audiences can appreciate these films as they were originally projected. Naturally, complications in resurrecting older films often require companies to upgrade films which have deteriorated. Not every film can be restored to its pristine state. Nevertheless, these new iterations surpass their abysmal pan and scan predecessors. Spanish director José Luis Merino's influential and above-average Iberian horse opera **"Requiem for a Gringo"** (*Réquiem para el gringo*, Italy, 1968) qualifies as an example of an upgrade from both its original VHS tape and DVD releases as **"Duel in the Eclipse."**

A Brief Introduction to José Luis Merino and his Films

Writer & director José Luis Merino enjoyed a long and successful career making genre films of every description between 1958 and 1990. As a testament to his popularity and longevity, the Madrid filmmaker directed 32 films and lived to age 92. Spanish film scholar Rafael de España has praised Merino as "a competent specialist in genre cinema after an unsatisfactory beginning, with apologies of provisional or vehicles for singers."[1] España's apologies concern Merino's first two directorial efforts, "**Those Times of the Coupe**" (*Aquellos tiempos del cuplé*, Spain, 1958) and "**The Tramp and the Star**" (El vagabundo y la Estrella, Spain, 1960), which were both musical comedies. Afterward, Merino went on to make seven other westerns, including "**Requiem for a Gringo.**" "**Kitosch, the Man Who Came from the North**" (*Frontera al sur*, Italy, 1967), about the Royal Canadian Mounted Police, was his first foray into the western. "**More Dollars for the MacGregors**" (*Ancora dollari per i MacGregor*, Italy, 1970) about competing bounty hunters in the Old Southwest followed. "**Seven Ride toward Death**" (*7 cabalgan hacia la muerte*, Spain, 1979) was Merino's final western, produced after the sun had set on the Spaghetti western. Although he was not the director, Merino contributed the story and screenplay for Paolo Bianchini's "**Gatling Gun**" (*Quel caldo maledetto giorno di fuoco*, Italy, 1968). Merino's three other westerns occurred before the American Civil War when Mexico ruled those lands. Drawing on Johnston McCulley's masked avenger of justice from the 1919 novel "*The Curse of Capistrano*," Merino helmed a trilogy of costumed western swashbucklers: "**Zorro's Latest Adventure**" (*La última aventura del Zorro*, Italy, 1969), "**Zorro, the Invincible**" (El Zorro de Monterrey, Italy,1971) and "**Zorro, Rider of Vengeance**" (Zorro il cavaliere della vendetta, Italy,1971).

Merino encountered no difficulties in adapting the adventures of other larger-than-life heroes from different genres. "**Robin Hood: the Invincible Archer**" (*Robin Hood, l'invincibile arciere*, Italy, 1970), Edgar Rice Burroughs' white jungle messiah in "**Tarzan in King Solomon's Mines**" (*Tarzán en las minas del rey Salomón*, Spain, 1973), the seafaring swashbuckler "**Pirates of Blood Island**" (*La rebelión de los bucaneros*, Italy, 1969), and "**Slaughter on the Khyber Pass**" (*La furia dei Khyber*, Italy, 1970), about the Imperial British Army in India are but a few examples.

He helmed three World War II, behind-enemy-lines mission epics: "**The Battle of the Last Panzer**" (*La battaglia dell'ultimo panzer*, Italy, 1969), "**Hell Commandos**" (*Comando al infierno*, Italy, 1969), and "**When Heroes Die**" (*Consigna: matar al comandante en jefe*, Italy, 1970). Furthermore, he received credit for the screen story to León Klimovsky's "**A Bullet for Rommel**" (*Hora cero: Operación Rommel*, Italy, 1969).

Merino also made horror films, such as "**The Hanging Woman**" (*La orgía de los muertos*, Spain, 1973) featuring cult Spanish horror star Paul Naschy in a cameo, and "Scream of the **Demon Lover**" (*Il castello dalle porte di fuoco, Italy*, 1970). Merino "developed a cult following among horror film fans" for these scary movies.[2]

Merino's last film saw him dabbling in an entirely different genre. Merino shared co-directorial duties on "**Superagents in Mallorca**" (Superagentes en Mallorca, Spain, 1990) with Antonio Cornejo. This contemporary espionage yarn dealt with a group of special agents searching for a missing British agent who had been investigating weapons which had been genetically engineered.

All filmmakers deserve some recognition for their achievements. One day perhaps a conscientious film historian will give Merino his due in Spanish cinema for not only his fellow countrymen but also for his own critical reputation.

A cursory glance at Merino's style shows a conspicuous difference between "**Requiem for a Gringo**" and his other horse operas. *Six Guns and Society*, Will Wright's groundbreaking structural study of western films, proves useful for classifying Merino's westerns.

Wright defines the four basic horse operas: the classical western plot, the vengeance variation, the transition theme, and the professional plot.[3] According to Wright's criterion, Merino's first western "**Kitosch, the Man Who Came from the North**" duplicates the model of a classical western, like George Steven's "**Shane**" (1953) and Michael Curtiz's "**Dodge City**" (1939). Wright describes the classical plot as "the story of a lone

U.S. Trans World vhs cover of **Requiem for a Gringo** under the title **Duel in the Eclipse**

Italian Poster for **Requiem For A Gringo**

stranger who rides into a troubled town and cleans it up, winning the respect of the townsfolk and the love of a schoolmarm."[4] A sprawling saga set in the Great Northwest about the Royal Canadian Mounted Police, "Kitosch" concerns a plan to smuggle a fortune in gold ingots in coffins for a long journey through hostile territory to a distant fort. The eponymous hero, Kitosch (George Hilton), is a trouble-prone, but plucky frontiersman who winds up guiding the wagon train to its destination. Kitosch finds himself drawn into a contentious situation involving the gold shipment, exposes a two-faced villain within their ranks, and saves a quartet of women masquerading as widows of the dead men strewn in those coffins. Unquestionably, "Kitosch" differs geographically as well as narratively from "Requiem." Meanwhile, Merino displays a competence in orchestrating large-scale action scenes, with hordes of renegades attacking an RCMP fort as well as the RCMP relief columns arriving in the nick of time to save Kitosch and the beleaguered defenders. The formulaic story is straightforward, with several surprises served up in classic cinematic fashion, but with none of "Requiem's" indulgent post-modern touches. The "Requiem" protagonist differs from Kitosch, because the former acts out of vengeance rather than the latter who supervises a mission.

"**More Dollars for the MacGregors**" came out two years after "Requiem." Apart from the surname MacGregor, this western shares little in common with Franco Giraldi's two, tongue-in-cheek, MacGregor horse operas, "**Seven Guns for the MacGregors**" (7 *pistole per i MacGregor*, West German,1966), and "**Up The MacGregors**" (7 *donne per i MacGregor,* Italy,1967), because Giraldi's films dealt with a rambunctious Irish family on the frontier. "More Dollars" focuses on a bounty hunter, George Forsyte (Carlos Quiney of "Zorro the Invincible"), who deceives wanted men into taking advantage of his wife, Yuma (Malisa Longo of "Blindman"), so he can get the drop on them. Unlike either "Kitosch" or "Requiem," "More Dollars" conforms to what Wright labels "a professional western." The two bounty hunters live off the rewards of wanted men.

According to Wright, professional heroes differ from classical heroes, because they are "willing to defend society only as a job they accept for pay or for love of fighting, not from commitment to ideas of law and justice."[5] Unlike "Requiem," the heroes and villains spend more time in the wilderness rather than in towns or on ranches. Like "Requiem," however, Merino maintains a serious tone throughout "More Dollars" and resorts to one brief flashback when the husband remembers his wife. The heroes and villains are standard-issue European western characters. They are lightning fast on the draw with their six-guns, more in the tradition of Sergio Leone's bounty hunters than those in standard American westerns. The action is divided up between two bounty hunters pursuing outlaws and the tragic death of Forsyte's wife. The "More Dollars" protagonists do not plot revenge using the weather and astrology like the eccentric "Requiem" hero. Furthermore, "More Dollars" stages none of "Requiem's" unusual duels. Basically, the heroes in "More Dollars" gallop around in the sun-drenched terrain and shoot it out with several villains. Interestingly, one of the short-lived villains wears a jaguar poncho

German Poster for **Kitosch, the Man who came from the North** (1967)

> *"Meanwhile, Merino displays a competence in orchestrating large-scale action scenes, with hordes of renegades attacking an RCMP fort as well as the RCMP relief columns arriving in the nick of time to save Kitosch and the beleaguered defenders. The formulaic story is straightforward, with several surprises served up in classic cinematic fashion, but with none of "Requiem's" indulgent post-modern touches. The "Requiem" protagonist differs from Kitosch, because the former acts out of vengeance rather than the latter who supervises a mission."*
>
> -Van Roberts

similar to the one worn by the "Requiem" hero.

Merino's third western "**Seven Ride toward Death**" is as interesting and offbeat as "Requiem." This sagebrusher deals with a contentious family that pursues a Native American after he kills the wealthy patriarch of a family, and the family swears vengeance. Similarly, "Requiem" and "**Seven Ride toward Death**" both concern revenge, but the family doesn't survive the fracas. Like "Requiem," "**Seven Ride toward Death**" conforms to Wright's vengeance variation. An agile Native American kills an affluent New Mexico rancher, Zachary Carter (José Luis Merino), about to marry a younger woman, Ann (Assumpta Serna), and the bride and family pursue the Indian recklessly into the wilderness. . Gradually, each of them succumbs to one of the seven deadly sins, while the Indian emerges unscathed and triumphant. Merino's underrated western shares something in common with British director Michael Winner's "**Chato's Land**" (1972), co-starring Charles Bronson, Jack Palance, and Richard Basehart. Merino keeps the family in the foreground, while he confines the elusive Indian to the periphery. While the early part of "**Seven Ride toward Death**" occurs in and around the landowner's hacienda, the rest of the film unfolds in the desert where the Indian exploits the best tactical use of the terrain to defeat the vengeance driven family.

An Analysis of "Requiem for a Gringo"

Ostensibly, "**Requiem for a Gringo**" is a vengeance western. Wright lists the thirteen elements of the revenge western.

1. The hero is or was a member of society.
2. The villains do harm to the hero and to society.
3. The society is unable to punish the villains.
4. The hero seeks vengeance.
5. The hero goes outside of society.
6. The hero is revealed to have a special ability.
7. The society recognizes a difference between themselves and the hero; the hero is given special status.
8. A representative of society asks the hero to give up his revenge.
9. The hero gives up his revenge.
10. The hero fights the villains.
11. The hero defeats the villains.
12. The hero gives up his special status
13. The hero enters society. 6

An analysis of Merino's film illustrates how he adhered to but at the same time departed from Wright's elements as the author applied them to John Ford's "**Stagecoach**" (1939) Anthony Mann's "**The Man from Laramie**" (1955), Marlon Brando's "**One-Eyed Jacks**" (1961), and Henry Hathaway's "**Nevada Smith**" (1966). The major difference between "**Requiem for a Gringo**" and those American westerns as well as Merino's other westerns is the anomalous protagonist. Imagine if French astrologer Nostradamus had strapped on a six-gun, donned a Stetson, worn a jaguar fur poncho, and then annihilated a gang of homicidal hellions with his astrological as well as meteorological knowledge of about their ill-fated future? Before you laugh, remember not all westerns—certainly of the European variety--must be identical. The features which make "**Requiem for a Gringo**" entertaining as well as influential are its strengths. Mind you, "**Requiem for a Gringo**" is neither John Ford nor Sergio Leone, but this is what sets it apart from other westerns.

Merino uses the introductory credit sequence of "Requiem" to foreshadow a clash between Good and Evil. This sagebrusher is not going to be traditional like either "**Shane**" or "**A Fistful of Dollars**" (*Per un pugno di dollari*, Italy, 1964). Indeed, as we shall see, Merino's film anticipated the Spaghetti western, Sergio Garrone's "**Django the Avenger**" (*Django il bastardo*, Italy, 1969), Antonio Margheriti's "**And God Said to Cain**" (*E Dio disse a Caino...*, Italy, 1970), Clint Eastwood's "**High Plains Drifter**" (1973) and "**Pale Rider**" (1985) as the first surreal, supernatural western. Merino inverts the negative and tinted it a pale blue, and then superimposed the credits over it in stark blood red. Our protagonist is shown plodding along a trail with a pack animal in tow. Merino juxtaposes the protagonist with a montage of the antagonists on charging horses, riding over the terrain, so they assume a sinister quality.

Composer Angelo Francesco Lavagnino's portentous orchestral score, featuring an eerie Thomas organ, imparts a Gothic vibe to the music. As the credits conclude, Merino reverts to real time, with natural, earth tone colors and blue skies. Not only do the opening credits sequence establish the imminent conflict between the good and evil, but it also implies "Requiem" may not be a conventional western.

Porfirio Carranza (Fernando Sancho of "**Minnesota Clay**") and his interracial gang of desperadoes pause before they cross the border into California with their loot. The paunchy bandit chieftain suspects Army patrols may have dispatched to intercept them. Dividing up his gang, separating his most valuable from his least valuable henchmen, he resolves to make their border crossing inconspicuous. Carranza explains, "But it wouldn't be wise for us all to cross over the border in one group. Army patrols would be sure to notice. We'll divide into small groups, and each group will have to cross over separately. That is the only safe way. In twelve days, we gather at the ranch of Ramirez." Tom Leader (Ruben Rojo of "**King of Kings**") voices the first sign of discontent when he inquires who will accompany whom. Not only does Carranza choose Tom, but he also summons a superstitious, half-breed, Charley Fair (Aldo Sambrell of "**Navajo Joe**"), garbed in buckskins with dentures and sadistic Ted Corbin (Carlo Gaddi of "**Violent Naples**"), decked out in a solid, form-fitting, black leather outfit, with two guns crisscrossing his abdomen, and a whip. In a moment fraught with foreshadowing, the bandit chieftain glances at the sky and observes, "The sky seems very strange." This scene corresponds to Wright's second element: The villains do harm to the hero and to society. Merino establishes the villains as apprehensive about the Army's interdiction. Moreover, Carranza's ominous admission prefigures the impending conflict with the protagonist.

Afterward, Merino introduces Ross Logan (Lang Jeffries of "**Fire over Rome**") as he rides into his family's hacienda. A white-clad peon welcomes him home after a prolonged absence, "You are here to stay now that the west is at peace?" Logan shrugs, "The west will never be at peace, but I'm tired, and I'm looking for my own peace." Logan's outfit reveals volumes about his character. Like the standard-issue Spaghetti western protagonist, he wears a beard and sports a poncho. However, this is no ordinary poncho, just as Logan is no ordinary western hero. Logan's poncho is made from the fur of either a leopard or a jaguar. Spaghetti scholars Kevin Grant, Lee Broughton, and Rafael de España have linked this poncho with Mayan culture.[7] The bond between the hero's identity and the animal symbolism of this fur poncho adds to his mystique. The Pure-Spirit, an animal symbolism website affirms this linkage.

"The jaguar is representative of power, ferocity, and valor; he is the embodiment of aggressiveness. For some, the jaguar represents the power to face one's fears, or to confront one's enemies. However, they are also associated with vision, which means both their ability to see during the night and to look into the dark parts of the human heart. The jaguar often warns of disaster, he does not offer any reassurance. Along with physical vision, jaguars are also associated with prescience and the foreknowledge of things to come." [8]

Top Left: The Great Fernando Sancho. **Top Right:** Italian Poster.
Bottom: German Lobby Card: Featuring Carlo Gaddi and Aldo Sambrell

Indeed, Logan exhibits these powers. Nevertheless, the filmmakers provide no satisfactory explanation for this exotic poncho, any more than they enumerate the number of years he has been absent or what he did. Logan's outfit imitates American western characters as well as Spaghetti western characters. He wears a shield shirt like John Wayne wore as the Ringo Kid in John Ford's "**Stagecoach**" (1939). Logan's yellow-striped, blue cavalry trousers suggests he has been recently mustered out of the Army. Presumably, Logan's pessimism about peace in the west may be attributed to his years in the Army, when he may have been contending with border vermin like Carranza.

Rafael de España sees Logan's poncho and mule as a homage of Clint Eastwood's Joe in Sergio Leone's "**A Fistful of Dollars**" (*Per un pugno di dollari*, Italy, 1964), while Logan's cavalry trousers are a homage to Franco Nero's eponymous character in Sergio Corbucci's "**Django**" (Italy,1966). España reveals that the name Django replaced the word Gringo in the title in Germany.9 Overall, the notion that Logan may have spent his absence patrolling the western frontier against bandits is implied by his take-no-prisoners attitude toward Carranza and his gang.

What Merino and his scenarists don't reveal about Logan is important. Apparently, during the length of his absence, his parents must have died, while his young brother has grown up enough that he is interested in girls. Not one word about Logan's parents is uttered, so we must presume they are dead. Similarly, little is known about the Ramirez ranch owners. Tom Leader mentions them briefly as does Samuels at his Hotel & Saloon, but details remain obscure. Basically, they are gone. Presumably, Carranza murdered them. Logan knows Dan has just ridden off to visit the girls at the Ramirez ranch. Apparently, Dan knows nothing about Carranza and his gang, otherwise he might have thought twice about riding into such a hornet's nest. According to Wright's first element, Merino has established Ross Logan as the hero who is or was a member of society. Logan is comparable to Ethan Edwards in John Ford's "**The Searchers**" (1956), because he has estranged himself from his family. The impending murder of his brother will prompt Logan to make family matters a priority. Ironically, the day he returned after his absence, Logan misses seeing his brother because Dan has just ridden off, to a fate he never expected.

Merino deploys Wright's sixth element: The hero has a special ability. The last thing an American western hero would have done upon his arrival at home is examine various astrological charts. An entire room on the second floor of the hacienda accommodates globes, charts, and other astrological paraphernalia. After he stores his gun belt in a chest, Logan studies a chart. Moments later, he steps onto the roof to peer into a telescope. He spots five armed strangers skulking about the premises. Fetching a Winchester and a crate of doves, Logan saunters onto the grounds. The five gunmen pause to watch him. Instead of shooting the doves, Logan shoots all five intruders without missing a single shot! These hellions had planned to rustle horses for Carranza from his ranch. Significantly, Logan never gave them a chance and killed them before they could retaliate. An American hero would have allowed them to shoot first before he killed them. A dying outlaw warns Logan to prepare himself for Carranza's wrath. He says Carranza is holed up at the Ramirez ranch. At this point, whether or not Logan suspects his younger brother's life is in jeopardy is debatable. Meanwhile, this scene demonstrates Logan's superb marksmanship. Moreover, it reaffirms Wright's second element the villains will try to harm to the hero.

Merino emphasizes this second element when he shows Carranza and his gang abusing the peons at the Ramirez ranch. No sooner has Dan (Carlo Simoni of "**The Battle of the Last Panzer**") ridden onto the premises than he witnesses Ted Corbin whip a helpless peon into submission because they found him armed with a gun.

Dan flees from the ranch. Charlie brings him back against his will. Carranza arranges a ritualistic duel between Dan and Ted. This is the first of three duels in "Requiem for a Gringo." Roped to separate pillars across the courtyard from each other, so they cannot move their arms, Dan and Ted stand poised with their guns in their holsters. Neither can draw until a bullet severs the rope linking them. Initially, Carranza told Tom to shoot the rope. Tom relents and offers his gun to Carranza. Carranza suffers a moment of doubt as Tom's revolver wavers in his fist. He fires and the rope snaps in two. Something left unsaid lurks between Carranza and Tom. Tom enjoys putting Carranza on the spot. Tom has been having an affair with Carranza's mistress Alma (Femi Benussi of "**Bloody Pit of Horror**"), but Carranza knows nothing about them. Eventually, he will discover of their treachery. When Dan empties his holster, he learns he has no bullets. Secretly, Tom removed the cylinders from Dan's two six-guns, so the youth cannot shoot Ted. Ted puts four slugs into Dan before the youth dies. Ironically, when Ted kills Dan, neither Carranza nor his gang have the remotest idea that they have just sealed their fate. Inevitably, Dan's murder places Logan on a collision course with these killers. Killing Dan reiterates Wright's second element because this prompts Logan to seek retribution.

A third of the way into "Requiem," Logan appears at the portal of the Ramirez ranch. Dan's body dangles from a noose. A board attached to Dan reads: "Warning. If you get too nosy, you might get your neck stretched." Instead of riding directly to the Ramirez ranch in the heat of the moment, Logan veers off to Samuels' Hotel & Saloon, the nearest place of its kind in thirty miles. He buys a drink and pays for a room. Like the peons at either ranch, those people at Samuels' Hotel & Saloon constitutes the society in "**Requiem for a Gringo**." The owner and his female attendant, Lupe (Giuliana Garavaglia of "**The Hanging Woman**"), are the only individuals between Logan's hacienda and the Ramirez ranch who are not associated with either ranch. The owner, Samuels (Ángel Álvarez of "**Django**"), warns Logan the Ramirez family is gone. Earlier, Tom Leader had told Dan that the Ramirez family was simply "out." Moreover, Samuels notifies Logan if he is looking for work at the Ramirez ranch that no jobs are available. Since Carranza has terrorized the area, Samuels has seen virtually nobody.

Later, four abrasive Carranza pistoleros barge into the saloon. One slaps around Nina (Marisa Paredes of "**High Heels**"), who had arrived ahead of them. He warns her to leave "this whore house," before Logan intervenes. Before Carranza's men realize it, Logan pins one gunman's hand to a post with his knife and leaves the other three dead on the floor. Afterwards, he kills the fourth whose hand had been pinned to a post with his knife without a qualm. Logan dispatches them with the same indifference to their humanity that he did to the first five at his ranch. Samuels surveys the massacre with misgivings. "That was a real pretty piece of shooting," he admits. "It's time someone stood up to these birds around here." Nevertheless, he fears reprisal. Indeed, he believes Carranza will burn down his establishment. Logan furnishes him some shrewd advice. "Tie them to their horses.

They'll go back to the ranch, and nobody will know where they were killed." This scene reiterates Wright's second element that the villains try to harm to society as well as the fifth element about the hero going outside society. In **"Requiem for a Gringo,"** the law doesn't shield society from Evil. The U.S. Army that worries Carranza is never present. Basically, Logan must take the law into his own hands like a vigilante. At the same time, this scene presents the seventh element of Wright's vengeance structure: Society—Samuels and Lupe—recognizes the difference between themselves and Logan as the hero, and they grant him special status.

Upstairs in his room, Logan notifies Nina in three days, on April 17, he will appear at the Ramirez ranch. She warns him Carranza will kill him. "You'd better go now," Logan advises, "Or you'll get caught in a storm." Nina is incredulous, "Storm, you said? It never rains around here in April." Logan reassures her. "It won't rain." A dramatic crescendo of lightning outside the hotel shatters the evening calm. This brief scene reminds us again about the hero's special status. Meantime, Merino and his scenarists have eliminated both elements eight and nine from Wright's model. Eight dictates a representative of society must ask the hero to renounce revenge, while nine has the hero repudiating revenge. Indeed, Ross Logan has no intention of forsaking vengeance!

During a celebration at the Ramirez ranch, Carranza's men interrupt him while he is arraying Alma's naked body with stolen jewelry. Essentially, she amounts to nothing but a trophy that he refuses to share. They show him the four dead pistoleros roped to their saddles. In a fit of rage, Carranza orders the deaths of four Mexican peons. The peons represent a part of society, and Carranza's men victimize them. Ted bullies Nina repeatedly, and he threatens to kill her if she refuses to have consensual sex. Later, when Nina returns to the Ramirez ranch, the gruesome sight of the four peons hanging from nooses shocks her. Merino reemphasizes Wright's second element: The villains do harm to society. Spaghetti western villains are most vile, despicable, dastards who love to rape, pillage and murder. By this time, it is clear that Carranza does whatever serves him. When Logan strikes, the collective villainy of Carranza and his lieutenants withers in the face of his cold stone violence.

The remainder of "Requiem" depicts elements ten and eleven. Logan keeps his appointment at the Ramirez ranch. He fights and defeats the villains. Initially, when one of Carranza's gunmen harasses him, Logan smashes a water bucket over his head without warning. Again, according to Wright's sixth element, Logan exemplifies his special ability that enables him to dispatch villains. Earlier, Charlie Fair had speculated about Logan's special ability. Charlie told Tom Leader and Ted Corbin that he planned to ride to Samuels' Saloon, "I heard the peons whispering something about a man staying there who has got magical powers. I want to find out just how powerful his magic really is."

Back at the Ramirez ranch, Logan surprises Carranza when he walks in and inter rupts him as he is plucking guitar strings. Logan wants to join Carranza's gang. Initially, Carranza demands Logan surrender his revolver just as he had forced Dan. Logan refuses, "You take away a man's gun, you take away his soul, and I'm quite fond of my mine." Carranza warns Logan he must kill a current gang member to join his outfit. After Logan steps outside into the courtyard, Kid Ericson and Carranza converse. "You know who he is?" The Kid asks. Carranza replies, "I don't know, but I got a bad feeling." The Kid suggests they get "rid of him." Carranza hesitates. "He could be a federal agent or a marshal or a sheriff. I want to know more though, make him talk. And afterwards, we'll say a mass, or a requiem for a gringo." Carranza has not only deluded himself into imagining Logan poses no problem, but also that he can kill him.

The climax of "Requiem" occurs in the courtyard. Merino establishes the arena for this scene as well as the heavy odds against Logan with an ambitious pan that isn't quite 360 degrees, but circles the setting. The camera frames Logan standing against the wall, sweeps past him, then traverses and tilts to reveal the rest of Carranza's gang. Finally, the camera completes its pan with a medium shot of Carranza. Merino and lenser Mario Pacheco have a knack for putting the audience in the right place in every scene. An earlier example is the scene where Ted Corbin whips the peon without mercy. Furthermore, in a stroke of editorial genius, Merino adopts a post-modern storytelling approach to the entire courtyard scene. Deliberately, Merino jumbles the chronology of the events and presents them out of order for maximum impact. Although he could have shown Logan killing Charlie Fair, Ted Corbin, and Tom Leader when their deaths occurred the day before, Merino resists this easy way out.
Everything starts as Logan demands a showdown with Ted. Nobody can find Ted. Logan challenges Charlie Fair. Charlie cannot be found. Finally, Logan asks for Tom. Tom can neither be found. At this point, Logan surprises an incredulous Carranza. He explains he has already killed them! Merino provides flashbacks of their respective deaths. Logan exploited Charlie Fair's superstitious nature and drove him into the mountains and ambushed him. Charlie wasted his ammunition out of fear, and Logan shot him out of the saddle. Logan put three bullets into Ted after he lured the gunman into an arroyo during a freak dust storm during their search for Nina. Our hero took advantage of Ted's perverted lust for Nina. The most chilling instance occurs when Logan brandishes his knife to cut off Corbin's gun hand. Pacheco frames Logan with his back to the sun so the brim of his hat obscures his face like an apparition. Lastly, he killed Tom while Tom and Carranza's cronies were shooting at the funeral procession of the four murdered Mexicans. Not only have Carranza's men harmed society, but they have also derided the Catholic Church. Logan assures Carranza all three men died like cowards.

Naturally, Carranza refuses to believe him. Logan corroborates each death with personal artifacts as evidence. When he discusses Tom's demise, Logan flashes the emerald from Carranza's chest that the bandit chieftain had given to Alma. . Realizing her treachery has been exposed, Alma struggles to save face. Carranza orders her death without a qualm in front of the gang at the hands of a machete wielding

African-American. Once he has delivered these revelations, Logan accuses Carranza of cowardice, too. Merino indulges himself in the longest zoom shot in cinematic history to reflect Carranza's own cowardice. The camera zooms in and out repeatedly, concertina style throughout this confrontation, imparting a sense of vertigo to the action. Carranza's men realize his cowardice when Kid Ericson refuses to shoot Logan. Instead, he offers his revolver at Carranza, just as Tom did during the rope duel. Overhead, the eclipse of the sun Logan has awaited occurs.

A gunfight erupts and ends during the eclipse interval. Not surprisingly, Logan leaves nobody alive and emerges unscathed. The third and lesser duel occurs when Logan shoots it out with Carranza. Logan warns Carranza he will kill him once his watch ceases to swing like a pendulum. Carranza refuses to fight Logan, just as Dan refused to draw on Ted. Nevertheless, Logan gives him a chance to use his sawed-off shotgun, but he fills the Mexican full of lead before he can fire it. An extreme long shot of the horizon concludes "Requiem." Logan is outlined against the sky riding his mule, with Nina following him like the youth did in a "Shane." Clearly, the hero has renounced his special status. Epitomizing society with a possibility for the future, Nina may settle down with Logan for the peace he sought before Dan's murder.

Criticism

Compared with most Spaghetti westerns, "**Requiem for a Gringo**" qualifies as an above-average but derivative example of the genre. Despite its modest budget and small cast, this ranks as Merino's most audacious western, populated with flawed but interesting characters, in a revenge-themed narrative pared down to the absolute essentials. Good and Evil are presented without subtlety. Perpetrating their evil deeds early, the villains constitute a menace to society. They murder five or more individuals and create a reign of terror when they occupy the Ramirez ranch. Naturally, none know the meaning of honor, courage, and forbearance. Spaghetti western villains are more treacherous than most American western villains. Spaghetti western villains betray each as if it were a destructive gene. Carranza replaces slow guns with fast guns, while his own gang cannibalizes their ranks without mercy. When they aren't killing each other, they terrorize and kill innocents with neither a qualm nor a question. Traditionally, lacking the hero's self-control, villains act on impulse without considering the consequences of their actions. This lack of self-control makes them shuck their irons first so they can destroy harmony. This lack of forbearance dooms them when they murder Dan. Implacable hero that he is, Dan's older brother Ross Logan wants payback. Like the quintessential Spaghetti hero, Ross Logan is good with a gun, and he doesn't always claim self-defense. He never lets his emotions interfere with his objectives. He makes no mistakes. Few Spaghetti western heroes can match Logan for his marksmanship and strategy.

The best Spaghetti westerns feature imaginative duels. The eclipse duel is the highlight of "Requiem." Literally, Logan eclipses Carranza and his gang, because the entire gunfight lasts the length of the eclipse. The first duel—the Rope Duel--is strikingly original for its elaborate formalism. Carranza relies on the Rope Duel to winnow out inferior gunmen past their prime. He recruits gunmen to kill his own men and provide turnover for his ranks. The final duel—the most personal of the three—far less complicated. Carranza has none of the advantages of the Rope Duel. Logan lets his watch swing until it stops and they shoot. The bandit chieftain whines about his bad luck. Earlier, Logan tangled with Carranza's gunslingers in showdowns that flaunted his special status. As revenge westerns go, Ross Logan kills them all and comes back alive! Amassing a double-digit body count, Logan kills more men than the outlaws themselves have slain since their arrival at the Ramirez ranch. Whether it be a formal duel or a showdown, Logan massacres Carranza and his entire gang!

Merino's western is not without its dramatic shortcomings. The hero's invincibility, a gallery of flamboyant but flawed villains, and a scarcity of exposition may seem like quibbles. Despite these apparent flaws, "**Requiem for a Gringo**" maintains a narrative momentum which never wanes. Simple, serious, straightforward and Spartan best describe "**Requiem for a Gringo.**" From start to finish, the action covers roughly twelve days. Before his gang and he enter California, Carranza announces the twelve-day deadline when they must rendezvous at the Ramirez ranch. Similarly, after he discovers Dan's body, Logan establishes his own three-day deadline. Originally, he had sought nothing more than to settle down and live in peace. The prospect of a peaceful life vanished when Carranza's men invaded his ranch. Afterward, Dan's murder compelled him to leave his ranch again, dispatch various villains at Samuel's Hotel & Saloon, and ultimately wipe out to the last man every adversary at the Ramirez ranch. The villains never stood a chance against Logan, because he was virtually omniscient and infallible.

As the protagonist, Ross Logan is strong and implacable. Asymmetrically, he maintains the upper hand throughout "Requiem." Nothing prevents him from exacting vengeance in Dan's murder. Usually, the standard-issue Spaghetti western hero must suffer grievous bodily harm before he triumphs. The "Fistful of Dollars" villains tortured and maimed Joe. Similarly, the hero of Sergio Corbucci's "**Django**" was brutally maimed. The villains battered the Craig Hill protagonist repeatedly in Paolo Bianchini's "**I Want Him Dead**" (*Lo voglio morto*, Italy-1968) in similar fashion. The villains in Mario Bianchi's "**Fast Hand**" (*Mi chiamavano 'Requiescat'... ma avevano sbagliato*, Italy-1973) maim the hero, so he can never hold an ordinary gun again. Generally, heroes are expected to run a gauntlet as a part of their exalted status. Ultimately, Ross Logan is invulnerable, and audiences need not worry about his welfare since he has planned everything ahead of time. Lang Jeffries gives a dour but monolithic performance, in his first and only western that reinforces the nature of his stern, heroic stature. Haunted by violence but seeking peace, Logan straps on his gun again, devoid of emotion to avenge his brother's murder. Remember, Logan had not seen Dan for years, but he knows how Dan would behave under the Carranza's conditions. Essentially, Carranza never had a chance because Logan is the personification of vengeance. The dramatic trade-off is the audience need not fear for Logan's welfare, because he cannot die.

Lobby Card: Femi Benussi and Lang Jefferies

Typically, villains are the driving force behind any melodrama. They create chaos and disrupt the status quo. The hero can only straighten things out in the end. Carranza ignited that fuse when he crossed the border. He wants to reduce the number of his gang, so the fewer receive a greater percentage of the loot. When he occupies the Ramirez ranch, he establishes himself up as an authority figure. Carranza is murderous. He orders the deaths of Logan's brother, the four innocent peons, and ultimately Alma without a second thought. Meantime, Carranza grows weak and passive. Once he is comfortably ensconced at the Ramirez ranch, Carranza doesn't budge. His only ace-in-a-hole is the shotgun he keeps stashed nearby when Tom challenges first and later during his showdown with Logan. His henchmen do his killing for him. Later, Logan criticizes Carranza, "Killing peons is like kicking a dog when you are afraid." Neither Carranza nor his men adequately challenge Logan. First, Carranza cannot maintain discipline and respect among his own henchmen. For example, Tom and Alma make a mockery of him behind his back. Moreover, Tom wants to kill Carranza, but the logistics frighten him. Inexplicably, Carranza suffers from an inferior complex. He accepted Tom's challenge without rebuke to cut the rope with a single shot so the duel between the Dan and Ted can commence. Indeed, he maintains his position as leader, but Tom keeps plotting to double-cross him. Second, Carranza doesn't respond well to challenges. When the four dead horsemen show up at the ranch, he cares only about killing innocents rather than hunting down Logan. Third, Carranza's three henchman are just as cowardly. They follow his orders. At one point, they do Carranza's bidding and eliminate several gang members. When the last bunch of gang members show up, Tom, Charlie, and Ted massacre them gleefully as if they were competing for the most kills.

Finally, Carranza's sniveling death scene exposes his ultimate frailty. One has only to wonder how such a man has survived in such a cutthroat world. Similarly, Charlie Fair's superstitious nature completely unhinges him when he spots a black cat. Ted allowed his lust for Nina to distract him and he died for it. Tom ranks a notch above both in despicability, especially when he shoots the corpses of the peons at point blank range.

Consequently, Carranza and his henchmen qualify as second-rate villains. "Requiem" might have been better had Carranza been a more challenging villain. Fernando Sancho parlayed a career out of playing scores of iconic, larger-than-life, patriarchal Spaghetti western villains. His brawling, scenery-chewing performances are reminiscent of American character actor Wallace Beery. Before he played Carranza, Sancho played a similar adversary, 'El Sancho' Rodríguez, in Luigi Capuano's **"Blood Calls for Blood"** (*Sangue chiama sangue* (Italy, 1968). Like Carranza, he killed his own men for greater shares of loot. Unlike Carranza; 'El Sancho' went out shooting. Fernando Sancho adds clout to any Spaghetti western. Similarly, Aldo Sambrell rose among the ranks to become another seminal Spaghetti western villain. Sambrell's villains were more treacherous than Sancho's villains. Initially, he appeared in Sergio Leone's Dollars trilogy and then scored as the chief villain in Sergio Corbucci's **"Navajo Joe"** (Italy, 1966) who raped, murdered, and scalped Burt Reynolds' Native American wife. As Ted Corbin, Carlo Gaddi makes an unforgettable impression. Although he is more sadistic rather than anything else, Ted Corbin imitates the black-clad gunslingers in Giulio Questi's **"Django, Kill!...If You Live Shoot!** (*Se sei vivo spara*, Italy-1967), with his own black outfit. Corbin is trouble from start to finish, and Gaddi's hatchet face enhances his villainous intensity. As Tom Leader, Rubén Rojo is constantly at odds with Carranza. He knows how to treat a woman, and he knows Alma prefers him over Carranza. Leader is the least psychotic of Carranza's henchmen. Although he dresses like a gentleman, little about him is civilized. After all, he shoots dead people! As the bad girl, Femi Benussi is the equivalent of a prostitute in an American western. She uses her beauty to beguile Carranza into giving her jewelry. Benussi gives a believable, two-faced performance as she alternates between Carranza and Tom. Meantime, as Nina, Marisa Paredes struggles to keep herself calm in the middle of all the violence. Lacking the bad girl's seductive ways, Paredes relies on her unadorned hairstyle and quiet demeanor to be the good girl. Ultimately, she may provide the peace that Ross Logan had sought for when he came home.

Merino and his writers provide little information about some plot points. Literally, Logan materializes at his ranch as if he appeared out of the blue. The protagonist's fascination with astrology and meteorology is never explained. Merino and company don't dwell on Logan's past. Similarly, it is enough that we are told the Ramirez owners are gone. Why did Carranza choose the Ramirez ranch? At some point, Tom calls Carranza a cousin of the Ramirez, but nobody substantiates this claim. Revenge motivates Ross Logan when Ted murders Dan. Logan doesn't have a crisis of conscience over it. Greed and jealousy create dissention within Carranza's ranks.

Tom Leader suffers from indecision which explains his reluctance to double-cross Carranza. Although the answers to these questions might prove illuminating, Merino and company address none of them because each is largely irrelevant to the headlong momentum of the film. "Requiem for a Gringo" remains an above-average Spaghetti western, and in retrospect the larger-than-life quality of its hero may have influenced later films, such as **"Django the Bastard,"** **"And God Said to Cain"** as well as Clint Eastwood's **"High Plains Drifter"** and **"Pale Rider."**

Wild East Productions have proven themselves the leader in resurrecting venerable Spaghetti westerns, and their Blu-ray presentation of this 1968 horse opera makes it undeniably a collector's item. Since I own fifty Wild East DVD titles, I know whence I write. With their release of **"Requiem for a Gringo,"** they have reproduced the cover picture from the Transworld Entertainment VHS release of "Duel in the Eclipse," with the evil Carranza cradling his six-gun in two hands and smoking a cigarillo. The audio is crisp, clear, and evocative. A prime example of the audio quality occurs after Logan has returned home and ascends the stairs. Although you cannot see his boots, you can hear the scrape of his booted feet. Since all Spaghetti's were post-synced, the sounds are vivid and appeal to your imagination. Naturally, the pictorial content, lensed in the 1.66 format looks even better than the earlier VHS offering. Wild East's version of "Requiem" credits Merino as the only director. Controversy has engulfed this western as early as its own publicity items that Eugenio Martin co-directed this film. *The Internet Movie Database* lists him as a co-director, even though most prints assign direction to Merino. Eugenio Martin has said he had nothing to do with "Requiem." This author messaged Martin's wife Lone Faerch through Facebook, and she relayed the question to him. Martin's answer again was he had nothing to with "Requiem."10 Were he alive today, director José Luis Merino would be gratified that Wild East has given his sixth film a new lease on life.

Aldo Sambrell and Carlo Simoni. **Requiem for a Gringo.** German Lobby Card

Above: French Program for **Requiem for a Gringo**
Left: Image used on both the Trans World Vhs and Wild East Productions releases
** All photos used in this review courtesy of Eric Mache**

Carlo Gaddi, Aldo Sanbrell and Carlo Simoni: **Requiem for a Gringo**

End Notes

1. Rafael de España, Sin dólares no hay ataúdes. 50 ejemplos del western mediterráneo (Barcelona,   Filmografías Esenciales, 2019) (Spanish Kindle Edition)
2. "Jose Luis Merino," in Wikipedia: The Free Encyclopedia; (Wikimedia Foundation Inc., updated 7 July 2019, at 01:02 (UTC). [encyclopedia on-line]; available from https://en.wikipedia.org/wiki/Jose Luis Merino; retrieved 27 January, 2020.
3. Will Wright, Six-Guns and Society, A Structural Study of the Western (Los Angeles: University of California Press, 1975), 29-123.
4. Wright, Six Guns and Society, 32.
5. Wright, 85.
6. Ibid, 69.
7. Kevin Grant, Any Gun Can Play: The Essential Guide to Euro-Westerns (London: FAB Press, 2011), 182; Lee Broughton, Review of "Requiem for a Gringo, CineSavant, Nov 19, 2019, available from https://trailersfromhell.com/requiem-for-gringo/ retrieved 27, January, 2019; Rafael de España, Sin dólares no hay ataúdes.
8. Jaguar Symbolism, Pure Spirit Animal Communication and Training Solutions, [database on-line]; available http://pure-spirit.com/more-animal-symbolism/306-jaguar-symbolism; retrieved 27, January, 2020.
9. España.
10. Van Roberts, Interview with Lone Faerch and Eugenio Martin, 19 January, 2020, Facebook

PAOLO BIANCHINI:
THE PROFESSIONAL

-Michael Hauss

"**P**aolo Bianchini only directed a small number of westerns, four in fact. And although his westerns make no one's top ten or twenty list and to besides the hardened fan of the genre, his name is unrecognizable. Those four films though are excellent examples of the genre and show a professional at work helming those films. Bianchini was born in 1931. He began as an assistant director in 1953 and worked in that capacity until 1966. The number of films that Bianchini served as an assistant director on varies, with IMDb only reporting twenty, and the book *Dizionario del cinema italiano*, placing the number closer to sixty."   -M.H.

Paolo Bianchini directed his first film in 1966, that being the Euro-spy thriller, **Our Men in Bagdad** (*Il gioco delle spie*, Italy, France, 1966). Of note, **Our Men in Bagdad** was co-produced by Hoche Productions out of France and Summa Cinematografica out of Italy; Summa Cinematografica was most notable for being one of the production companies behind the wonderfully bizarre Giulio Questi film **Death Laid an Egg** (*La morte ha fatto l'uovo*, Italy, France, 1968). It would take two more years and three films in between before Bianchini directed his first western, **God Made Them... I Kill Them** (*Dio li crea... Io li ammazzo!*, Italy) in 1968. Those three films sandwiched between his directorial debut and his first western show the progression of his professional style. Bianchini's second film, **The Devil's Man** (*Devilman Story,* Italy, 1967), which stars the American actor Guy Madison is a sci-fi thriller that is more akin to a 1930's serial. **The Devil's Man** includes scenes from the producer of the film Gabriele Crisanti's 1965 film **I Predoni del Sahara** (Italy). Crisanti would also produce Bianchini's next three films, **Massacre Mania** (*Hipnos follia di massacre*, Italy) in 1967, **Superago and the Faceless Giant** (*L'invincibile Superman*, Italy, Spain), and **God Made Them... I Kill Them**, both 1968. **Massacre Mania**, aka **Hypnos**, starred Robert Woods, the actor who would appear in Bianchini's most significant western **Gatling Gun** (*Quel caldo maledetto giorno di fuocok*, Italy, Spain, 1968) aka **Damned Hot Day in Dallas**. [1]

"Paolo and I became immediate friends when hired to do a film called 'Hypnos' under his direction. It was a totally different film than others I had done, and I accepted to do it with reluctance. Paolo Bianchini was one of the most enthusiastic, flexible, collaborative, and creative directors I worked for... though, of course, there were a few others, as you know, that I held in high esteem. I enjoyed Paolo's company so much, that when Dr. Amati of Fida Films asked me to put together another Western for him, I immediately thought of Paolo for the directorial job and to collaborate on a script for it. The ultimate result was 'Gatling Gun'... and what fun we had making it. John Ireland loved Paolo, too. I wasn't aware that he made other Westerns after that one, but it was a great success, so I assumed he probably did... We sort of lost touch afterward, because I went away to do other work before I returned to America. Paolo is still in my heart... Great guy...talented director...creative writer!"

-Robert Woods-

God Made Them... I Kill Them

This 1968 film stars the American singer/actor/political activist Dean Reed in the lead as a *gunslining*-dandy who is hired by a Wells City to protect their gold shipments. The film was written by Fernando Di Leo, who was involved in the writing of numerous noteworthy westerns including but not limited to: **A Fistful of Dollars** (*Per un pugno di dollari*, Italy, Spain, W. Germany, 1964), **A Pistol For Ringo** (*Una pistola per Ringo*, Italy, Spain, 1965), **For A Few Dollars More** (*Per qualche dollaro in più*, Italy, Spain, 1965), **Django** (Italy, Spain, 1966), **Massacre Time** (*Le colt cantarono la morte e fu... tempo di massacre*, Italy, 1966), **Sugar Colt** (Italy, Spain, 1966), **Navajo Joe** (Italy, Spain, 1966), **Hate for Hate** (*Odio per odio*, Italy, 1967) and **The Ruthless Four** (*Ognuno per sé*, Italy, W. Germany, 1968).

Di Leo is more noted these days for his work writing and working behind the camera on Italian crime films, most notably for his two classics from 1972, **Caliber 9** (*Milano calibro 9*, Italy) and **The Italian Connection** (La mala ordina, Italy, W. Germany)

God Made Them... I Kill Them unfortunately relies more on trickery and deception, including some elaborate weaponry and a hero who is cold and aloof, cultured, snobbish, which leads to a disconnect between hero and audience. With Reed's perfectly pomaded hair, his character's sophisticated pompous attire, and upper-class snobbery and mannerisms, he is ultimately just a shallow construct, who lacks the commonness of the genres best character constructions. Reed would play a similar character in the Yul Brenner classic western **Adios, Sabata** (*Indio Black, sai che ti dico: Sei un gran figlio di...,* Italy, 1970). In that film, Reed stars as another dandy fellow, but more down and dirtier; the director of the film Gianfranco Parolini (as Frank Kramer), made the character more grounded, always kept in place by the craftier Yul Brenner 'Indio Black' character. In **Adios, Sabata**, Reed's Ballentine character, has a healthy counterbalance in the refined and intelligent Indio Black, who Ballentine can never outfox, a man also of high society and taste, but also of the people. Slim Corbett (Dean Reed) is introduced seducing a married woman in his private suite as they consume oysters, when a note arrives for Slim wishing for him to come to Wells City to discuss a deal. This introductory scene is placed there to notate that the flamboyant Slim Corbett was a red-blooded male- who, while a sophisticated dandy, still pulled his trousers on or off like all his Italian western forebearers.

The Slim Corbett character can be linked back to Col. Mortimer in **For A Few Dollars More**, in his use of gadgetry- And to the excellent 1966 film which Fernando Di Leo had a hand in writing, **Sugar Colt**, which is vastly superior to **God Made Them... I Kill Them**, but has a similar, refined lead character in the Hunt Powers authored Sugar Colt. **Sugar Colt** boasts a great turn by Hunt Powers. The Powers' Sugar Colt character is elegant and sophisticated, a lover of women and the beautiful things in life. Still, Powers, with his physicality and mannerism, never crosses over into parody, which at times the Slim Corbett character trespassed in to. Unfortunately, the figure provides a disconnect, and including comedic scenes does little to help the already shaky narrative foundation. And let us face facts most spaghetti westerns using a comedic angle in their narratives are, for the most part, unsuccessful.

After Slim Corbett arrives in Wells City to discuss the job, it does not take long for him to cut down six thugs, who were laughing at his expense, concerning his well-equipped carriage and his stylish clothing. The town wants Corbett to help put an end to the robberies concerning the town's bank and gold supply. But when Slim requests $1000 a week and living expenses, they are beside themselves with anger, and Slim does little to endear himself to them, conducting his business in a rude, standoffish way. Judge Kincaid (Ivano Staccioli), who requested Slim to come to town, is an old friend of Slim's and feeds him info even as the rest of the town leader's eventually turn on Slim for his whore-mongering and off-putting ways.

The strongest and richest man in town, Don Luis (Peter Martell), is behind the robberies, employing many men, including the sheriff (Piero Lulli), to pull off and keep the robberies secret; with an eye to an upcoming huge gold shipment from the U.S. government, being sent to aid the town's growth. Slim befriends a local *jack of no trades* named Job (Fidel Gonzalez). Job proclaims himself to be the laziest man in the parts but aids Slim as he tries to get to the bottom of things in town. Slim seduces two saloon girls Doris (Agnes Spaak) and Dolly (Rosella Bergamonti), and they fight over his attention, but Dolly turns against him, aiding the evil Don Luis. After the stage carrying the gold intended for Wells City and all the members killed off by the sheriff and Dark (Bruno Arie), the tables get turned on Slim, and he's fingered for the robbery. But Job and Slim had been a witness to the robbery, and Job followed the sheriff and Dark, finding out where they hid the loot and abscond-sed with it. Slim gets tossed into jail after the strongbox from the robbery is found in his room after being planted there by the men of Don Luis. Once Job explains to Judge Kincaid what he and Slim had seen, the Judge goes to the jail and forcibly frees Slim. Job is captured and taken to the estate of Don Luis and tortured, but he will not say a word about the gold or Slim. The ending has Slim singlehandedly wiping out the gang who work for Don Luis. The finale features a severely wounded Slim (stabbed by a blade in Don Luis' retractable cane) outsmarting the cunning Don Luis- who curses Slim as he dies because he "*cheated*" him in his little game of death.

God Made Them... I Kill Them is Dean Reed's second appearance in an Italian western, the year before he had appeared in the film **Buckaroo: The Winchester Does not Forgive** (*Buckaroo (Il winchester che non perdona*, Italy, 1967). Reed, as he does in Buckaroo, sings the vocal song for **God Made Them… I Kill Them**. Reed just never makes the Slim character relatable (aided by a quite embarrassing dance number, as Slim cuts the rug with Doris and Dolly) to the viewer! And that hurts the movie overall, and even his redemption and playing through the pain at the end of the film is not enough to make the characterization stand out in a field littered with the likes of Clint Eastwood, Gianni Garko, Anthony Steffen, and numerous oth-ers. One never feels an affinity for the Slim character and his abrasive personality; and the comedy bits are honestly just annoying. The rest of the cast is outstanding, and although Peter Martell does chew the scenery up a bit much, he is dependable and allows the film a worthy antagonist. Martell's Don Luis is the evil town boss, which was a plot device used in countless Italian western and Hollywood westerns for good measure. Don Luis has the sheriff on his payroll, another commonly used device. The producer of this film Gabriele Crisanti had found some success with his spy films, obviously inspired by the James Bond films, and had tried to incorporated a bit of that slick secret agent into the Slim Corbett character, suppling him with gadgetry and a healthy libido. But regardless of the issues with the film, the direc-tion was not one of them, and quite honestly, one can say that Bianchini directed professionally with a fluid style that kept the film moving as it does not bog down for a minute. And while the protagonist is unfortunately unlikeable, the film is for the most part entertaining as hell and moves by at a blistering pace.

God Made Them... I Kill Them. Top to Bottom: Dean Reed as Slim, Fidel Gonzales as Job and Piero Lull as Sheriff Lancaster

The cinematography by Sergio D'Offizi is constrained to a point as most of the film takes place within the interiors of Wells City, which was the back-lot at Tirrenia Studios in Pisa. Don Luis' estate is the fabled Villa Mussolini, where countless western scenes were shot, including very effectively in **Days of Violence** (*I giorni della violenza*, Italy, 1967). The score by Marcello Gigante fits the action onscreen to perfection and does nothing but enhance it. The streets of Wells City are always in a mudded-up mess,

Peter Martell (Pietro Martellanz) as Don Luis

and by the foggy breath coming from some of the actor's mouths in the town scenes, winter was upon the area, bringing into one's mind the film **Django** and its cold wintry muddy makeup.

The rest of the cast is first class, including the corrupt sheriff Lancaster, essayed by the great Piero Lulli, best remembered as Oaks in Giulio Questi's surreal western **Django Kill... If you Live Shoot**! (*Se sei vivo spara*, Italy, Spain, 1967). The versatile actor Ivan Staccioli here as Judge Kincaid helps hold this film together with his authoritative presence; Staccioli accrued ninety-two acting credits, including nice turns as Blackie in Giuliano Carnimeo's, **Have a Nice Funeral, My Friend... Sartana will Play** (*Buon funerale amigos!... paga Sartana*, Italy, Spain, 1970) and as Clinton in the odd Robert Woods starring film **Kill the Poker Player** (*Hai sbagliato... dovevi uccidermi subito!'* Italy, Spain, 1972). Fidel Gonzales is the comedy relief, and although portraying a Mexican- is in no way a typical stereotype. However, he is as he says "*lazy*," but he is honest and loyal to Slim Corbett, even in the face of death. The two girls who entertain Slim at the hotel in Wells City are played by the beautifully paired, Agnes Spaak (Doris) and Rosella Bergamonti (Dolly). Slim's married conquest at the beginning of the film Suzanne, is played by Linda Veras, best known in Italian western circles as Penny Bannington in **Run, Man, Run** (*Corri uomo corri*, Italy, France, 1968). But to me her turn as Jane a sexual conquest to nagging girlfriend of the William Berger character 'Banjo' in **Sabata** (Italy, 1969), is her finest performance in an oater

Peter Martell, while at times overplaying the Don Luis part in the film, was a fine actor who had a strong animal magnetism that came through on screen. Martell, aka Pietro Martellanza, appeared in numerous westerns, including but not limited to, **Black Tigress** (*Lola Colt*, Italy, 1967), **Long Days of Hate** (*I lunghi giorni dell'odio*, Italy, 1968), **The Unholy Four** (*Ciakmull - L'uomo della vendetta*, Italy, 1970) and **Gunman of Ave Maria** (*Il pistolero dell'Ave Maria*, Italy, Spain, 1969). As the story goes, Martell was supposed to appear alongside Bud Spencer in **God Forgives... I Don't** (*Dio perdona... Io no!*, Italy, Spain) in 1967 but broke his foot during a fight with his girlfriend right before the film was to start and was replaced with Terrence Hill, and the rest, as they say, is history.

The production companies behind this Italian film were Cinecris (also produced **Massacre Mania**) and Cineriz. An interesting side-note on Cineriz; among their many outstanding credits- they were the company that first distributed the Akira Kurosawa film **Yojimbo** (Yôjinbô, Japan, 1961), in Italy in 1963.

While I think that **God Made Them... I Kill Them** is a good movie; it misses its mark with the inclusion of doses of humor, and at times a way over the top villain (aided by a sadistic dwarf!) and an unlikeable hero. As noted above, the *Sugar Colt* character plays a bit of a dandy, but he has a noted past, and when the time comes, he uses his brains and brawn as much as he does his fast guns. All we know about Slim Corbett is that he is a hired *gunslinger* and an expensive one at that. Paolo Bianchini handles the directorial chores of his first western with skill and precision.

The film was fraught with money issues, and according to Gabriele Crisanti, it was Bianchini who added the comedic bits and doomed the picture financially as no one was interested in comedic westerns at that time. Bianchini was arrested along with Reed for staging a demonstration against the Vietnam War during filming . By all accounts, Reed was a professional on the set and got along well with his director, the only issues being production related. [2]

Dean Reed was born on September 22, 1938, in Denver, Colorado. He began as a pop singer, but during a trip to Latin American in the early 60s, his political views changed, and he became a proponent of socialism; he was sometimes referred to as the "communist cowboy." A massive star in Latin America, Eastern Europe, and the Soviet Union Reed eventually settled in East Germany. After a visit to the United States in 1985, he expressed a desire to return to America, but before he could, he committed suicide by drowning on June 13, 1986. His Italian westerns are as follows: **Buckaroo** (1967), **God Made Them.... I Kill Them** (1968), **The Nephews of Zorro** *(I nipoti di Zorro*, Italy, 1968), **Adios, Sabata** (1970), **Twenty Paces to Death** (*Veinte pasos para la muerte*, Italy, Spain, 1970) and **Karate, Fists, and Beans** (*Storia di karatè, pugni e fagioli*, Italy, Spain, 1973).

Paolo Bianchini's approach to directing would changed significantly for his next western **I Want Him Dead** after the comedic effects added to **God Made Them... I Kill Them** marred the finished product; **I Want Him Dead** would have none of that type of nonsense. Bianchini learned much from his first western, and when it came time to helm his second oater, he would produce a damn near perfect revenge western.

I Want Him Dead
Less than a minute into the film Clayton (Craig Hill) while resting with his sister Mercedes (Cristina Businari) [3] after a long day's ride to visit a friend who he is to buy land from, shoots down three men, who one would assume were there looking to rob Clayton of his savings, or there with rapist designs. Clayton stops in town, leaving his sister at the local saloon/hotel to rest as he heads out to meet his friend to complete the already decided on purchase of some land for $4000.

The problem is that the money Clayton made driving horses and cattle for the last few years is confederate currency, and as his friend says, it is virtually worthless with a truce between the north and the south looming. So, his friend suggests he go back to town and exchange those dollars for "pesos or Union dollars." After Clayton arrives back in town, he finds his sister dead and the killer has left behind a distinctive pouch. Clayton asks the bartender to call the sheriff and questions him about the pouch, finding out it belongs to a man named Jack Blood (Jose Manuel Martin) who works for the wealthy Mallak (Andrea Bosic). A drunk sitting at the bar sarcastically replies to Clayton that people die every day, to which Clayton responds with a backhand, sending the drunk flying. After recovering from the sudden assault, the man reaches for his gun, and Clayton draws, shooting him dead. All the violence is sudden in **I Want Him Dead**, even the color-tinted opening credits with its quickly cut excerpts from the film, all displaying one of any number of violent outbreaks or deadly conclusions. The world within Clayton travels in is corrupt and brutal; the Civil war, although waning, is still raging around him, and most of the men he encounters are disillusioned, injured, or sadists. The women are raped, ridiculed, placed into servitude, and abused.

> *"After a gunslinger's sister is kidnapped and murdered, his plans for vengeance become entangled in a plot to assassinate two generals to prolong the Civil War. "I Want Him Dead" is arguably one of Craig Hill's best westerns. A tight story, great direction, and acting and one of the best scores of the genre make it one of the best films in the Euro-western genre." -Tom Betts*

The man that Clayton killed at the bar was the brother of the sheriff, and within his office, Clayton is administered a severe beating (the first of many), for the killing. The sheriff tells Clayton he didn't care what he has to say about his "tramp" sister. Clayton is not a man though so easily kept down and manages to kick the gun out of the sheriff's hand and gets a jump on the sheriff and his two deputies, locking them up in a cell as he exits, telling the sheriff he is only out to kill Jack Blood.

Jose Manuel Martin as Jack Blood

Clayton, with the info garnered from the bartender, goes to have a look around the estate of Mallak. The wealthy Mallak is an arms dealer, sitting on a large stockpile of weapons and ammo, and if the truce happens, then he will stand to lose a significant amount of money. So, Mallak concocts a plan for Jack Blood and his gang to blow up the meeting place of a contingent of north and south leaders laying down the parameters of the upcoming terms of surrender. Mallak thinks that the killing of the generals in attendance will cause the war to ramp back up again, at least long enough for him to empty his cache of arms and ammo. While snooping around at Mallak's, Clayton is assisted by two women Almoa (Lea Massari) and Marisa (Licia Calderon), both in servitude to Mallak and both abused by the men around the estate. Mallak's plan has Jack and his men intercepting a confederate transport and taking the place of the those soldiers who were to be to guards at the meeting. Blood's men then in disguise as confederates are to blow up the building hosting the reception of the two generals. Clayton tries to save Marisa after she is caught spying on Mallak. In an exchange of gunfire, Marisa is fatally shot, but before she expires, she tells Clayton and Almoa about Mallak's plan to have Jack Blood assassinate the generals. Almoa, realizes that if she is left at the estate, she is as good as dead. She begs Clayton to take him with her, with the promise to lead him to the small cabin where Jack and his crew are, awaiting the time to embark on their job. At the cabin, Clayton thinks he can take Jack Blood and his men in with his pistol but is categorically wrong when they get a jump on him and beat the living hell out of him and leave him alive but tied to a chair with the cabin afire. Almoa, who had stayed safely back, rushes into the cabin and frees Clayton. At this point, the characters realize they need one another, giving the film another dimension. Almoa, initially desperate for help in freeing herself from the binds of Mallak, has now become emotionally attached to the stoic Clayton and he to her. **I Want Him Dead**, provides that emotional relationship between a man and a woman, something that many of these films did not attempt. It adds another layer to the film and helps sooth some of the rough edges as the violence is sudden and quite frequent.

The romance angle is an absolute necessity in this film, if not included, it would have been an excessively violent revenge film that would be a redundant affair awash in attendant violent impulses all the while presenting a soul-crushing pessimistic attitude. While in some movies, the nihilistic balls to the walls works, those are few and far between, and the ones that do work are usually spurred on by great acting, solid storytelling, and or artistic direction. A film like **Django** and its violent nihilism works because of the exceptional performance of Franco Nero along with a comic book styling and Sergio Corbucci's direction. **Black Jack** (Italy, Israel, 1968), another nihilistic affair, is a brilliant film because of a fantastic turn by Robert Woods as the titular character who burns the screen up with his fierce demented performance. There is nihilism in one the best the genre has to offer, **The Great Silence** (*Il grande silenzio*, Italy, France, 1968) which also boasts a romantic angle, but has the bad guys winning out in the end (well, depending on the ending)!

Clayton goes from the proverbial frying pan into the fire when he is accosted by the sheriff and his two deputies after finding Almoa a safe place to hide before he heads off to confront Jack Blood. In a scene similar to their earlier encounter, Clayton slaps the gun in the sheriff's hand, killing one deputy, and Clayton grabs the now dislodged weapon and finishes off this business before setting course for his final confrontation. The ending consists of two different showdowns- The first Jack Blood and Clayton and the other between Mallak and Blood's goons. Jack Blood versus Clayton is an excellently staged and executed fight scene thats a precursor to the outstanding Mallak-Gang finale. The ending ties things up beautifully and eliminates the last despicable characters and allows a bit of light into an otherwise bleak production. In the end, after Clayton recovers the money Mallak, was to pay Jack Blood with, he finally buys his plot of land and we learn that he cannot read and would rather not learn how to, staying to a point blissfully ignorant of the changing, industrial world encroaching around him, a man of instinct and simplicity, a man of the west!

Craig Hill's Clayton character shares a lot of similarities to his character Hank Fellows in what I believe is Hill's best Italian western Italian, **Taste of Killing** (Per il gusto di uccidere, Italy, Spain, 1966). Both are simple men who cannot read, but they understand how to use a gun and the value of money- Fellows even saying the only thing he can read is what follows behind a dollar sign. Each man is one dimensional in their pursuits, Hank in his pursuit of the almighty dollar and Clayton in his quest for revenge. Besides that, the films are both strikingly beautiful films and professionally directed. Tonino Valerii, the director of **Taste of Killing**, used in his film **A Bullet for the President** a similar pretense that was used in **I Want Him Dead**, in the trying to reignite the Civil war.

The film is nihilistic through most of its runtime but finally relents and allows good to overcome evil. Hill's Clayton is never presented as anything more than a simple hard-working man, a man just trying to save up enough money to buy a plot of land. Clayton and Almoa are thrust together out of necessity and are together at the end, firmly emotionally attached to each other after their perilous journey.

SAM PROTIV BANDE

GLAVNE ULOGE:
CRAIG HILL
GEORGE MARTIN
FERNANDO SANCHO

TONINO VALERI   NICO FIDENCO

Above: Craig Hill as Hank Fellows in **Taste of Killing** (1966)

Right: Croation Poster for what is arguably Craig Hill's best Italian Western **Taste of Killing** aka Lanky Fellow

I cannot say enough about how exquisite the direction by Bianchini is, as is the breathtaking cinematography by Ricardo Andreu. Many shots are startling in their clarity and construction. The master shots and the long shots in this film are particularly effective, giving life to the whole of the scenes. One must also make a note of the many wonderfully executed punch-ups. The gunmanship on display is also striking in its efficiency and sudden deadly eruptions. The brutal beatings that the Clayton figure sustains in the film are rather hard to watch and even harder to understand is his near-immortal therapeutic abilities.

The film is a violent opus that is clear in its vision and singlemindedness, delivering a damn near perfect revenge film. Maybe a bit too violent and redundancy are the things that hold this film back from the upper echelon of the genre, but I believe those things do not overly weigh the film down. This film is just a straight-forward revenge film that unfolds at a blistering pace. The inclusion of a significant female into the narrative gives the film an emotional character to help expand what would have been a rather one-dimensional film. A man of integrity who is motivated by vengeance helps rid the world of some undesirables and- in the process saves the states from more bloodshed that would have spelled if Jack Blood and his men would have successfully carried out Mallak's evil plan.

To this writer, you can put **I Want Him Dead, Hands of a Gunfighter** (Ocaso de un pistolero, Italy, Spain, 1965), and **Taste of Killing** at the top of Craig Hill's performances in the Italian western genre. Sadly, Hill would not appear in many other western films of note, appearing in average to below-average fare. The reason a lot of these films are so entertaining is the assembled casts. And this production is loaded with some amazing talent, including, Frank Brana, Andrea Bosic, Rick Boyd, Jose Manuel Martin, Lea Massari, and Jose Canalejas. Lucio Bompani was the production manager on **I Want Him Dead** and he ties the film back again to **Taste of Killing**, a film on which he was the executive producer. The film boasts one of the most exceptional scores in the genre by Nino Fiedenco and a scorching vocal song called "*Clayton,*" by Lida Lu, lyrics by Giuseppe Cassia.

Rick Boyd is one of the most recognizable faces in popular Italian film- he seemed to have the edgy psychopath down pat. Just a few of his many western appearances include: **Cjamango** (Italy, 1967), **A Sky Full of Stars for a Roof** (*E per tetto un cielo di stele*, Italy, 1968), **Adios, Sabata** (1970) and **Have a Good Funeral, My Friend... Sartana will Pay** (*Buon funerale amigos!... paga Sartana* , Italy, Spain, 1970). The Yugoslavian actor Andrea Bosic was prolific in the Italian western genre- His turn as Abel Murray in **Day of Anger** (*I giorni dell'ira*, Italy, W. Germany, 1967) is one of his most noteworthy, two other credits (among many) worth noting are: the superb heist-western **Two Faces of the Dollar** (*Le due facce del dollar*, Italy, France, 1967) and **Two Pistols and a Coward** (*Il pistolero segnato da Dio*, Italy, 1967). Frank Brana is a legendary Italian actor who appeared uncredited in all of Leone's '*Dollar*' films and **Once Upon A Time in the West** (*C'era una volta il West*, Italy, USA, 1968). Besides those films, what jumps out at this writer is Brana's rather nasty turns in **Django Kill... If You Live Shoot!** and **Fasthand** (*Mi chiamavano 'Requiescat'... ma avevano sbagliato*, Italy, Spain, 1973). Jose Manuel Martin was a participant in many fine Italian westerns, including being memorably choked out by Alex Cord's character Alex McCord in **A Minute to Pray, A Second to Die** (*Un minuto per pregare, un istante per morire*, Italy, USA, 1968). A few of the other significant oaters Martin appeared in include: **Gunfight at High Noon** (*El sabor de la venganza, Italy, Spain*, 1964), **A Pistol for Ringo** (*Una pistola per Ringo*, Italy, Spain, 1965), **Taste of Killing** (1966), **Five Giants from Texas** (*I 5 della vendetta, Italy, Spain*, 1966) and **A Bullet for the General** (*Quién sabe?*, Italy,1966).

The highly acclaimed actress Lea Massari appeared in this film her only Italian western as Aloma and turns in an emotional performance as a strong yet loving character. Getting an actress, the caliber of Massari for this production was considered quite a coup by the production companies.

Jose Canalejas has another one of those well-known spaghetti mugs, appearing in numerous westerns in credited and uncredited turns. Canalejas appeared in some of the greatest Italian westerns ever made including, in Leone's first two '*Dollar*' films, **Django, Taste of Killing, The Ugly Ones** (*El precio de un hombre: The Bounty Killer*, Italy, Spain, 1966), **The Hellbenders** (*I crudely*, Italy, Spain, 1967) and **The Mercenary** (*Il mercenario*, Italy, Spain, 1968) Craig Hill relocated to Europe in the early 1960s to find work, there he worked steady in various genres, finally settling down in Spain in 1978, where he remained until his death in 2014 at the age of eighty-eight. Hill began his Italian western career with some great films, including **Hands of a Gunfighter, A Taste for Killing,** and **I Want Him Dead**, but his choice of oaters thereafter was not up to par with these early efforts. Hill's complete Italian western career: **Hands of a Gunfighter** (1965), **A Taste for Killing** (1966), **Fifteen Scaffolds for a Killer** (*15 forche per un assassin*, Italy, Spain, 1967), **Rick and John, Conquerors of the West** (*Ric e Gian alla conquista del West*, Italy, 1967), **Adios Hombre** (*7 pistole per un massacre*, Italy, Spain, 1967), **Bury Them Deep** (*All'ultimo sangue*, Italy, 1968), **I Want Him Dead** (1968), **No Graves on Boot Hill** (*Tre croci per non morire*, Italy, 1968), **And the Crows will Dig Your Grave**

(*Los buitres cavarán tu fosa*, Italy, Spain, 1971), **Drummer of Vengeance** (*Il giorno del giudizio*, Italy, UK, 1971), **The Masked Thief** (*In nome del padre, del figlio e della Colt*, Italy, Spain, 1971), **An Animal Called Man** (*Un animale chiamato uomo*, Italy, Spain, 1972), **My Horse... My Gun... Your Widow** (*Tu fosa será la exacta... amigo*, Italy, Spain, 1972), **Return of the Holy Ghost** (*Bada alla tua pelle Spirito Santo!*, Italy, 1972), **Stay Away from Trinity... When he comes to Eldorado** (*Scansati... a Trinità arriva Eldorado*, Italy, 1972) and **Court Martial** (*Corte marziale*, Italy, 1974).

I Want Him Dead was an Italian-Spanish co-production filmed in Almeria, Spain (exteriors) and S.C.O. Studios (interiors), Rome, Italy. Production companies include Centauro Films out of Spain, consisting of Joaquin Romero Marchent, Agustin Aredina, and Felix Duran, and Inducine of Rome, which was headed by the two listed producers on the film Corrado Ferlaino and Enrico Verga. Credited as the writer on this film is Carlos Sarabia, and he only has this one credit, and according to Marco Giusti, "on the script preserved at the Experimental Center in Rome, there is only the name of our Adriano Bolzoni." Carlos Sarabia possibly being a fictional writer named to stay in line for some co-production requirement. Bolzoni would make sense as he was highly respected and contributed to the likes of A **Fistful of Dollars**, **Minnesota Clay** (Italy, France, Spain, 1964), **My Name is Pecos** (*2 once di piombo*, Italy, 1966), **Requiescant** (Italy. Monaco, W. Germany, 1967), and **The Mercenary**, among numerous others.

The film **My Name is Pecos** has a similar protagonist in Pecos Martinez to Clayton in **I Want Him Dead**, a man who has one thing on his mind, vengeance- exacting revenge for a murdered family member(s). **My Name is Pecos**, a gutsy straightforward revenge flick- is aided by a great turn by the always intense Robert Woods-- And like **I Want Him Dead** is a film full of violence and is a non-wavering vengeance train on a single-minded collision course of retribution.

Gatling Gun
With one western under his belt in 1968 and a successful one at that, Bianchini was selected to helm a western starring Robert Woods (who had appeared in Bianchini's 1967 film **Massacre Mania**, aka **Hypnos**) called **Damned Hot Day of Fire** aka **Gatling Gun**. *Loaded* with an all-star cast, an interesting if too far-reaching story, one would imagine that the film would be Bianchini's best western, possibly topping his great **I Want Him Dead**. Ah, but **Gatling Gun** misses its mark here and there, but is wildly entertaining and just outside the genres upper echelon- And if the truth be told, is not as good as **I Want Him Dead**.

All the components were assembled for this to be a great western, including such superb thespians as Robert Woods, John Ireland, Evelyn Stewart, Claudie Lang, Gerard Herter, George Rigaud, Roberto Camardiel, Furio Meniconi, Rada Rassimov and a professional director and crew.

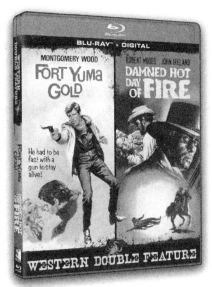

Left: Dorado Films DVD release of **Gatling Gun**
Right: Mill Creeks release of **Fort Yuma Gold** (Per pochi dollari ancora , Italy, France,1966) and Damned Hot Day of Fire aka **Gatling Gun**

Captain Chris Tanner is accused and found guilty by a military tribunal of the murder of three government officials- And Richard Gatlin (Ennio Balbo), who was developing a secret weapon for the North, a rapid-fire machine gun, is missing. Whether the weapon was completed or not, the military is not sure, but they feel if it was that Chris was trying to exploit it for financial gain. But we the viewer know that Chris was not the perpetrator of the crimes, they were pulled off by two men working for the bandit Tarpas (John Ireland). Those men are rewarded upon their return by being killed, including one who receives a knife to the gut, flicked from between the toes of Tarpas! After killing the two men Tarpas turns to a mystery man and says, "I *hate* witnesses!" Rada Rassimov of The **Good, The Bad, and The Ugly** fame, appearing here as Maria gets drowned in a bubble bath within the first few minutes of the film; Maria is one of the three whom Tanner is supposed to have murdered. Tanner's boss Pinkerton (Tom Felleghy) though believes that Chris is innocent and concocts a plan to free him from prison. Tanner takes over the identity of a Jeremiah Grant (Furio Meniconi), whom Pinkerton essentially cons into trading places with Chris. Pinkerton can eventually release Grant on the offense that Pinkerton has charged him with, the understanding being that Tanner is to return before thirty days with evidence to prove his innocence, and Grant will be released before facing the gallows as Tanner. So, Tanner heads to La Cruzas to meet up with a northern sympathizer, Doctor Alan Curtis (Roberto Camardiel). Tanner, while in the area, will stay with Grant's family, which consists of two brothers, one reserved and thoughtful, and the other a hothead! The younger brother detests Chris because he thinks he killed his brother. When the rage takes over the boy, he drags Tanner behind his horse, and later in the film, his anger causes the death of his brother and himself when he reaches for a gun against impossible odds. The shadowy figure Tarpas works for is revealed to be Ryckert (George Rigaud); one of the men thought to have been killed amongst the government officials but has faked his death and has concocted a plan to extract one million dollars from the Union States for the safe return of Gatlin. Tarpas though figures that he will play both sides, thus offering the Confederate's the Gatling Gun for one million dollars in jewels. Tanner begins to snoop around and with the help of the Doctor begins to put the pieces together, including the fact that Ryckert was not dead and buried. One thing behind Tarpas's motivation to acquire such wealth is he believes that if he can cover his ex-*flame* in jewels, then he can win her back, but Martha Simpson (Claudie Lange), wants nothing to do with the "*Half-breed*" Tarpas anymore. Tanner uses Simpson to garner information on Tarpas to which she happily supplies after a vigorous lovemaking session. When Tanner asks Martha, "If he (Tarpas) is her man?" she replies, "I'd rather marry a pig… Could you see me- I couldn't see me marrying a half-breed, could you, Jerry?" When Tanner calls Tarpas a "poor Half-breed," Martha tells him that Tarpas will not be poor for long and when he does become rich, he is ready to cover her body in Jewels. Tarpas will have two million dollars soon but reiterates that even though he might be the richest man on earth, he will always be a "half-breed." When Tanner turns to leave, Martha Simpson asks if she will see him again? Tanner replies, "I wouldn't want to contaminate the perfect example of the pure race. You see, my Grandmother was a Cherokee Indian!" Once Tarpas finds out that Martha has spilled her guts to Tanner, he drags her before Ryckert, who returns the favor with a bullet to her abdomen. Tanner, of course, gets to the bottom of things with the help of Doc and eliminates the bad guys.

John Ireland plays the part of Tarpas, and its really an odd turn by the great actor. Tarpas is ruthless, but madly in love with the woman he once was in a relationship with- she now rejects because of his Mexican American heritage. Ireland has his character pull his shoes off repeatedly and goes about scratching his feet madly. As if this foot scratching was his definition of an uncouth *Half-breed*. Overall his portrayal is a mixed bag, ruthless, crude, lovelorn and sentimental. All Tarpas wants to do is buy his old girlfriend back, covering her with the jewels he will be getting from the Confederates for the Gatling gun. The film **Requiem for a Gringo** has a similar pretense with Fernando Sancho's character Carranza wanting to cover his (unbeknown to him) two-timing girl in jewels. Jose Luis Merino, the director of **Requiem for a Gringo** (among others), was one of four writers on **Gatling Gun**, which also included Paolo Bianchini, Claudio Failoni, and Franco Calderoni. [4]

The great Robert Woods does an outstanding job in the lead, giving the film energy and keeping the narrative together, which was seemingly ready to unravel at any minute. The scale of the film is vast, and while **I Want Him Dead** is a straight-forward revenge affair, **Gatling Gun**, is a film of a much larger scale. Chris Tanner is doing detective work, which infuses the film with an interesting angle and keeps the film fresh. Like **I Want Him Dead**, this film also has the Civil war raging in the background, never directly presented in battle scenes but included in an offhanded manner.

Paolo Bianchini does a solid job directing, including some beautiful night scenes, highlighted by a great staged shootout at a cemetery. One would find it hard to imagine that no one in Dallas would know Jeremiah Grant, whose family farm was just outside of town. The cinematography by Francisco Marin Harrada is one of the highlights of the film, especially in the above-mentioned cemetery scene.

Gatling Gun was filmed in Madrid and on the Cinecitta Americano set. A Spanish-Italian co-production. The producer was Edmondo Amati. The Production companies involved, Atlantida film out of Madrid and Fida Cinematografica, Rome. The cast is filled with some of the finest Italian popular actors. Evelyn Stewart plays the confederate Belle Boyd, Stewart appeared in numerous westerns including **Blood for a Silver Dollar** (*Un dollaro bucato*, Italy, France, 1965) and **Adios Gringo** (Italy, France, Spain, 1965). The gorgeous Claudie Lange as Martha Simpson appeared most notably in **$100,000 per Killing** (*Per 100.000 dollari t'ammazzo*, Italy, 1968) and **To Hell and Back** (*Uno di più all'inferno*, Italy, 1968). Who can forget the German actor Gerd Herter's sadism in full effect in **The Big Gundown**? But Herter's best performance in a western I believe is in the superb heist picture **Two Faces of the Dollar** (*Le due facce del dollar*, Italy, France, 1967).

Roberto Camardiel plays the doctor Alan Curtis, he also appeared as a doctor in **Adios Gringo** and **Adios Hombre**. Camardiel has the distinction of his character in **Arizona Colt** (Italy, France, 1966) being called "*Whiskey*" and his character in **Arizona Colt Returns** (*Arizona si scatenò... e li fece fuori tutti!*, Italy, Spain, 1970), referred to as "*Double Whiskey.*" The Spanish born Camardiel, though, is undoubtedly best remembered for his roles in **A Fistful of Dollars** as the clerk in Tucumcari and as Zorro (or Sorrow) in **Django Kill... If You Live Shoot!**. Speaking of **Django Kill... If You Live Shoot!**, the most infamous scene in Giulio Questi's film is the digging the gold bullets out of the evil Oaks (Pierro Lulli); Chris Tanner digs a bullet out of his hand in a garish close-up. Look for Fidel Gonzales, who played Job in **God Made Them... I Kill Them**; he appears uncredited briefly at the beginning of **Gatling Gun,** as the helper of Gatlin.

The score by Piero Piccioni is not a typical Italian western score, mixing somber organ-heavy tunes along with jazzy accompaniments.

In Italy Gatling Gun preformed moderately well at the box office, the highest grossing of Bianchini's westerns there. Gatling Gun had its premiere in Italy on December 13, 1968. Bianchini's other 1968 westerns God Made Them... I Kill Them premiered in Italy on April 29 and I Want Him Dead on June 15, which also first premiered in Italy. [5]

A very competent film that in my opinion needed to be tightened up a bit and the scope is maybe too wide. The Tarpas character is more caricature than a fleshed out character. Has some great scenes and some moments of pushing the plausibility too far! But, besides some easily overlooked flaws, the film is highly entertaining!

Gatling Gun aka **Damned Hot Day of Fire** was released on home video in the United States on VHS under the title, Machine Gun Killers. The front cover depicts soliders from the civil war. The film while set during the conflict between the states did not show any battle scenes, only intrigue behind the lines. The *Meteor Video* release of the film was only 86 minutes, even though the back stated the runtime as 98 minutes. The back cover lists the actors as: John Irland (John Ireland), Robert Woods and Everlyn Stewart (Evelyn). Meteor Video released the film in 1988.

Hey Amigo! A Toast to your Death

After three Italian westerns in 1968, Bianchini would revisit the genre only once more that being the 1970 poverty row affair **Hey Amigo! A Toast to your Death** (*Ehi amigo... sei morto!,* Italy, 1970). It is almost as if Bianchini tried to go back and make another **I Want him Dead**, replacing one aging American actor Craig Hill for another in Wayde Preston. Both actors were most famously known for their roles in American television series, Hill for **Whirlybirds** (1957-1960) and Preston for **Colt .45** (1957-1960). And although **Hey Amigo! A Toast to your Death** is a rather cheap-looking affair in comparison to **I Want Him Dead** and **Gatling Gun**- It has some wonderfully bizarre moments, an unflinching Wayde Preston in the lead and Marco Zuanelli as the treacherous El Loco, who turns in an intriguing multidimensional performance.

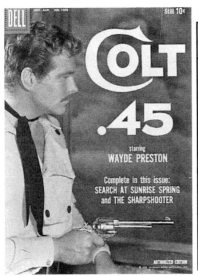

Wayde Preston Italian western Filmography:
A Long Ride to Hell (Vivo per la tua morte, Italy, Spain, 1968), **Today it's me... Tomorrow You!**, (Oggi a me... domani a te!, Italy, 1968), **Wrath of God** (L'ira di Dio, Italy, Spain, 1968), **God Will Forgive my Gun** (Dio perdoni la mia pistola, Italy, 1969), **Tierra Brava** (Pagó cara su muerte, Italy, Spain, 1969), **A Man Called Sledge** (Italy, USA, 1970), **Sartana in the Valley of Death** (Sartana nella valle degli avvoltoi, Italy, 1970), **Hey Amigo! A Toast to your Death!** (1971)

Wayde Preaston starred in The Warner Brothers produced television series **Colt .45** from 1957 until 1960. Dell Comics released nine comic book tie-ins from August 1958 until 1961

And yet again, we have a protagonist who is dead set on revenge and will not veer from that course. And harking back to **God Made Them... I Kill Them**, Preston's character, has a Mexican sidekick, this one named El Loco (Marco Zuanelli) who saddles up next to him. But Job (Fidel Gonzales) in God Made Them is a sympathetic character, blindly assisting Slim Corbett; El Loco (Marco Zuanelli) is a cunning man who while lazy like Job, is malicious and deceptive. The beginning of the film shot at De Laurentiis Studios in Rome shows the western town is in severe disrepair. Just check the way it looks in this film compared to the way it appeared only a few years prior in **A Minute to Pray, A Second to Die** (*Un minuto per pregare, un instante per morire,* Italy, USA, 1968).

Italian Poter for **Hey Amigo! A toast to your Death!**

A group of bandit's rides into town and gathers up all the residents, holding them hostage. They force the postmaster 'Doc' Williams to help them rob the arriving stagecoach which is carrying gold. The townsfolk call Doc a "coward" and accuse him of being part of the bandit gang because he is allowing them to rob the stagecoach without incident. Doc, though, knows that the ruthless gang will have no qualms about mowing down the townsfolk if they do not play along. He must swallow his pride for the safety of the town. When the stage arrives, Doc goes out to meet it and tries to alert the stagecoach crew of the bandits, but the bandits open fire, cutting down the men. Doc survives the onslaught. When one of the women whose husband was killed in the attack asks Doc what he is going to do, he says, "*Now I'm going to kill! Kill them all.*" From there, Doc rides out in pursuit of the gang, dressed in all black, from his pistolero days one would assume. As Doc sets out on his mission of vengeance, it reminds us of Clayton from **I Want Him Dead.** Here we have another man seeking revenge on a mission of death and will not be sidetracked for any reason.

The bandits are a despicable lot, including the leader Burnett, played by the great Rik Battaglia who is ably assisted by Aldo Berti, who plays the sadistic rapist Black, a character that has much in common to and is dressed similarly to his character in **Go with God, Gringo** (*Vaya con dios gringo*, Italy, Spain, 1966). Doc rides into an accompanying town, and there is alerted by El Loco, after buying him a bottle of tequila and calling him "*hombre*" that three men were positioned around town to kill him. After Doc shoots the men down (paid to kill Doc by Burnett), he is thrown in jail for thirty days and is sprung by El Loco, who uses a wire metal with which he saws the bars on the window, a tool he also plays some electrified guitar sounds on throughout the movie. When Doc asks El Loco why he is helping him out, El Loco replies, "Cause you're the only person to call me 'hombre.' I do not know if you know this, Amigo, but everyone around here thinks I'm crazy. They must think so because I love the air, the sun, liberty, and all those things! The only thing I don't care about is money!" El Loco's tone changes once Doc reveals that there were $100,000 gold dollars taken from the stage.

The two men part ways with Doc racing off on his trusty steed and El Loco on his slow, prodding mule, but El Loco decides to follow Doc. The ever-stoic Doc finds the bandits holed up in a deserted town. Black notices Doc's horse tied up outside the ghost town, and when the inevitable gunfire begins, Black slips into the church where the money is hidden and makes off with it. El Loco, who has arrived in the ghost town, shows his true colors after being caught by Burnett's men, offering Burnett some information for cash. He informs Burnett that Doc is out of jail and in pursuit of the gang. Burnett pays El Loco back by hanging him by his neck, making him stand on grain sacks (resembling the Tuco hanging scene at the end of **The Good, The Bad and The Ugly**), which Burnett shoots holes in and heads out to confront Doc. El Loco is eventually freed by Doc, just as he is about to expire when Doc shoots the rope that suspends him.

After a very nicely designed shootout in town, including a rather flamboyant end to the Burnett character, Doc sets out on foot (along with El Loco on his mule) after Black, who had taken off on his horse. A point that popped into my head as Doc walked through the countryside was, why didn't he go back into the ghost town and take one of the bandit's horses? After a long, arduous trek, Doc and El Loco arrive at a farmhouse and find a woman clutching the body of a dead man. In a fog-shrouded, bordering on a psychedelic flashback, we get the story of how Black killed the woman's husband and then raped her. After the men bury the woman's husband, they hear a gunshot, and as the two men ride away, in a perfectly framed shot, shown are two newly placed crosses. After securing a horse, Doc realizes that Black has changed direction and is heading back to town- And Black has rape on his mind- looking for the woman (Anna Malsson) whom he attempted to molest in the opening scene! Although never given a proper name or her relation to Doc, one can only assume she is Doc's woman. Black, arrives back in town and confronts the woman in her home, tying her to her bed.

When Doc arrives back in town- he hears the woman screaming and kicks in her door. The door lands atop the momentarily startled Black. The two men begin fighting which spells out into the street. Black will not divulge where the gold is, even after the severe beating he sustains and having his head submerged in water, just as was done to Doc in the opening scene. Before Black can say anything, a shot rings out, and he falls to the ground dead. Doc smells a rat and sets out to locate the gold. He visits the ghost town and finds E Loco there playing the organ in the church, but no gold.

Doc, after he leaves El Loco in the ghost town, is stopped by a small group of Mexicans' who ask him where "Burnett's gold" is. After dispatching the gang, Doc stops El Loco as he rides toward Mexico. Doc yells out, "You going Loco?" Which is the first time Doc has referred to him as Loco! That being symbolic in that Doc knows that El Loco is not his "hombre." Throughout the film, El Loco has said that if he got hold of some money, he would return to Mexico! Doc cuts open El Loco's saddlebags and out pours the stolen gold dollars. Doc says, "Burnett's gold," which would point to El Loco as being the one who sent the Mexican bandits after Doc. The dejected El Loco rides off without even one dollar.

The film **Three Silver Dollars** (*Dai nemici mi guardo io!*, Italy, Spain, 1968) jumps to my mind after watching this film. In that film, the Gringo Alan Burton (Charles Southwood) is helped out of various situations by a Mexican named Hondo (Julian Mateos). Why Hondo is helping Burton out is because he wants to gets his hands on a silver dollar that Alan has in his possession- the dollar has some numbers etched in it- if all three silver dollars (Hence the title) are located and placed together, then it reveals the location of a buried treasure. But the Hondo character is a violent man, who is only playing the part of good Samaritan; El Loco though, is never shown to be vicious, but we must assume him the person who shot Black in the back from afar or paid to have it done.

The film is a low budgeted affair and it shows but being the professional that he is Bianchini turned the film into an enjoyable experience with some inventive camera angles, grungy scenery, and dreamlike scenes intermittent. Clocking in at eighty-four minutes the films unfolds at an extraordinary pace and while small in scope is a highly enjoyable romp. Wayde Preston changes expressions seldom and goes about the business of vengeance with a stoic, dour expression. Mixing the faux-cheery yet malicious personality of El Loco along with Preston's Doc gives the film a certain unstable atmosphere as the viewer can see through the fake façade of El Loco and wonders what lengths his desire for gold will send him. Besides the Doc, El Loco, Burnet and Black character no other character is in the forefront for any time. Its about those four characters and the actors who are portraying them; the whole of the film essentially relying on them to make it work. And one could not go wrong with the likes of Rik Battaglia and Aldo Berit as the two main villains. Battalia who had a long career appearing in many different genres was a natural as a villain, who can forget his sadistic turn in Black Jack, where he appeared as Skinner. Berti as the sidekick Marinero to Frank Wolff's Aguilar in **A Stranger in Town** (*Un dollaro tra i dent*, Italy, USA, 1967) is the role that probably is ingrained in the minds of most Italian western fans, especially in the U.S. where **A Stranger in Town** along with **The Stranger Returns** (*Un uomo, un cavallo, una pistola*, Italy, W. Germany, USA, 1967) were in constant rotation on *TNT*. Wayde Preston participated in eight Italian westerns including, **A Long Ride from Hell** (1968), **Today it's me… Tomorrow it's You!** (1968), **The Wrath of God** (1968), **God will Forgive my Gun** (1969), **Tierra Brava** (1969), **A Man Called Sledge** (1970), **Sartana in the Valley of Death** (1970), **Hey Amigo! A Toast to your Death** (1970. Preston after retiring from acting became a flight instructor in California.

Renato Savino wrote the story for **Hey Amigo! A Toast to your Death** and the screenplay along with Roberto Colangeli. Savino also wrote the story/screenplay for **Chapaqua's Gold** *(L'oro dei bravados*, Italy, France, 1970) and **His Name was King** (*Lo chiamavano King*, Italy, 1971) and the story for **Vengeance** (*Joko invoca Dio... e muori* , Italy, W. Germany, 1968) and **Hey Amigo! A Toast to your Death**. Savino was the production manager on **Vengeance** and Hey Amigo! Mario Zuanelli also appeared in the westerns: **Once Upon a Time in the West** (uncredited), **Sabata, Sartana's Here… Trade your Pistol for a Coffin, Chapaqua's Gold, His Name was King, Beyond the Frontiers of Hate** (*Al di là dell'odio* , Italy, 1972) and **Son of Zorro** (*Il figlio di Zorro*, Italy, Spain, 1973). Filmed at De Laurentiis and Elios Studios. Produced by Gatto Cinemagrafica. Mila Vitelli Valenza did the costume design, Valenza was of course the wife of the legendary low-budget auteur Demofilo Fidani. The music by Carlo Savina is testosterone fueled electric guitar riffs, but it does become redundant as the film progress; the vocal theme song is a macho piece of

Aldo Berti as "Black" in **Hey Amigo!**.

bravado sung by the great Don Powell, "Hey Amigo! you're dead." [6]After his last western Bianchini would direct in various genres, before working exclusively in television as a director from 2003-2009. Bianchini directed the drama, **Bright Flight** (*Il sole dentro,* Italy, 1972), as recently as 2012 and is currently at work on a comedy called **Frammenti**. Paolo Bianchini was a professional at work in his Italian western films, and although working with limited budgets turned out quality product. I think that **I Want Him Dead** without a doubt belongs in the second tier of Italian westerns. **Gatling Gun** is a remarkably intricate and complex film that although a bit vast in its scope is wildly engagingly and utterly entertaining. **God Made Them... I Kill Them**, is hampered by an unlikeable protagonist and its small scope. **Hey Amigo! A Toast to Your Death**, although riddled with money problems, is a straightforward revenge flick with flashes of brilliance and for what Bianchini was forced to work (low budget, dilapidated back lots) with in this film, it really showcases his technical prowess in the directors chair!

End Notes

[1]. **Massacre Mania** aka Hypnos can be found on a few sources, including a Greek VHS, sans English sub or dub. I have never seen an English sub or dub of this film. Even Robert Woods, the main actor in the movie himself, has never seen an English sub or dub of it.

[2]. From Marco Giusti's invaluable book, *Dizionario del Western all'Italiana.*

[3]. Cristina Businari, Miss Italy, 1967.

[4]. "Of the many names that sign script and titles, Bianchini says only Claudio Failoni and Franco Calderoni who with them had really written the subject and screenplay, Calderoni was a journalist who had worked to find news about the weapon protagonist of the film, the **Gatling Gun** of the American title." Marco Giusti- Dizionario del *Western all'Italiana.*

[5]. Box office in Italy only: **God Made Them... I Kill Them** 356.966.000 Lira, **I Want Him Dead** 278.773.000 Lira, **Gatling Gun** 380.190.000 Lira, **Hey Amigo! A Toast to your Death!** 184.030.000. - *Spaghetti Western Bible.*

[6]. Gatto Cinematografica was composed of Renato Savino and Otello Colangeli. *Dizionario del Western all'Italiana*

*To read Eugenio Ercolani's (author of *Darkening the Italian Screen*), take on Paolo Bianchini please turn to page # 99

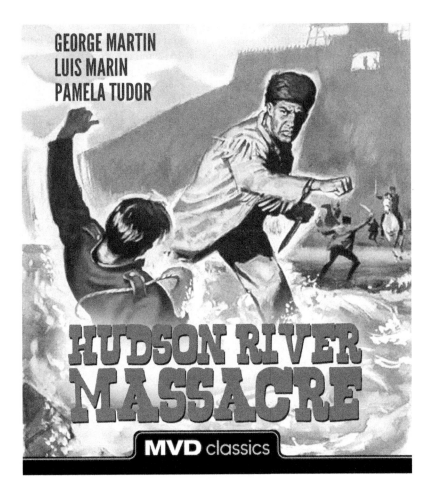

Hudson River Massacre *aka Canadian Wilderness (I tre del Colorado, Italy, Spain, 1965) was released by MVD classics in February of 2020. It stars the great Spanish actor George Martin (Francisco Martínez Celeiro), along with Pamela Tudor, Diana Lorys and Giulia Rubini. Directed by Amando de Ossorio, who is best known for helming the four films in the* **"Blind Dead"** *series of films. de Ossorio also directed George Martin in another oater, that being the 1964 film* **Tomb of the Pistolero** *(La tumba del pistolero, Spain, 1964). While Amando de Ossorio's western* **Tomb of the Pistolero** *(his only western directing credit besides* **Hudson River Massacre***) is not very good, his* **Hudson River Massacre** *with this release by MVD Classics has changed this reviewers opinion of it drastically.* *Turn to page 152 for a review of this MVD Classics release.*

Chuck Cirino Interview

I think one would be hard pressed to find a person more versatile in the film world than Chuck Cirino. I first became aware of Chuck when I heard his fantastic work on the soundtrack of Chopping Mall (USA) back in 1986. Chuck Cirino is not only a composer; he is essentially a jack of all trades when it comes to working behind the scenes: hell, he even works as an actor. I know Chuck is a fan of Ennio Morricone and Italian westerns in general and I jumped at the chance to interview him.

M.H. Were you a fan of westerns growing up?

C.C. I was not a fan of westerns growing up until I saw FISTFUL OF DOLLARS. Then I became a fan of Italian Westerns, but not yet a fan of American Westerns. Once Peckinpah got started making movies I began to appreciate American Westerns more. I still believe Americans, for the most part do not make great westerns. They get it right about 10% of the time. The best American Western in my opinion is DANCE WITH WOLVES.

M.H. What is your favorite Italian western?

C.C. My favorite western is THE GOOD, THE BAD AND THE UGLY.

M.H. When did you first become familiar with Italian westerns?

C.C. I became familiar with Italian Westerns when my high school friend, Jeff Siesser dragged me to see a double bill of FISTFUL OF DOLLARS and FOR A FEW DOLLARS MORE. I was hooked and mesmerized at that point.

M.H. How would you rank the Leone westerns?

C.C. Leone westerns in the order I love them:
1. *The Good, the Bad and the Ugly*
2. *For a Few Dollars More*
3. *Fistful of Dollars*
4. *Once Upon a Time in the West*
5. *My Name is Nobody*
6. *Duck You Sucker*

M.H. What is your favorite non-Leone westerns?

C.C. My favorite non-Leone spaghetti western is SABATA. But there are several others that rate right up there with it including, THE MERCENARY, NAVAJO JOE, DEATH RIDES A HORSE, THE BIG GUNDOWN, FIVE MAN ARMY and of course the TRINITY pictures.

M.H. Who is your favorite actor that appeared in Italian westerns?

C.C. My favorite western actor must be LEE VAN CLEEF. I cannot imagine him in anything other than a western. He's got the looks and the attitude. My favorite Italian (born) western actor is TERENCE HILL. He never fails to give a great performance and usually makes me laugh in the process.

M.H. What made the Italian western unique in your eyes?

Lee Van Cleef as Sabata

C.C. What made the Italian Western unique in my eyes is the music, the art direction, the costumes and the set design. The plots are often about revenge, fortune and glory... I love that. The attention to details on every level is what makes the Italian Western great.

M.H. Favorite vocal song?

C.C. My favorite Italian Western score with a vocal song is THE RETURN OF RINGO. The line... "We are fearless men..." gets to me every time. My favorite Italian Western score without a vocal is THE GOOD, THE BAD AND THE UGLY.

M.H. Most underrated Italian western?

C.C.. I believe the most underrated Italian Western is SABATA. I love all the gimmicks used in that film. From the silver dollar being thrown to trigger yet another weapon to the parkour jumping Native American character. Great film with great music!

Left: USA Release. **Right:** 7" Japanese Release, **A Fistful of Dollars**

Dennis Capicik's Italian Westen- Round-UP of Reviews!

A MAN CALLED DJANGO (W Django!, Italy, 1971)

In what was their fourth and final spaghetti western collaboration, the always-popular Anthony Steffen and director Edoardo Mulargia were simply going through the motions here, and in spite of the film's relatively skillful technical credits and enjoyably brisk pace, it also confirms your conviction that, by the early 'Seventies, spaghetti westerns were beginning to show signs of repetitiveness and exhaustion.

One of the countless unofficial rip-offs of Sergio Corbucci's **Django** (1966), that also borrows substantially from a number of other, bigger-budgeted films, including—inevitably!—the highly-respected works of Sergio Leone, the film opens with Django (Anthony Steffen) wandering into the town of La Puerta, which has been taken over by both Mexican and American bandits to serve as their (quote) "hideout". Immediately upon his arrival, Django gets a lit stick of dynamite thrown at his feet by an unnamed bandit (Remo Capitani). Rather than faze the recipient of this unexpected 'welcoming gift' in the least, Django proves his mettle by ever-so-calmly-and-cockily lighting his cigar on the burning fuse before tossing the TNT right back at him. Following this brazen act of defiance, Django is given an enthusiastic welcome by Paco (Donato Castellenata), one of La Puerta's last remaining residents and owner of the local saloon, who proclaims, "It does my heart good to see the likes of you in this town!" As it happens, Paco's promiscuous wife Lola (Esmeralda Barros) is having an affair with Jeff (Stelio Candelli), the leader of the occupying gang. In a fortuitous circumstance, Django rescues Carranza (Glauco Onorato) from being lynched (which results in one of the film's many elaborately-staged gunfights) in the hopes that Carranza can help him locate three outlaws who, two years earlier, had raped and killed his wife. Django and Carranza then go hunting for this trio of perpetrators, all of whom are now prominent gunrunners along the U.S. / Mexican border.

AMCD is highlighted by a number of shaky alliances and double-crosses. 'Clint clone' Steffen is at his usual squinty-eyed best, and his laconic demeanor plays well alongside Onorato's colorful Carranza character, creating a dynamic that was clearly modeled after Eastwood's and Wallach's uneasy, mutually-distrustful partnership in Leone's **The Good, the Bad and the Ugly** (*Il Buono, il brutto, il cattivo*, Italy, 1966). In what turns out to be one of many references to Leone's oeuvre within Nino

64

Stresa's derivative script (including the 'music box' motif from Leone's **For A Few Dollars More** [*Per qualche dollari di più*, Italy, 1965]), **AMCD's** playful nature is obvious right from the very beginning when, after witnessing Django's handy handling of that lit stick of TNT (a classic riposte to a hurled insult if ever there was one!), Paco exclaims excitedly, "A trick like that is worth a *fistful of dollars* in my book!" As an interesting aside, Spanish character actor Fernando Sancho had also played Carranza characters in both Umberto Lenzi's earlier Nino Stresa-scripted western **Go For Broke** (*Tutto per tutto*, Italy, 1968) and José Luis Merino's stylish **Requiem for a Gringo** (*Réquiem para el gringo*, Spain/Italy, 1968).

In keeping with his usual unidimensional approach to the material, Steffen's black-clad bounty hunter 'rides' (note quotes) into town with that by-now-customary overconfidence displayed by innumerable western heroes/antiheroes before him... even if he has been reduced to just his saddle *sans* any horse to go with it (*See screen shot above- MH*). With nothing but revenge on his mind, Django is indifferent to just about everything else, including the spoils of his bounty-hunting ("What's the use of savin' it, sheriff? I could be dead tomorrow!"), and he only appears to be in his element when he's either scheming or gunning-down the film's vast array of duplicitous characters.

Overlooking the film's all-too-obvious imitative streak, **A Man Called Django** is nevertheless energetic and engaging, which is a testament to Mulargia's effectiveness as a director, whose reliance on non-stop action keeps things moving along whenever the narrative threatens to slow down too much. Populated by a large number of then-prominent Italian actor/stuntmen—including Gilberto Galimberti, Benito Stefanelli, Omero Capanna and former "Superargo" himself, "Ken Wood"/Giovanni Cianfriglia—**AMCD's** ludicrously high body count most certainly keeps them all busy as they stage a seemingly endless amount of shootouts, fisticuffs and all sorts of other spry and spritely acrobatics. All this was efficiently-lensed by veteran DP Marcello Masciocchi (who also lent his talents to both **A Stranger in Town** [*Un dollar tra I denti*, Italy, 1967] and **The Stranger Returns** [*Un uomo, un cavallo, una pistola*, Italy, 1967]) at Italy's famed Elios Studios (a once-popular studio backlot used for many, usually lower-budgeted westerns, whose rundown appearance here actually serves the film well, further establishing a town on the brink of collapse).

Utilizing what appears to be the cost-efficient 2.35:1 Techniscope format, Masciocchi takes full advantage of said format's wide frame in a number of well-composed shots. As with most modestly-budgeted movies such as this, he in turn minimizes camera movement to a number of simplistic pans, so as to avoid laying costly dolly tracks. Nevertheless, his efficient work here belies the humble origins of the production, which is also enhanced greatly by Piero Umiliani's score, that hits all the right notes.

This film is often identified by its unauthorized English-language title, **Viva Django!** (a literal translation from its original Italian title of *W Django!*; the "W" [twin crossed V's, signifying "Viva"] representing a symbol used by Italian resistance fighters during WWII). **A Man Called Django** never made it onto either U.S. or Canadian VHS videocassette, although it did turn up on Venezuelan tape as **Un Hombre Llamado Django** (in English, with Spanish subtitles), a release which sometimes popped-up on the shelves of North American ethnic video stores in larger metropolitan areas. During the digital era, though, it's had a fairly healthy presence on DVD, including an official Italian release from Surf Video, a rather handsome "Hardbox" edition from Germany's New Entertainment (which included German, Italian and English audio options), and as part of a multipack set from TGG Direct. The less said the better about Dagored/Abraxas' bootleg DVD edition from 2005, which, while it did at least come with English soft-subs and was presented widescreen (of sorts), its fuzzy/murky transfer print (which ran a mere 79½ minutes rather than the full 94) was evidently struck from a sub-par videotape source, and the disc was subsequently unceremoniously discontinued for reasons of copyright infringement. These days, what is by far the best and cheapest option on disc remains Timeless Media/Shout! Factory's "Django Double Feature" DVD from 2012 (in which **AMCD** is paired-up with Miles Deem's equally-enjoyable Django and Sartana's Showdown in the West [*Arrivano Django e Sartana... è la fine*, Italy, 1971]), which includes an excellent transfer (in its correct aspect ratio of 2.35:1) of the film's original English-language export version, which looks about as good as standard definition allows.

Although nothing you haven't seen before, **A Man Called Django** is, thanks to some solid tech credits and Mulargia's experienced professionalism, a swiftly-paced and surprisingly watchable film, which should please most fans of Anthony Steffen's numerous Italo westerns.

REQUIEM FOR A BOUNTY KILLER (*La ammazzo' come un cane... ma lui rideva ancora,* Italy, 1972)
Here's a film whose obscurity is well-deserved. It's a poorly-developed, late-in-the-game revenge oater, which represents low-end exploitation director Elo (Angelo) Pannacciò's sole, decidedly humble contribution to the SW genre (well, *sort* of, but more on that later). To its benefit though, in what was a by-then-typical revenge set-up, **Requiem for a Bounty Killer** unfolds in the most unconventional of ways. Bordering on the surreal and displaying an almost modernesque aesthetic, this fact alone may make the film of interest to more forgiving viewers of Italo trash films or seasoned aficionados of spaghetti westerns.

Lifted from any number of similar revenge-driven westerns, the rudimentary plot revolves around rancher Nick Barton (Michael Forest) who, after discovering most of his family has been murdered and his daughter Suzy (Susanna Levi) raped, seeks vengeance on those responsible, which in this case turns out to be Ramson (Antonio Molino Rojo) and his bandits. Kimble (Steven Tedd), one of Ramson's associates who was also privy to the nasty goings-on, severs his ties with the murderous group when he emphatically remarks, "I want nuthin' to do with killin' defenceless girls!" This act of defiance in turn puts a price on his own head.

Much like Charles Bronson had hummed into a 'tin sandwich' in Sergio Leone's **Once Upon a Time in the West** (*C'era una volta di West*, Italy/USA, 1969), Kimble, who is also known as "The Whistler" due to his penchant for tooting his reed flute (!) attempts to do much the same here, but not surprisingly, his musical interludes don't have one iota of the emotional resonance found in Leone's film. Case in point, when Kimble visits one of his 'regulars', a prostitute somewhere on the outskirts of town, she complains, "Why do you always want it like *this*?" as he goes about playing his flute whilst she proceeds to, um… play his other flute! Dressed in an all-black leather duster and sporting a 'Seventies-styled shag haircut with big, bushy sideburns to match, Kimble's rather rebellious appearance compliments his bounty hunter image well, but despite his assertion that he's merely a (quote) "tumbleweed" who goes where the wind blows, this is but just a façade. Oblivious to the fact that he was a witness to the massacre, Barton hires him to help track down Ramson and his men, an opportunity that Kimble then sneakily takes advantage of to kill off his former accomplices in the name of vengeance/justice (two words which are virtually *interchangeable* in the realm of the Western, perhaps most especially of the 'spaghetti' kind!).

Unsettled by his twitchy disposition and nervous, eerily psychotic giggle, most everyone in the film is distrustful of Kimble, who at one point callously proclaims, "I do what I want!" after offing a potential squealer. His personality growing progressively darker, Kimble's presence is hereinafter accompanied by a series of sinister, horror movie-tinged tonalities that creep into the soundtrack, further accentuating his mounting psychosis. At one point, the crazed Kimble even slashes some guy's throat in a scene right out of any contemporary *giallo*. Incidentally, Daniele Patucchi's easy-listening opening theme also wouldn't be out of place in any number of Italian thrillers.

In a rather strange development, Michael Forest's Barton character, who, given the film's main narrative thrust, is all-but-relegated to a marginal role at best, sometimes disappears for large sections of the film; a tactic director Pannacciò (here hiding behind the pseudonym "Mark Welles") would also utilize when hiring American 'name' talent on some of his later films (i.e., his **EXORCIST** rip-off **Cries and Shadows** [*Un urlo dalle tenebre*, Italy, 1976], starring ex-Hollywood film noir great Richard Conte in his final role). First seen riding together to the strains of a syrupy ballad ("*A man is made of love and pain...*"), Suzy and the family doctor (Chet Davis), set out to look for Barton, only to get mixed-up with a bunch of corrupt deputies in town ("You see Barton's daughter? She could make things tough... We never should have kept her alive!"). Fortuitously enough though, Suzy's doctor happens to be just as handy with a rifle as he is with a stethoscope when he kills one of the deputies. In a calculated move, Ramson incriminates Kimble for the murder of the sheriff's deputy, except Kimble proves to be a formidable foe, but his luck soon turns against him when his involvement in the film's opening massacre is ultimately exposed, leading to an unexpected—and weirdly hypnotic—finale, which only adds to the films already strange, languorously-paced tone leading up to it.

Possessing lowly production values similar to any of Miles Deem (a.k.a. Demofilo Fidani)'s final spaghetti westerns, **RFABK's** production history appears to have been every bit as muddled as its disjointed storyline. In spite of the onscreen credits, actor "Ray O'Connor" (an alias commonly used by Remo Capitani) doesn't appear in the finished film, while Spanish actor Antonio Molino Rojo, Fidani bit-player "Chet Davis" and Pannacciò regular Susanna Levi go completely uncredited. According to reviewer "Morgan" over at the *Spaghetti Western Database*, parts of this film were (quote) "shot back-to-back with another Pannacciò production, **Una cuerda al amanecer**, directed by Manuel Esteba, which also featured Rojo and may very well account for his uncredited appearance in the present film. Confusing matters even further, in 2008, director Luigi Petrini was interviewed by Alessio Di Rocco in Dossier Misteri d'Italia 3 of the Italian genre magazine *Nocturno* (Issue 70, May 2008), wherein Petrini claimed that *he* was the actual director of said film, after having had a falling-out with Pannacciò.

Released onto Greek videotape by Hi-Tech Video (in English with Greek subtitles, no less!), and running a scant 74 minutes, this remains the only known version to exist on home video. Once again, according to reviewer "Morgan", this **Requiem for a Bounty Killer** version was apparently (quote) "released in 1979 in an extended 90 minutes' version with 14 years rating (sic)." But the film's most mysterious incarnation as **Porno-Erotic Western** (or *Porno Erotico Western*) was also (quote) "released by Pannacciò the same year", but has yet to appear on home video anywhere in the world. After interviewing the film's DP Maurizio Centini, Di Rocco confirms in a forum post at *gentedirispetto.com* on May 31st, 2008 that **PEW** included (quote) "scenes from two westerns Pannacciò had produced in the early 1970s (that would be **Lo ammazzo** and **Una cuerda**), with additional "pushed scenes" (*"di scene spinte"*) shot by Pannacciò at Gordon Mitchell's western town."

Looking over the credits of the current film under review, which shares much of PEW's cast, crew and shooting locations at Gordon Mitchell's (self-built) aforementioned backlot (known as Cave Film Studios), this might go far in explaining both the absence of O'Connor, Rudy and Bien as well as explain **RFABK's** scant duration, as it may have been shorn of the 'new' explicit sex scenes that were shot for **PEW**. This hypothesis makes sense, given the current version's choppy appearance during many of its potentially salacious scenes.

As demonstrated by this film's darker tone, director Pannacciò was ultimately better suited to helming a number of esoteric horror films throughout the decade, and later still, under the alias "Angel Valery", he even ventured into the netherworlds of Italian porn.

WATCH YOUR BACK, HOLY GHOST! (*Bada alla tua pelle Spirito Santo*, Italy, 1972)

Not to be confused with Giuliano Carnimeo's more upmarket Gianni Garko headliner **His Name Was Holy Ghost** (*Uomo avvisato mezzo ammazzato... parola di Spirito Santo*, Italy, 1972), this in fact turns out to be the second film following ...**And His Name Was Holy Ghost** (*...e lo chiamarono Spirito Santo*, Italy, 1971), the first—and best—entry in Roberto Mauri's modest, loosely-connected *Holy Ghost or Spirito Santo* trilogy.

A Union colonel (Tom Felleghy) on his way to guard a valuable cache of state gold at Fort Phoenix is ambushed and killed by a mysterious gunman during the film's opening. Later, when interrupted transporting a wagonload of gold ingots from Fort Phoenix to Fort Knox, it becomes readily apparent that Union soldier 'Holy Ghost' has stolen the gold for himself when a fellow soldier (Salvatore Billa) tracks him down as a result of (quote) "serious crimes against the Union." While escorting him back to Fort Phoenix, the Union cavalcade is taken by surprise thanks to the self-proclaimed (quote) "future King of Mexico", Diego d'Asburgo (Remo Capitani) and his colorful gang of bandidos, who are affectionately identified in the film's credits as (quote) "The Four Magnificent Rogues of the West." Garibaldi (named as such for the real-life Italian general Giuseppe Garibaldi [1807-1882], who contributed to the unification of Italy in 1861), the most imposing of Diego's men jokingly refers to himself as "Garibaldino" ("Little Garibaldi"), and even brags about having served under the famed heroic general back in the old country, but was later forced to leave Sicily due to committing a (quote) "honor killing." This lively motley bunch of misfits also includes the hunchbacked Irishman (Aldo Berti), who is better known as "Bogey" due to his proclivity for constantly picking his nose ("bogeys" is another word for "boogers" in certain parts, you see!), plus a gun-toting, snickering priest (Omero Capanna) and "The Pirate" (Augusto Funari), who, rumor has it, is the (quote) "last descendent of Morgan the Pirate!"

Naturally, Diego and his bandit buddies steal the aforesaid gold for themselves, only to soon discover—much to their collective disappointment, natch—that the ingots are

BADA ALLA TUA PELLE SPIRITO SANTO!

Watch Your Back, Holy Ghost!

as fake as three-dollar bills. Later, while visiting him known as "The Banker" (José Torres), Diego's unassuming informant, who struggles to earn his keep, is promised his (quote) "share in lead" for providing them with bad intel prior to the heist, but he is given some respite after assuring Diego that the next shipment out of Fort Phoenix will be the real deal. However, along the way, Holy Ghost discovers that the Colonel at the fort (Craig Hill) is *not* who he appears to be…

Although restraining itself from devolving into all-out slapstick, **Watch Your Back, Holy Ghost** (the film's Italian title more accurately translates as "Watch Out for Your Hide, Holy Ghost") was nonetheless—*big surprise!*—clearly influenced by the sudden meteoric popularity of Enzo Barboni's then-recent *Trinity* duology, which, in the inimitable Italo exploitation way, spawned slews of cash-in imitators, some highly entertaining, many comparatively abysmal. Striving for mild amusement here, **WY-BHG**'s comedic elements mostly revolve around the unkempt and overly-excitable Diego and his lively bunch of buffoonish bandits, whom he describes as "The best sons-of-bitches in the west!" Other than for a brief barroom punch-up where Holy Ghost gets mistakenly called "Hallelujah" (an obvious nod to one of George Hilton's memorable character turns), none of them ever do too much other than chase after Holy Ghost. Infantile humor is provided by most of Diego's men, whilst Diego's flatulence ("Majesty, it stinks like shit in here!") also tries to garner a few fitful laughs; which, admittedly, it does.

Aside from some dubious, underlit day-for-night photography during the film's climactic gunfight (which may just be a side effect of the cheapo Italian "Kiosk" DVD from Fabbri Editori, seeing as how DP Giuseppe Pinori's work is, for the most part, perfectly functional here), it's all capably put together, and benefits most from Carlo Savina's solid score. Long after seeing his name in the opening credits, you might almost have forgotten that charismatic American actor Craig Hill is in the film, which is a real shame, especially considering some of his other stellar work within the genre, including the likes of Paolo Bianchini's **I Want Him Dead** (*Lo voglio morto*, Italy, 1968), or even his later—completely over-the-top—role in "Dick Spitfire"/Aristide Massaccesi's **Run Man Run… El Dorado is Coming to Trinity** *(Scansati… a Trinità arriva Eldorado*, Italy, 1972) wherein, as the heavy of the piece, he really chewed the scenery.

Vassili Karis—first seen in the present film driving a Union wagon—is, in comparison to Capitani, very reserved as the film's antihero, but ideally suited to play the conniving Holy Ghost, whose outer guise is also not what it appears to be. His love interest is provided by "Daria Norman"/Maria Francesca as Suomi, the daughter of a local rancher he once helped out, who, in turn, returns the favor on a few occasions while he works his way through all the usual double-crosses, dirty deals and switcheroos.

Largely forgotten if consistently watchable nevertheless, **WYBHG** nicely counterbalances its straight-ahead action with just enough comedic moments, without the latter ever becoming too distracting. Director Mauri and most of the cast and crew would return in quick succession for the film's below-discussed sequel **Holy Ghost and the 5 Magnificent Rogues** (1972).

HOLY GHOST AND THE 5 MAGNIFICENT ROGUES (*Spirito Santo e le cinque magnifiche canaglie*, Italy, 1972)

The last (and least) of Roberto Mauri's tenuously-linked Holy Ghost 'trilogy', this nominal, quickly-thrown-together effort is debatably the shabbiest entry in what was already a rather threadbare series to begin with.

Governed by the aptly-named Mr. Powers (American actor Lincoln Tate), the town of Springfield hires the quick-witted Holy Ghost (Vassili Karis) to kill a ruthless, enterprising bandit known as "The Loner." Likened to The Scarlet Pimpernel or a (quote) "poisonous snake with all the abilities of a chameleon", Holy Ghost insists on one stipulation: to hire his (quote) "trusted colleagues"—the so-called five magnificent rogues of the film's title—to help him in his pursuit of this elusive lone bandit.

This time out, in its attempt to add more for even less, the filmmakers resort to broader and more frequent forced comedy, even going so far as to add one more 'rogue' (well, at least per the film's title, anyway) into the mix. As Holy Ghost embarks to reunite his old gang for another fling, many of the larger-than-life characters from **Watch Your Back, Holy Ghost** (1972) are reintroduced, including Remo Capitani as the histrionically *italiano* Diego d'Asburgo ("I'm a-still a pretender to the Mexican throne!"), whose chronic flatulence here continues unabated; Aldo Berti also returns as the nose-picking Bogey, and, in keeping with the preceding *HG* entry's lingering sense of silliness, he's invented a (quote) "[*bust-developing*] cream for women with small breasts", which he continually tries to pawn-off on most of **HGAT5MR's** tertiary female players. Although "Ken Wood"/Giovanni Cianfriglia briefly reappears as Garibaldi in a few key scenes (including a drawn-out, over-the-top dream sequence that makes a sly observation on just how low the genre had sunk in the post-*Trinity* era), most of his cobbled-together scenes were simply either lifted verbatim or else were slightly-repurposed inserts taken from the previous film.

In one of *HG* #3's numerous, uh, diverting—I hesitate to say distracting—subplots, the ever-overconfident Garibaldi has a fateful (i.e., fatal) run-in with The Loner. Vowing revenge ("*sangue chiama sangue* / blood calls for blood"), his wife Consuelo

Vassili Karis appeared in all three of Roberto Mauri's **Holy Ghost films**

72

(Angela Bo) gets in touch with his cousins Carmelo (Salvatore Billa) and Torreto (Giacomo de Michaelis) from Corleone, a pair of Mafia hitmen armed with that deadly firearm-of-choice of Sicilian shepherds and hitmen alike, the *lupara* (i.e., sawn-off shotgun). Adding to this distinctive cast of characters—who were clearly meant to play to domestic Italian audiences, indicating that foreign sales for the film weren't expected by its producers—it's no surprise that composer Carlo Savina also has some fun here, and decides to mix that other Sicilian trademark into the soundtrack, the Jew's harp or jaw harp (known as the scacciapensieri in Italy, or, more specifically in the Sicilian dialect, the *Turi 'u mericanu norma*). In another broadly-sketched comic aside, The Pirate (this time out played by frequent stuntman Riccardo Petrazzi, misspelled "Pedrazzi" in the credits) finally gets to skipper his own boat… which turns out to be nothing more than a decrepit old ferry barge (it's more like a basic raft, really). Unlike Lee Van Cleef in the post-spaghetti Hollywood oater **Barquero** (1970), however, he can't even assist a lowly shepherd (played by an uncredited Salvatore Baccaro—the future "Sal Boris" a.k.a. "Boris Lugosi" himself!) to cross the river without causing the 'barge' to sink.

Yank guest-star Lincoln Tate is given a sizable-enough role herein as top honcho of Springfield, who mostly takes part in the more standard 'straight' western ingredients, managing (luckily for him!) to completely avoid most of the sophomoric slapstick moments (that said, Tate had been up to his ears in 'em the previous year on Mario Garriazzo's and Richard Harrison's daft-as-a-mule-on-*loco*-weed 'western parody' **Acquasanta Joe** [Italy, 1971]). Meanwhile, pretty leading lady "Daria Norman"/Maria Francesca also returns, and, in what seems like a thankless role at first as Mr. Powers' cousin, she too gets caught up in all the double-dealing, which provides one of the nutty narrative's more original twists.

Released to Italian theatres a mere five months after **Watch Your Back, Holy Ghost**, **HGAT5MR** was announced under a variety of shooting and/or export titles, including "**Gunmen of the Holy Ghost**", "**Return of the Holy Ghost**", and even as "**Holy Ghost and the Magnificent Five Scum**" ("scum" merely being an alternate Anglo translation of the Italian word "*canaglie*"), and its overly rushed approach is most certainly evident in the finished product. In what amounts to one of the more impressive low-budget 'Kiosk' releases, the Italian DVD from Hobby & Work is relatively sharp in its detail, even if the colors do appear a little washed-out at times. Enhanced for 16x9, the disc comes (not surprisingly, considering the 'Italocentric' nature of much of **HGAT5MR's** content/comedy) in the Italian language only; good news is that a nice English fan-subbed copy has become available for those willing to do a little legwork to get it. Sloppily-pieced-together by Adriano Tagliavia, the film's overabundance of lowbrow antics is certainly not for everyone, but, in the end, it's a diverting enough time-waster with plenty of mindless gunplay and some nice onscreen camaraderie on display between Karis and Capitani.

[Author's Note: Many Thanks to Steve Fenton and Michael "Ferg" Ferguson for sharing some pertinent info relating to these four films, and also to Michael Anderson for allowing me access to his vast spaghetti western collection, including English subtitled copies of both the Holy Ghost films reviewed here.—DC]

WHAT IS THE PRICE OF POWER?
A BULLET FOR THE PRESIDENT!
-VAN ROBERTS

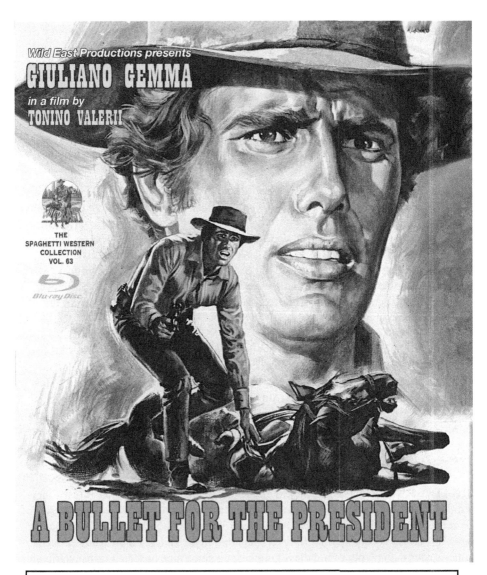

Wild East Productions presents
GIULIANO GEMMA
in a film by
TONINO VALERII

THE
SPAGHETTI WESTERN
COLLECTION
VOL. 63

Blu-ray Disc

A BULLET FOR THE PRESIDENT

"The villain's frame Jack Donovan for Garfield/Kennedy's assassination. Jack's racial heritage is the counterpart to Lee Harvey Oswald's Communist sympathies. They tarred and feathered Oswald for being a Communist, and they did the same with Jack because he was an African-American."   *-Van Roberts*

PROLOGUE

The last thing anybody would expect to find in a Spaghetti western is a recreation of President John F. Kennedy's assassination as he cruised the streets of Dallas, Texas, in 1881 rather than 1963! The President and the First Lady are shown being transported in an open carriage, rather than an open limousine, while two assassins stand poised on an elevated platform, comparable to Dealey Plaza's grassy knoll, with their Winchester rifles aimed at him. As preposterous as this premise sounds, Tonino Valerii's Spaghetti western "**A Bullet for the President**" (Un proiettile per il presidente, Italy, 1969) depicts this incident as well as others in a way that subjects the tragic events of November 22, 1963, to greater scrutiny than either President John Garfield's impromptu assassination in 1881 or the Warren Commission's findings. Two crucial issues about the legacy of this film may never emerge from the fog of history. We may never know exactly how much Valerii and uncredited scenarist Ernesto Gastaldi rewrote Massimo Patrizi's original screenplay. Italian scholar Roberto Curti wrote that Valerii told him Patrizi had the JFK idea in his script, but Valerii and Gastaldi "fleshed out the plot around it." According to Curti, "Gastaldi was more trenchant and said they (Valerii and he) rewrote the story from scratch." Unfortunately, in his research, Curti never found Patrizi's original script.[1] Furthermore, we may never know what prompted Patrizi to recreate the Kennedy assassination as the basis for a Spaghetti western rather than a contemporary political thriller, like Oliver Stone's "**JFK**" (1991). Incredibly, not only have Valerii, Gastaldi, and Patrizi assimilated this reimagined history so it contains a semblance of credibility, but they also argue the Kennedy assassination qualified as a conspiracy! This speculation clashes with the Warren Commission's conclusion that Oswald acted alone as Kennedy's assassin in 1964.[2] In 1979, the United States House Select Committee on Assassinations also scrutinized the Kennedy assassination and decided a conspiracy was behind JFK's death. Nevertheless, the Justice Department declared "no persuasive evidence can be identified to support the theory of a conspiracy in ... the assassination of President Kennedy."[3]

Ostensibly, Patrizi rewrote history because President James Garfield was the chief executive who was gunned down in 1881. In truth, Garfield's assassination occurred hundreds of miles away from Texas in Washington, D.C., where disgruntled office seeker Charles J. Guiteau shot him in a crowded railway station. Little about Garfield's assassination would have raised questions about a conspiracy, since the deranged assassin was arrested, convicted, and hanged. Everything about Kennedy's assassination, however, has conjured up a multiplicity of conspiracy theories. Countless volumes have been published about Kennedy's murder in broad daylight. Americans have wondered if Lee Harvey Oswald was either a puppet or a patsy for an anonymous group of killers. Watching "**A Bullet for the President**," you must suspend your disbelief to accommodate this gimmicky premise which conflates the identities of Garfield and Kennedy. Indeed, not only were Garfield and Kennedy both reform presidents who championed civil rights for African Americans, but they also served only one term in the White House. Presumably, Patrizi chose Garfield's assassination because it corresponds to the timeline for most Spaghetti westerns.

French lobby card: **A Bullet for the President**

Unlike Garfield, President Lincoln was shot and died less than a week after Confederate General Robert E. Lee had surrendered at Appomattox Courthouse to Union General Ulysses S. Grant. President William McKinley was assassinated in 1901, a little more than ten years after the U.S. Census Bureau officially listed the frontier as settled. The Superintendent of the Census Bureau issued this statement because "he could no longer locate a continuous frontier line beyond which population thinned out to less than two per square mile."[4]

Garfield and Kennedy were not the only historical figures in Valerii's film. Vice President Chester A. Arthur, who became president after Garfield's assassination, is conflated with Kennedy's own Vice President Lyndon B. Johnson. Arthur finds himself in a dilemma because the cabal of killers who ordered Garfield/Kennedy's assassination possess incriminating documents that will end his political career if he refuses to capitulate to their demands. In his controversial biography *The Dark Side of Lyndon Baines Johnson*, author Joachim Joesten alleges LBJ participated in graft and corruption with criminal syndicates, big Texas oil producers, and politicians.[5] Essentially, the Texas conspiracy of killers in "A Bullet for the President" allowed their ideology to generate differences. They want to either ensure African Americans never enjoy full citizenship privileges under the U.S. Constitution or incite a second Civil War. The saintly Vice-President Arthur is at the mercy of these conspirators who carefully groomed him for his post because they don't want the changes that Garfield wants to make.

Apart from the politicians, "**A Bullet for the President**" portrays two other significant participants in the assassination. As the Lee Harvey Oswald character framed by the conspirators for the assassination of Garfield/Kennedy, Jack Donovan is not only an African American, but he is also an avid supporter of the president! Jack Ruby is the last actual non-political character involved in the assassination and the unrepentant, Southern extremist Wallace exhibits a greater hatred for the Federal government than his co-conspirators. Wallace is reminiscent of the murderous patriarchal Confederate Colonel Jonas (Joseph Cotton of "**The Tramplers**") in Sergio Corbucci's "**The Hellbenders**" (I crudeli, Italy, 1967) who massacres thirty Union troops escorting a wagon loaded with a million dollar shipment of tattered bills and steals that fortune to finance a second insurrection.

Like Jack Ruby, Wallace engineers Oswald/Jack Donovan's demise during an ambush after Jefferson's deputies had evacuated him from Dallas and were taking him to Fort Worth to protect him from vigilantes. Valerii's film differs in two important respects from the Kennedy assassination. First, nobody exonerated Oswald for his complicity in the shooting. Garfield's bodyguard Arthur McDonald clears Jack Donovan as President Garfield/Kennedy's assassin. Second, the conspiracy of Texas politicians as well as Wallace destroy themselves when they argue about possession of the documents to blackmail Arthur.

An in-depth comparison between the actual characters and their fictitious counterparts lies beyond the scope of this article. Nevertheless, Valerii, Gastaldi, and Patrizi have included several bits of trivia which allude to the Kennedy assassination. For example, when the President and his wife arrive in Dallas, she receives a bouquet of red roses rather than yellow roses. When Garfield's bodyguard McDonald inquires about the symbolism, a newspaper journalist informs him red roses "usually mean hate." Later, during the assassination itself, blood from Garfield's wound splashes across Mrs. Garfield's dress just as Kennedy's wounds stained Jackie Kennedy's dress. Vice President Chester A. Arthur stands out as a sympathetic character under duress by his fellow conspirators. Indeed, once President Garfield dies, Arthur warns the ringleaders that he plans to embrace Garfield's liberal agenda and act beholding to nobody

"**A Bullet for the President**" qualifies as the first and only presidential assassination movie in the Spaghetti western genre. Some may argue that Eugenio Martin's subsequent presidential assassination saga "Captain Apache" (1971) featured an attempt on the life of President Ulysses S. Grant. As it turns out, Grant's double was aboard the train during the attack, and he didn't suffer a scratch. Anyway, Valerii's film remains far more politically charged as well as sophisticated than Martin's competent horse opera. The closest example of another Spaghetti western depicting a historical episode is Paolo Bianchini's "I Want Him Dead" (Lo voglio morto, Italy, 1968) about an attempt to sabotage Union and Confederate truce talks near the end of the war.

Although Bianchini and his scenarist Carlos Sarabia may not have realized it, Northern and Southern officials convened a meeting, known as The Hampton Roads Conference, aboard a steamboat at Hampton Roads, Virginia, on the eve of the end of the war. Since defeat of the Confederacy was a foregone conclusion, the truce talks achieved nothing. Presumably, Bianchini and Sarabia used the Hampton Roads Conference as a basis for their Spaghetti western. Unfortunately, they do not take advantage of the historical precedents, and the plot is not based loosely or otherwise on what happened at Hampton Roads. On the contrary, in "A Bullet for the President," the filmmakers appropriated history and used it as an allegory to depict a criminal conspiracy.

Valerii and Gastaldi chronicle life, liberty, and the pursuit of happiness in the state of Texas after Reconstruction ended in 1877. The Compromise of 1877 mandated the withdrawal of all remaining U.S. troops from the Southern states. Not surprisingly, white supremacists regained dominance over African Americans. Neither Gastaldi nor Valerii provided this historical subtext as exposition. Nevertheless, the Compromise of 1877 served as a milestone because it restored home rule for those former Confederates. The Confederates and the white supremacists who orchestrated President Garfield's assassination in "A Bullet for the President" are those same people who regained power in 1877.6

POLITICAL SPAGHETTI WESTERNS
As a general rule, most political Spaghetti westerns, labeled Zapata westerns, take place between 1862 and 1916. Typically, these Zapata westerns involved foreigners, such as either American or European interlopers, who empowered peasants to whittle away at the tyranny of their Draconian governments. Zapata writers, producers, and directors appropriated Mexico as the setting for these films. Italian historian Roberto Curti has written that these filmmakers set their movies in Mexico and other Third World countries "as a way to explore issues that were deeply felt in" Italy.7 These metaphorical films could be made without inciting controversies at home because they were westerns. Typically, Zapata westerns spouted Leftist, Marxist rhetoric in their narratives which would never have been permitted in a Hollywood western.

These westerns began at the time of the French occupation under the Emperor Maximillian in the late 1860s and endured during subsequent, corrupt Mexican presidential administrations until World War I. The French had wrested control of Mexico from President Benito Juarez in 1862, because the country could not pay its debts. The French never recouped their losses, and the United States pressured Napoleon III to evacuate his troops in 1866. Later, in 1868, Juarez executed Maximillian. Although neither of these were Spaghetti westerns, Robert Aldrich's **"Vera Cruz"** (1954) and Don Siegel's **"Two Mules for Sister Sara"** (1970) showed American mercenaries taking advantage of this situation. Gianfranco Parolini's Spaghetti western **"Adios, Sabata"** (Indio Black, sai che ti dico: Sei un gran figlio di..., Italy, 1971) depicted the collapse of Maximillian's regime.8

After Juarez died, Mexican General Porfirio Diaz presided over the country from 1877 to 1911. Diaz's reforms marginalized the campesinos. Several political Spaghetti westerns and American westerns occurred against the background of the Diaz regime. Affluent land-owner Francisco Madero led a revolution in 1910 against Diaz and sent him into exile. Later, General Victoriano Huerta staged a military coup against Madero. Huerta had Madero murdered. The national outcry doomed Huerta's militarist regime. Mexicans abhorred Huerta even more than Diaz. Venustiano Carranza led another revolution, with rural bandits Pancho Villa and Emiliano Zapata serving as two of his generals. Villa and Zapata later broke with Carranza in 1914. Carranza triumphed over Villa in 1915, and U.S. President Woodrow Wilson formally sanctioned the Carranza government.[9]

Hollywood movies about the Mexican Revolution date back to Jack Conway's "**Viva Villa!**" (1934), Elia Kazan's "**Viva, Zapata**" (1952), George Sherman's "**The Treasure of Pancho Villa**" (1955), Richard Fleischer's "**Bandido!**" (1956); Richard Brooks' "**The Professionals**" (1966), Sam Peckinpah's "**The Wild Bunch**" (1969), and Luis Puenzo's "Old Gringo" (1989). Spanish westerns about the Mexican Revolution included Eugenio Martín's "**Pancho Villa**" (West German, 1972) and José María Elorrieta's "**The Vengeance of Pancho Villa**" (Los 7 de Pancho Villa, Spain, 1972). Prime examples of politically oriented included Sergio Corbucci's "**Django**" (1965), Sergio Sollima's "**The Big Gundown**" (La resa dei conti, Spain, 1966) and "**The Big Gundown**" sequel "**Run, Man, Run**" (Corri uomo corri, Italy, 1968), Damiano Damiani's "**A Bullet for the General**" (Quién sabe?, Italy, 1967), Giulio Petroni's "**Tepepa**" (1969), Corbucci's "**The Mercenary**" (Il mercenario, West Germany,1968), and Corbucci's "**Companeros**" (Vamos a matar, compañeros, Italy, 1970). Sergio Leone's "**Duck, You Sucker**" (Giù la testa, Italy, 1972) would cap this subgenre of Italian westerns.

The Mexican Revolution figured peripherally in "**Django**" with bandits turned revolutionaries, while the political elements grew in prominence in later films. "**The Battle of Algiers**" scenarist Franco Solinas contributed to several Spaghetti westerns, and traces of his Marxist rhetoric appear in "**The Mercenary**," "**A Bullet for the General**," "**Tepepa**," "**The Big Gundown**," "**Run, Man, Run**" as well as Gillo Pontecorvo's non-western adventure "**Burn!**" (Queimada, Italy, 1969), about a 19th century aristocratic British mercenary who foments a revolution in the Caribbean island of Queimada to stimulate the British sugar trade. Laurence Staig and Tony Williams, in *Italian Western: The Opera of Violence*, dismiss these political westerns as "just another gimmick employed by directors to add a new novelty to their films."[10] American westerns produced in Spain that covered the Mexican Revolution without Marxist ideology included Buzz Kulik's "**Villa Rides**" (1967), Don Taylor's "**The 5-Man Army**" (1969), Tom Gries' "**100 Rifles**" (1969), Paul Wendkos' "**Guns of the Magnificent Seven**" (1969); Paul Wendkos' "**Cannon for Cordoba**, ," (1970) and Robert Parrish's "**A Town Called Hell**" (1971), originally entitled "**A Town Called Bastard**."

Championing the rights of the downtrodden, however, Valerii doesn't advocate another revolution on American soil as do Corbucci, Petroni, Damiani, and Sollima on Mexican soil. Instead, Valerii presents one of the earliest JFK conspiracy theories in the guise of a western. Once you accept the way the Italians revised history in "**A Bullet for the President**," you get a western which has endured the test of time with a premise like none other. Nobody has ever made such a western as Valerii's seminal film, and nobody may ever make one as insightful and entertaining as "A Bullet for the President."

Content with narratives about frontier crime, most Spaghetti westerns rarely churned up dust over political and economic issues either of which might overshadow or undercut the cathartic spectacle of the action. Typically, political films promote messages, something producers dread because messages distract audiences from the entertainment value of a film. Meanwhile, few Spaghetti westerns set on the American frontier trafficked in overt, Leftish, Marxist political rhetoric concerning economic issues, such as the divide between entrepreneurial privileges and proletariat rights. Inevitably, racism enters the mix owing to the differences in cultural heritage and religious beliefs of the entrepreneurs and the proletariat.

For example, Sergio Leone's timeless masterpiece "**Once Upon a Time in the West**" (1968) illustrates the driving force of Manifest Destiny on Mr. Morton, the crippled railroad baron who dreams of building a transcontinental railroad. Nevertheless, Leone could have approached the subject matter from the perspective of the railroad owner's rights versus the rights of the wage laborers. Leone's film would have been neither as memorable nor as dramatic if he had concentrated on the clash between owners and workers. Instead, he focused "**Once Upon A Time in the West**" on the competition between those who forged the railroad and those who controlled the land and the contentious predicament between the two.

Consequently, Tonino Valerii's "**A Bullet for the President**" which openly addresses Marxist Dialectical materialism remains the exception to the rule regarding political Spaghetti westerns set in the United States. Basically, Valerii's ambitious horse opera contemplates the socioeconomic issues of class, labor, and race more than any other Spaghetti western dared. The Dallas town hall meeting between President Garfield and the wealthy businessmen, such as Pinkerton, provides this key moment. Inevitably, this expository scene is necessary because it explains why Pinkerton and his cronies want to assassinate the president. Adapting Massimo Patrizi's original screenplay, Valerii and scenarist Ernesto Gastaldi, have succeeded in minimizing the rhetoric sufficiently so it does not eclipse the spectacle. Nevertheless, this allegory about the Kennedy assassination and the elaborate transposition premise does indeed constitute the gimmick that Staig and Williams complained about in Spaghetti westerns. Before we venture farther with "**A Bullet for the President**," a few words about director Tonino Valerii are insightful.

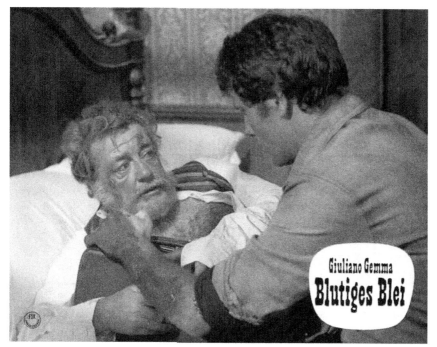

German lobby card of **A Bullet for the President**

TONINO VALERII VS SERGIO LEONE

Sergio Leone reigns as the maestro of Spaghetti westerns. He reinvented the Italian western as a profitable genre with "**A Fistful of Dollars**" (Per un pugno di dollari, Italy, 1964), "**For A Few Dollars More**" (Per qualche dollaro in più, Italy, 1965) "**The Good, the Bad, and the Ugly**" (Il buono, il brutto, il cattivo, Italy, 1966) and "**Once Upon A Time in the West**" (C'era una volta il West, Italy, 1971). However, Leone did not make the first Spaghetti western. Actually, Leone's father Roberto Roberti, aka Vincenzo Leone, directed the first Spaghetti western, a silent oater entitled "**The Indian Vampire**" (La vampira Indiana, Italy, 1913). Suffice to say, Sir Christopher Frayling has chronicled the rise of the European western as well as the emergence of Sergio Leone as its greatest practitioner. Anybody searching for specifics should peruse Frayling's groundbreaking scholarship.[11] Nevertheless, a few words are useful for the sake of perspective. European filmmakers had dabbled in horse operas as early as the silent film era, but their efforts by the early 1960s were largely influenced by Hollywood. As well made as some of the early Spaghetti westerns were, these films did not spur a stampede of westerns onto the silver screen like Sergio Leone's "Dollar" trilogy did. Indeed, Leone imitated the works of legendary American western film directors such as John Ford, Raoul Walsh, George Stevens, Anthony Mann, Robert Aldrich, Nicholas Ray, and John Sturges.

Nevertheless, Leone took the western, gave the saddle-sore genre a reboot, and forged new stars while revitalizing veterans. Ostensibly, Clint Eastwood, Lee Van Cleef, and Charles Bronson became legends as a result of the Leone treatment, while Leone ushered Henry Fonda back into the limelight with "**Once Upon A Time in the West**" and "**My Name Is Nobody**" (Il mio nome è Nessuno, Italy, 1973). A constellation of American western actors descended on Europe, but they never enjoyed the superstardom of those mentioned above. Some actors—such as Richard Harrison, Gordon Mitchell, Craig Hill, Gilbert Roland, and Guy Madison—added years to their careers. Most Italian directors who followed in Leone's footsteps imitated his ideas. Some emerged as significant rivals in their own respect—Sergio Corbucci, Sergio Sollima, Enzo Barboni, Gianfranco Parolini, Giuseppe Colizzi, and Tonino Valerii—because they adapted the genre to suit their needs. Enzo Barboni was not the first to poke fun at the Spaghetti western. That honor is accorded to Duccio Tessari for his tongue-in-cheek western "**A Pistol for Ringo**" (Una pistola per Ringo, Italy, 1965). Nevertheless, Barboni would make a worldwide superstar of Terence Hill for his portrayal of a filthy but funny gunslinger and produced the most profitable Spaghetti western in history: "Trinity Is Still My Name," much to Leone's chagrin.

Tonino Valerii acquired a reputation for himself with serious Leone-esque westerns, but his style of filmmaking differed from the maestro. Valerii's proscenium arch framed mise-en-scene utilized fewer distracting close-ups and far more medium shots and long shots. His filming methods resemble Orson Welles' brand of deep-focus filmmaking. The audience gazes on Valerii's westerns, and they scan the imagery for what is important. Leone does not allow his audience the luxury of appreciating the spectacle. He makes his salient points with extreme close-ups, sprawling long shots, and busy medium shots. The lyrical kaleidoscope of Leone's clashing montage of images when assembled and projected to an audience italicizes the narrative. You do not so much watch a Leone Spaghetti western as you react with awe to the mesmerizing poetry of his editing. Valerii shuns Leone's flamboyance and exhibits a pragmatism that foregrounds the narrative without displaying Leone's cinematic wizardry.

Indeed, Valerii stages gunfights with comparable operatic impact as Leone, while Leone relies on the heightened stylization at 24 frames per second. Comparably, Sam Peckinpah treated standard issue shoot'em ups with his own brand of stylization, relying on slow-motion to amplify the horrific consequences of a shootout. Peckinpah gunfights were designed to make the audience cringe as blood blossoms from torn bodies with a masochistic eroticism, while Leone gunfights achieve a similar poetry without exposing an audience to a Grand Guignol display of blood and gore.

Like Orson Welles, Valerii empowers his narratives with a static beauty without resorting to either Leone's sleight of hand editing or Peckinpah's erupting blood squibs slowed down in time to appreciate their ghastly splendor.[12]

The Internet Movie Database provides a list of Tonino Valerii's works with Sergio Leone. He served as an uncredited assistant director and scenarist on "**A Fistful of Dollars**" (1964) and then again as a credited assistant director on "**For A Few Dollars More**" (1966). Afterward, Valerii took the helm and directed "**A Taste of Killing**" (Per il gusto di uccidere, Italy, 1966), "**Day of Anger**" (I giorni dell'ira, Italy, 1967), then "**A Bullet for the President**," largely known overseas as "**The Price of Power**," "**Dirty Dozen**" style American Civil War western "**A Reason to Live, A Reason to Die**" (Una ragione per vivere e una per morire, West Germany, 1972), before Leone chose him to direct the Terence Hill comedy "**My Name is Nobody**." Valerii's five Spaghetti westerns form a coherent as well as sturdy quintet. Not until distinguished Italian film historian Roberto Curti rescued Valerii's reputation from relative obscurity with his insightful text—*Tonino Valerii: The Films*, (2016), with Sir Christopher Frayling's foreword and Ernesto Gastaldi afterword, did Valerii's eminence as a filmmaker emerge. Valerii's importance had languished because many scholars felt that producer Sergio Leone's influence overshadowed Valerii's directorial contribution to "**My Name is Nobody**." Spaghetti western enthusiasts who take the genre seriously should peruse Sir Christopher Frayling's landmark Sergio Leone biography *Something To Do with Death* as well as his various texts about Spaghetti westerns in general to acquaint themselves with a greater critical appreciation of the genre.[13]

"A BULLET FOR THE PRESIDENT"

Now, we can classify Valerii's third Spaghetti western. Ironically, recent arguments about Sergio Leone's influence on Valerii as a director rear their ugly heads again with "**A Bullet for the President**." Valerii wound up using the same sets which Leone had left intact after he completed "**Once Upon a Time in the West**." Actually, these sets served a purpose because everything has a strictly American flavor rather than a distinctly Hispanic flavor. Nobody wears ponchos, and everything occurs in Texas. Essentially, you don't see any Mexican cantinas, and Mexicans are nonexistent. Although "Bullet" is an Italian western, it differs in several respects from the standard-issue Spaghetti, because revenge is not the dominate theme. Moreover, the protagonist is not a bounty hunter. Instead, Bill Willer (Giuliano Gemma of "**A Pistol for Ringo**") is the disgraced son of a rancher. Will Wright's book *Sixguns and Society: A Structural Study of the Western,* classifies the four main plots of successful oaters: the classical plot, the vengeance variation, the transitional plot, and the professional plot.

"Bullet" adheres largely to Wright's classical plot, while revenge takes a back seat to the action. Kevin Grant in his encyclopedia, *Any Gun Can Play: The Essential Guide to Euro-Westerns,* diminishes the importance of vengeance and observes "an individual's quest for revenge is at once trivial and imperative since, by coincidence, the fate of a nation rest on its outcomes." Wright's classical hero is a "lone stranger who rides into a troubled town and cleans it up, winning the respect of the townsfolk and the love of the schoolmarm."[14]

Mind you, Valerii's film doesn't follow all the classical plot's functions. For the sake of reference as well as analysis, Wright's classic plot features 16 functions.

1. The hero enters a social group.
2. The hero is unknown to the society
3. The hero is revealed to have an exceptional ability.
4. The society recognizes a difference between themselves and the hero; the hero is given a special status.
5. The society does not completely accept the hero.
6. There is a conflict of interests between the villains and the society.
7. The villains are stronger than society; the society is weak.
8. There is a strong friendship or respect between the hero and a villain.
9. The villains threaten the society.
10. The hero avoids involvement in the conflict.
11. The villains endanger a friend of the hero.
12. The hero fights the villains.
13. The hero defeats the villains.
14. The society is safe.
15. The society accepts the hero.
16. The hero loses or gives up his special status.[15]

"A Bullet for the President" dispenses with various classical plot features while modifying others. For example, function number eight doesn't apply. The heroes and the villains have never had a strong bond of friendship. Similarly, none of the heroes fulfill function number ten: The hero avoids involvement in the conflict. Christopher Frayling contends along with Austin Fisher that "Spaghetti westerns do not fall neatly into Hollywood categories."[16] Collectively, President James Garfield, Bill Willer, and Arthur McDonald constitute the three heroes. However, this heroic trio never avoids involvement. First, President James Garfield (Van Johnson of "Battleground") behaves like a classical hero.

He enters the troubled town of Dallas, Texas, on a solemn mission to promote his liberal ideology. He wants to alter the economic relationship between the haves and the have-nots. Unlike the usual classical hero, the idealistic Garfield is known already to everybody in Dallas, and they abhor him enough to want to kill him. They have plastered the town with mug shot posters of Garfield emblazoned with the words Wanted for Treason. Moreover, the governor of Texas savors the potential outcome of Garfield/Kennedy's death when the President appears to be late arriving at the station. When Arthur worries about the President's delay, the smug governor shrugs, "Here today, gone tomorrow. What is that old saying? When a president dies, there's always another to take his place." The governor is openly referring to Arthur. Should the President die, Arthur would replace him as the nation's chief executive. Despite his own bodyguard's ominous words, Garfield has arrived to champion his reforms.

German lobby cards: **A Bullet for the President**

Garfield's bodyguard Arthur McDonald (Warren Vanders of "The Revengers") explains, ". . . your new reform programs have set the powers that be against you, beginning with the governor of the state." Garfield the idealist is nonplussed. "I want to talk to the people who work fourteen hours a day. I'm not looking for the support of those who exploit them." Later, he adds, "I have no personal enemies, only enemies of my ideas, and no bullet can stop an idea." Eventually, it dawns on Garfield how mistaken he is. Earlier, he gaped incredulously at the Texans' reactions to his beliefs: "My ideas are twisted and distorted almost beyond recognition." A Texas native himself, McDonald admonishes Garfield. He explains Texans "still feel like heroes from the Alamo. A loaded gun is their symbol of manhood." Later, Bill Willer corroborates McDonald's warning and reminds Garfield that "only one thing counts around here." Bill nudges his holstered revolver when he utters those words. Willer's words fall on deaf ears. Garfield came to Texas in his own words "so that violence will give way to equality, justice."

Garfield doesn't fear violence. Nevertheless, Willer reminds Garfield about the power of the gun, "It can put a stop to anyone, even a President."

Still from **A Bullet for the President**

Second, Bill Willer qualifies as the more conventional hero. The son of a local rancher, Bill's best friend is an African American, Jack Donovan (Ray Saunders of "Magnum Force"), who served alongside him during the American Civil War. Technically, the Union Army remained segregated, and the only whites in black units would have been their officers. Like Jack, Bill was an enlisted man. Clearly, this represents an instance of the filmmakers invoking dramatic license, because Jack has to be an African American for the purposes of the assassination. Unlike his father, Pa Willer (Antonio Casas of "The Texican"), who served with the Confederacy, Bill enlisted in the Union Army, but he refused to kill his father.

Since he didn't kill his father, Bill wound up in a Union prison for treason for the duration of the war. As it turns out, Garfield was the officer who presided over Bill's court martial. Later, these two protagonists are revealed to have "an exceptional ability." President Garfield labors under the delusion he can reason with the defiant Southerners who run Dallas. Meantime, Bill has his own exceptional ability. He knows what the Dallas conspirators see when they see the President. According to function four, the city fathers recognize a difference between themselves, the President, and Bill Willer. Each man in his own right attains a special status. Function number five applies more to Bill than either Garfield or McDonald. In a southern town, everybody hates Bill Willer because he wore the blue uniform of the Union Army, while his father clothed himself in Confederate gray. Later, after the depraved Sheriff Jefferson frames Jack Donovan as Garfield's killer, Willer vows to kill the lawman.

Meanwhile, Willer doesn't conduct himself like a traditional Spaghetti western hero. He is no Sergio Leone bounty hunter who shoots first and refuses to ask questions afterward as long as he is paid his bounty. For example, when Bill interrupts the Sheriff's deputies from wiring the bridge up with explosives, so they can blow it up when the President's train crosses it, he announces his presence by kicking a rock to attract their attention. Afterward, he displays his superior marksmanship and kills three of them on the trestle and one underneath who has just lighted the fuse. Not long afterward, Garfield's presidential train grinds to a halt as McDonald, armed with a derringer, discovers Bill has thwarted an attack on the president. Garfield finds something about Bill familiar, but he doesn't clearly remember him. Bill warns him about the inhospitable climate in Dallas. "But be careful. This could be your last trip." Willer handles most of heavy lifting in "Bullet," but Arthur McDonald is no shrinking violet.

Initially, lurking on the periphery until Garfield's assassination, Arthur McDonald enters the fracas like a genuine Spaghetti western hero. McDonald plays both sides against each other, catching Willer off guard, while he wins Sheriff Jefferson's confidence as well as the Texas conspirators. An apprehensive Chester A. Arthur fears the specter of blackmail that Pinkerton and his cronies hold over him like puppet strings. McDonald assures Arthur that he will retrieve those documents. Bill and McDonald clash when Bill tries to get a confession from one of Jefferson's deputies. McDonald takes the sheriff's deputy at gunpoint, and Bill suspects that Garfield's bodyguard may have switched sides. Later, they clash over those blackmail documents. After he obtains the blackmail items, Bill wants to reveal their contents to the world. As the wiser of the two in the politically-savvy ways of Washington, McDonald convinces Bill to relinquish them. Even more than either Garfield or Bill, McDonald acts like a hero, unknown to society, with an exceptional ability which allows him to preserve Arthur's innocence. These three amount to a heroic triptych.

Collectively, Pinkerton (prolific Fernando Rey of "**The French Connection**"), the wealthy president of the Southwest Bank and ringleader of the cabal; corrupt Dallas Sheriff Jefferson (Benito Stefanelli of "**Wanted**"); the racist Texas Governor (Julio Peña of "**The Castilian**"), Pinkerton's sagacious attorney (Ángel del Pozo of "**El Condor**"), and former Confederate officer Wallace (Michael Harvey of "**Duck, You Sucker**") comprise the villainous conspiracy. Wright's seventh function in the classical western model applies to them: "a conflict of interest" exists "between the villains and society." [17] In this instance, President Garfield and the 14 hour a day proletariats represent 'society,' because he wants to institute changes beneficial to the working classes. As the leading citizens of Dallas, Pinkerton, the Governor, their attorney, and Sheriff Jefferson appear eminently respectable. Conversely, Wallace remains a stalwart, unreconstructed Southerner who agitates for another Civil War. They plot to assassinate President Garfield, but they leave the details up to Sheriff Jefferson. One of Jefferson's loose-lipped deputies took Bill's father, who fought for the Confederacy, into his confidence and shared information about the plan to blow up the president's train on Tuesday at a bridge outside of Dallas.

Pressbook insert for the U.S. release of **A Bullet fot the President**

The first villains we see are Sheriff Jefferson and his abrasive deputies treating Jack Donovan like a punching bag. Initially, Pa Willer wants Jefferson to lock up his son, so Bill will have an alibi and cannot be charged with murdering the president. He fears that his son will try to kill Garfield because Garfield sentenced him to four years in prison for dereliction of duty. Later, we learn that Bill holds no grudges against Garfield. After he discovers the deputy who leaked the information to Willer, Jefferson escorts Pa Willer back to his ranch. Pa enters to find Wallace awaiting suspiciously for him. After the initial conviviality of drink, Wallace surprises Pa and skewers him with a red-hot poker. Predictably, when he finds his father's corpse, Bill vows to kill the four who murdered him.

Meantime, the other conspirators arrange for President Garfield to review his policies at a town hall meeting. Topping Garfield's reforms is a proposal to make the affluent--the twenty percent of society--pay greater taxes. This source of revenue will help the eighty per cent of society—the people working for the affluent—enjoy a better life. Interestingly, the target audience that Garfield sought to address do not attend the town meeting. Indeed, they were probably at work during the town hall meeting and were not allowed to attend. Naturally, Pinkerton insists that if they pay their African Americans a high wage, they will sacrifice revenue, too. Garfield affronts them with his abrupt comment, "You'll have to be satisfied with a little less profit." At this point, it seems a foregone conclusion that Garfield picked the wrong time and place to defend his progressive policies.

Afterward, while touring the streets of Dallas, Garfield is shot from behind by two assassins on an overpass near Cotton's house where Donovan has been recuperating from his leg wound. Jack has a rifle that he took away from Cotton. He opens fire on the assassins. No sooner has the well-meaning Jack blazed away at the assassins than he finds himself not only at gunpoint but also accused of being Garfield's assassin! Surprisingly, Garfield advocated greater rights for African Americans, so it will look ironic that a black man would assassinate the president.

Initially, the villains remain a step or two ahead of our heroes. Not only do they kill Garfield, but also, they dispose of Jack. As the counterpart of Jack Ruby, Wallace arranges an ambush to silence Jack, and he shoots him five times at close range. This point blank murder approximates what the real Ruby did when broke through a cordon at Dallas police headquarters and shot Oswald to death. Meantime, everything is proceeding well enough for Pinkerton and company until Wallace demands the blackmail materials on Vice President Arthur. The conspiracy collapses when the impetuous, hot-tempered Wallace double-crosses Pinkerton and his cronies. Once he gets the blackmail materials, Wallace shoots Pinkerton to death. Meantime, Bill spends most of his time contending with the evil Sheriff Jefferson, while the wily McDonald approaches Pinkerton to cut a deal. Once more, the villains start out with greater clout than the heroes and threaten society, but their efforts are destined to miscarry.

Giuliano Gemma and Van Johnson on the set of **A Bullet for the President**

The villains in "**A Bullet for a President**" make few mistakes. Although they outnumber the heroes, they fail to maintain group solidarity within their own ranks. Defeating the villains proves to be a grim task for Willer and McDonald. Willer loses his old friend Jack Donovan, but McDonald exonerates the African American during an inquest scene and exposes Sheriff Jefferson's perfidy. Ultimately, after McDonald clears Donovan's name, Sheriff Jefferson crashes through a window during a legal hearing in the town saloon. Straddles a horse, he escapes with Bill in close pursuit. Although our heroes failed to shield the President, they manage to kill most of the conspirators that the conspirators don't kill themselves. The classical plot's fourteenth function dictates that society is now safe. Ultimately, we must wonder what McDonald plans to do with those blackmail documents Bill handed over to him. Since the status quo has been restored, the inference is McDonald will make certain nobody can use them against President Arthur. Furthermore, Arthur will follow in Garfield's footsteps with his progressive agenda as he threatened he would when he left the conspirators.

CRITICISM

Tonino Valerii's "**A Bullet for the President**" ranks as an anomalous Spaghetti western masterpiece because it transposes one of the 20th century's most infamous assassinations with a 19th century assassination and integrated them seamlessly into a speculative shoot'em up! No other Spaghetti western attempted such a feat with the audacity of this film. For this reason alone, Valerii's film should make every-body's top ten list, for its artistry, its artifice, and its audacity. Spaghetti western aficionados and critics hold it in high regard. Howard Hughes is more ambivalent than most. He argues, "The film is not without its faults." Nevertheless, he ad-mires its gimmick. "The politicizing is cleverly handled and the film is truly epic in scope—Valerii's equivalent of "Once Upon A Time In the West . . ." [18] In his book *10, 000 Ways to Die: A Director's Take on the Spaghetti Western*, author Alex Cox praises Valerii's film as "a well-made, thought-provoking western thriller, with very few failings." [19] Kevin Grant calls "**A Bullet for the President**" "an audacious critique of American history."[20] Christopher Frayling summed it up with one word "extraordinary."[21]

This political Spaghetti western about an affluent elite who assassinate an American President and dream of fomenting a second Civil War is no half-baked, slapdash, superficial saga. Valerii orchestrates the expository scenes about the motives of both heroes and villains around dynamic set-pieces. The showdown at the bridge with Bill killing the four deputies is exciting stuff. Valerii stages the assassination with close attention to replicating details from the Kennedy shooting. The newspa-per man who conceals a rifle in his crutch to rescue Bill is another surprising scene. Pitting a heroic group against a villainous faction, this film emerges as a complicat-ed but never convoluted western.

Despite its gimmicky premise, Valerii doesn't sidestep the issue of race. Race is of central importance to the plot. The villains are primarily racists who fear the loss of cheap black labor. This motivates them to frame Jack Donovan for Garfield's murder. Just as the actual Oswald was stigmatized by his Communist sympathies, Donovan's racial heritage condemns him to death! Pinkerton speaks on behalf of the wealthy citizens of Dallas, when he denounces the outcome of Garfield's progressive policies and its fall-out for their plantations. "Your plan is to stir up discord because you need their labor up north." Furthermore, the filmmakers condense their narrative about a conspiracy underlying the Kennedy assassination into 108 minutes, with enviable brevity. Comparably, Oliver Stone's controversial "JFK" (1991) took three times that length to present its conspiracy premise!

Interestingly, "**A Bullet for the President**" was the second film about the Kennedy assassination. Exploitation director Larry Buchanan released his film "**The Trial of Lee Harvey Oswald**" (1964) shortly after the assassination in April 1965, but he complained it was pulled from theaters owing to its controversial subject matter. "**Common Law Wife**" writer & director Buchanan approached the assassination from a 'what if' standpoint. Basically, Jack Ruby never killed Oswald, and Oswald went on trial. The prosecution argues Oswald's Marxist beliefs induced him to kill Kennedy. Advocating an insanity plea, Oswald's defense attorney contends his client suffered from psychological problems that led him to kill Kennedy. Buchanan shoots most of the action from the perspective of the jury with occasional cutaways of assassination newsreel footage. Ultimately, the audience must decide if Oswald was a cold-blooded killer or mentally disturbed. Valerii's film surpasses this simple, but safe black & white potboiler that reportedly was withdrawn from release. Moviegoers would have to bide their time for the next six years after

"**A Bullet for the President**" was released before the next Kennedy conspiracy thriller. David Miller's "**Executive Action**" (1973) contemplated the assassination from the perspective of the conspirators and relied on documentary footage to forge its own sense of verisimilitude. Nine more films would be produced about the assassination along with several documentaries, but none have a premise with a gimmick like "A Bullet for the President."

Parsimonious producer Bianco Manini, who made one of the best political Spaghetti westerns about the Mexican Revolution, "**A Bullet for the General**," must have felt he had bitten off more than he could chew with Valerii's sprawling, conspiracy theory, horse opera. According to Italian scholar Robert Curti, Valerii encountered production problems working with the frugal Manini. Furthermore, Gemma told Curti he was never fully paid for the film. Curti also said the JFK assassination "had a huge resonance in Italy, but I think the element that had the filmmakers rework it for Il prezzo del potere was the conspiracy angle, which was so close to all the events that were taking place in the country and outside in that period."

Despite budgetary shortfalls, Valerii succeeded in making "**A Bullet for the President**" appear every bit as impressive as it does. Nothing about this western may be described as claustrophobic. Lenser Stelvio Massi's widescreen, Technicolor, cinematography enhances the scope of scenes both interior as well as exterior. If you watch carefully, you can see orchestrated equestrian and pedestrian traffic in the streets during the Donovan inquest that gives the illusion the people outside are going about their daily routines. Another part of that it is the left-over "**Once Upon A Time in the West**" sets. Valerii and Gastaldi never let the action slacken and bog down, and the characters never lurch off on loquacious tangents. Valerii never lets the exposition interfere with the orchestration of its spectacle. The film unfolds in an orderly fashion, presenting the narrative in a coherent but aggressive manner that commands attention.

The opening credits materialize over a venerable map of Texas and the territories surrounding it to give audiences a clear idea where the action transpires. Apart from establishing the physical setting, the map serves a dual purpose. "A Bullet for the President" is rooted in a historical past, and Valerii's film is no fantasy shoot'em up set in an unspecified corner of the southwest. The highly detailed map imparts a vestige of reality that "Bullet" requires for its verisimilitude. Furthermore, we can tell by composer Luis Bacalov's beautiful but subdued orchestral score with some shrill harmonica riffs that this western is not going to be a superficial sagebrusher. From the start, we know the atmosphere in Dallas is conspicuously antagonistic to Garfield's arrival. Deputy Sheriffs are burning a portrait of Abraham Lincoln in the town square. The Lincoln portrait signifies the political ideology which brought about a Union victory, an anathema to this Confederate enclave. Furthermore, it reminds us of Lincoln's assassination being the work of radical extremists, similar to those governing Dallas in the highest positions as bankers, politicians, lawyers, and the lawmen. Interestingly, images of Lincoln in either presidential portraits or carved busts are visible in Dallas, in the background of rooms or the periphery of the screen. The burning of Lincoln's portrait foreshadows the aims of the conspirators who want to kill Garfield. These individuals abhor the society that Texas has become with the Confederate defeat. Ultimately, burning Lincoln's portrait foreshadows the impending Garfield/Kennedy assassination. The first thing we hear is Pa Willers warning Sheriff Jefferson about a suspected attempt to blow up the president's train. The opening twenty minutes dwells in depth with the before, during, and after of the train incident. Bill's father dies because he accidentally learned about the attempt to kill the President. Wallace rears his ugly head fuming with hate in general for the Union and specifically for Garfield as the president. During the train incident, Bill and Jack hightail it on horseback to intercept the train. Jefferson's deputies surprise and ambush them. They wound Jack in the leg, but Bill plays possum. Slumped lifelessly over his horse, Bill topples into the dust as one deputy tips him off his steed. When he thuds against the dirt, Bill surprises both deputies, empties his holster, and kills both men! Rather than delay and help Jack, Bill does Jack's bidding and rides off to thwart an attempt to blow up the train.

Later, Bill ushers in Doctor Strips (José Calvo of "**A Fistful of Dollars**") tend to Jack's wounds. Although J.B. Cotton (Ángel Álvarez of "**Django**") agreed to hide Jack, he wastes no time in notifying Jefferson about his unexpected guest. When Jefferson and Cotton are conferring about Jack Donovan, Jefferson glances up at the window of Jack's room where the African American has taken refuge and then looks across the street at the overpass. During that moment in the street after dark, Jefferson decides how Garfield will not only be assassinated, but also the patsy who will take the fall for the assassination! Moreover, Jefferson decides where the assassins will station themselves to shoot Garfield as well as the best way to frame Jack for the assassination! Several subtle touches such as this recur throughout "**A Bullet for the President**." The film follows functions eleven through sixteen of Wright's classical plot. Eventually, Bill kills Sheriff Jefferson in an interesting duel that takes place in the dark. The two opponents are allowed to have only one bullet in their respective revolvers and two lighted stogies. In the dark, the only way to know where an opponent is requires looking for the glowing tip of the stogie. Valerii stages this unusual showdown, so Bill can kill Jefferson. After all, once he knew that Pa Willers had heard about the bridge attack, Jefferson left it up to Wallace to deal with the elder Willer. In a sense, Jefferson is just as guilty of Pa Willer's murder as Wallace. Although the heroes do not thwart Garfield/Kennedy's assassination, they see trust unravel between the conspirators, and the villains wind up killing each other. Ironically, Vice President Arthur had warned the greedy Pinkerton that all of his gold wouldn't save his life. Once Pinkerton hands over the blackmail documents, Wallace kills him in cold blood at point blank range. Afterward, Willer confronts Wallace on the street in a showdown. Before they shoot it out, McDonald surprises Willer and guns down one of Wallace's cronies so Willer can kill the firebrand rebel conspirator.

Giuliano Gemma
Blutiges Blei

EPILOGUE

Any thought-provoking revelations about the production history of "**A Bullet for the President**" are as likely to appear as a breakthrough in the ambiguity surrounding the Kennedy assassination. Long out of the limelight, Patrizi has remained mum about Valerii's film, which turned a profit in Italy, while Ernesto Gastaldi is the only witness to this conspiracy classic who could reveal something significant. According to Roberto Curti, "Ernesto doesn't remember these things, he just wrote too many films, and sometimes he tends to embellish memories. But unlike others he's very candid and modest about his work." Curti assures me the copy of the final screenplay is identical to the movie. Still, it would be something to know what prompted Patrizi to reenact a 20th century, American, assassination as a dusty Spaghetti western. What could possibly have been achieved with such a crackpot notion? Valerii's film raises so many questions it is truly unfortunate that film critics and scholars have snubbed it because of its cultural heritage as a Spaghetti western. *Wild East Productions* has done an exemplary job with their Blu-ray presentation of this landmark western. The audio and video are both crisp and clear. Finally, Spaghetti western collectors need no longer scour compilation DVDs for a good copy of this movie!

Pages 94-95, German lobby cards for **A Bullet for the President**

END NOTES

1. Curti, Roberto. Interview. Conducted by Van Roberts, 2, January, 2020.

2. The Warren Commission Report: The Official Report of the President's Commission on the Assassination of President John F. Kennedy. United States Government Printing Office, Washington: 1964, p. 23.

3. "Letter from Assistant Attorney General William F. Weld to Peter W. Rodino Jr., undated" (PDF). Retrieved February, 2020.

4. George Brown Tindall, America: A Narrative History, 2d ed. (New York: W.W. Norton & Company, 1988), 773.

5. Joachim Joesten, The Dark Side of Lyndon Baines Johnson (London, Dawnay, 1968), 14-17.

6. Tindall, America: A Narrative History, 732-35.

7. Curti, Roberto. Interview. Conducted by Van Roberts, 4, February, 2020.

8. T. R. Fehrenbach, Fire And Blood: A History Of Mexico, 2d ed. (Da Capo Press, 1995), 424-425, 436-439.

9. Fehrenbach, Fire And Blood: A History Of Mexico, 449-460, 500-504, 517-546.

10. Laurence Staig and Tony Williams, Italian Western: The Opera of Violence (London, Lorrimer, 1975), 92-111.

11. Christopher Frayling, Sergio Leone: Something to Do with Death (New York: Faber and Faber, 2000), 30; Christopher Frayling, Spaghetti Westerns: Cowboys and Europeans from Karl May to Sergio Leone (London: Routledge & Kegan Paul, 1981).

12. Curti, Roberto. Interview. Conducted by Van Roberts, 4, February, 2020. After studying Valerii's cinematic style in this particular section, I messaged Curti about the Orson Welles & Valerii comparison, and he wrote back: "That's spot-on, Van! Tonino told me he took inspiration from the deep-focus shots in "**Citizen Kane**," I don't know whether it was a later embellishment on his part but Massi's cinematography is excellent, and he indeed uses deep focus in several shots."

13. Robert Curti, Tonino Valerii: The Films, with a foreword by Christopher Frayling and an afterword by Ernesto Gastaldi (North Carolina, McFarland & Company, 2016); Frayling, Something to Do with Death, 348-363.

14. Will Wright, Six Guns and Society: A Structural Study of the Western (Berkeley: University of California Press, 1975), 32-59; Kevin Grant, Any Gun Can Play: The Essential Guide to Euro-Westerns (London: FAB Press, 2011), 176.

15. Wright, Sixguns and Society, p. 48-49.

16. Christopher Frayling, Spaghetti Westerns, p. 51; Austin Fisher, Radical Frontiers in the Spaghetti Western: Politics, Violence and Popular Italian Cinema (London, I.B. Tauris, 2011), p. 81.

17. Wright, 45.

18. Howard Hughes, Spaghetti Westerns (Great Britain, Pocket Essentials, 2001), p. 67.

19. Alex Cox, 10,000 Ways to Die: A Director's Take on the Spaghetti Western (London: Kamera Books, 2009), p.248.

20. Kevin Grant, Any Gun Can Play, p.31.

21. Frayling, Spaghetti Westerns, p. 96.

New from Kino Lorber! Details to be released soon!

Augusto Caminito and Eugenio Ercolani

The Story of Paul Maxwell
Considerations on Paolo Bianchini
by Eugenio Ercolani

Since its reconstruction and subsequent rise in the mid to late fifties, the Italian film industry—among other things—famously became a forging factory of elusive chameleonic filmmakers, not easily or neatly definable: directors that managed to slalom their way through the loopholes, ever-shifting genres, and improvised producers with which the Italian filmic milieu had always been filled. Among those figures who've managed to slip and slide their way, decade after decade, through the mirrors and smoke of this impalpable and ambiguous world, one should include Paolo Bianchini.

The biographical information on Bianchini, Roman, born in 1931, is scarce and thinly spread, but what is clear from just a superficial glance at his filmography as a director is that Bianchini is a survivor, a testimony of which is the fact that he continued directing well into the new millennium (his last official credit is dated 2012) at a time in which most of his contemporaries had long retired. "Despite rarely including political elements within his films, Paolo was particularly efficient when it came to navigating strategically within the industry. Not a political director but politically savvy." These are the words of film mogul Augusto Caminito, known for producing such titles as Abel Ferrara's **King of New York** (1990), Lucio Fulci's **Murder Rock** (1984), Klaus Kinski's **Paganini** (1989), Tinto Brass' **Paprika** (1991); for having written more than 55 films; and for helming the infamous production nightmare entitled **Nosferatu in Venice** (1988). More importantly, with regard to what we are tackling here, Caminito, with others, penned Bianchini's directorial debut, Il gioco delle spie (**Our Men in Bagdad**, 1966). "Paolo was nice, a sweet man, and I was very fond of him. He had ideas, but most importantly he had a lot of energy. But he had loads of problems with women. He ran after all the waitresses in his neighborhood, creating a lot of issues for himself. He was married to Anna Maria, a very patient woman, very patient indeed. However, Paolo was, of all the people known in the initial phase of my career, the one most immersed in cinema, he had become the right arm of Luigi Zampa. By the time I got to know him I had started writing but he was already a step ahead, he was in the mix. Zampa was an incredibly important director, unfortunately a little forgotten now but very powerful at the time so being his assistant was a big break for Paolo. **Our Men in Bagdad** was a simple thing to put together; it was your typical James Bond inspired commercial operation which Paolo directed well, no flare but competently."

It is with Zampa that Bianchini begins working as far back as 1953, but throughout the same decade he flanks other directors such as Antonio Racioppi, Renato Polselli, and Roberto Mauri, and in doing so passes from the last spasms of the neorealist movement and the first of the new "commedia all'italiana", to the genres germinated from the "Hollywood on the Tiber" years and the consequent American presence on Italian soil, one representative film being **Costantino il grande** (Constantine and the Cross, 1961) by Lionello De Felice. It is worth mentioning that Bianchini was also the 1st AD on the seminal rural horror drama **Il demonio** (The Demon, 1963), that helped shape so many films on demonic possessions to come, the first of which was William Friedkin's classic **The Exorcist** (1973). After his debut with the aforementioned spy story, Bianchini will, for the most part and always in collaboration with others, participate in the writing of scripts for his own films, but in interviews he has often underlined the importance of having taken part in **Ad ogni costo** (Grand Slam, 1967) directed by Giuliano Montaldo.

The film boasts a star-studded cast—Edward G. Robinson, Robert Hoffmann, Janet Leigh, Adolfo Celi, Klaus Kinski, George Rigaud—and was a big commercial hit that turned out to be a game changer for most of the young talents involved.

Apparently, things were about to go down very differently, as Caminito explains: "I wrote **Grand Slam**, a first treatment, in the early sixties. It was among the first scripts I wrote. Nobody asked me to, I was dishing out as many stories as possible trying to get something sold. Paolo loved the script, he liked it a lot. When he read it, he hadn't yet made his first film as a director and was set on my little treatment. That story was conceived long before its realization, just around the time I met Bianchini and Maurizio Lucci. It was probably too expensive… anyway whatever the reason, it was forgotten until we decided to dust it off and hand it to Montaldo, years later, who eventually directed it. It was Giuliano that opened the door to Mino Roli, a seasoned screenwriter who didn't do much, but in general at the time he worked mainly for the theater, he wrote comedies. He coordinated the writing of the film."

It is undoubtable that Bianchini was never able to make the film, that pivotal title that could launch him to the next level. Between 1966 and 1973, often using the pseudonym Paul Maxwell, he directs ten films of various genres, among which comic strip extravaganzas, Decameron inspired sex comedies, and a proto-giallo, but it is in Westerns that Bianchini leaves his deepest mark. Caminito: "I was never credited for my work on his Westerns because it wasn't what I wanted to be known for. He liked the genre and I think managed to tap into some of the important ingredients and make a good Western, but he was a little uncertain in his directing, which is a shame. The scripts were written in record time. Those were years in which I would dish out a script every two weeks. I had two or three university students which would work, one in the living room, the other in the bathroom, on different projects. You had to find a twist, a narrative edge that worked and develop it as quickly as possible. I'm talking about low budget Westerns, and most of Paolo's ones were."

Quel caldo maledetto giorno di fuoco (Gatling Gun, 1968), starring Robert Woods and John Ireland, is generally considered his best effort within the genre. Two years after the outbreak of the American Civil War, Richard Gatling, creator of the machine gun he gave his name to, offers his invention to the Federal Government. President Lincoln secretly sends a commission to Las Cruzes, New Mexico, to meet with him and lead him to Washington. During the night two hitmen kill the three northern members of the commission and kidnap Gatling. The Federal Government blames and condemns agent Chris Tanner, accusing him of having revealed the plan's details. Sure of his innocence, the director of the Pinkerton Agency that Tanner works for manages to free him, and entrusts him with the task of ascertaining the truth. After many vicissitudes, Chris discovers that Gatling and the machine gun are in the hands of Tarpas, a Mexican bandit, and Rykert, a member of the Northern Commission. The plan of the traitor and his partner is to sell Gatling's weapon to the southerners and deliver the man to the northerners in exchange for a million dollars. The fairly straightforward story is made quite hectic and confused by directing and editing that play with time-lapses and give the film a certain dysfunctional feel. This is what most reviews tend to underline as the film's charm, seeing that the result is as unconventional, though undeniably interesting—Quentin Tarantino includes the film among his twenty favorite Italian Westerns.

Bianchini has said more than once that he remembers little to nothing about the film's production. Also, it is not rare to come across texts that hypothesize Sergio Corbucci's hand in the making, maybe inspired by the presence of a very explicit and gory scene of a bullet being extracted from a hand, but it is very unlikely there is any truth to this. Caminito: "I personally agree that it is his best film, but cinema is like that at times, especially Italian cinema. A bunch of random things are brought together, mixed with each other, and surprisingly they work… not only do they work but they become snapshots of the aspects of our country's life." In many ways this last definition seems to perfectly encompass the dysfunctional career of Paolo Bianchini.

Interview with Augusto Caminito by Eugenio Ercolani

Grand Slam (Ad ogni costo, Italy, Spain, W. Germany, 1967)

Darkening the Italian Screen

Interviews with Genre and Exploitation Directors Who Debuted in the 1950s and 1960s

EUGENIO ERCOLANI

Darker Things to Come
Interview with Eugenio Ercolani

M.H. First off let me put this out there, I am a huge fan of your book *Darkening the Italian Screen*. Tell us a bit about your background and how you decided to write this book?

E.E. Well, let me start by saying that really, you've been so enthusiastic about my book right from its release, and for your support I can't thank you enough. Anyway, moving on to your question, I guess Darkening was born by chance, which I realize is quite a vague and cheesy answer to give but allow me to elaborate. Ever since I was a child I wanted to be in films, make films, watch films, study them, immerse myself in that world and stay as close as possible to it, even if at first just at the periphery. I guess many go through a phase just before they decide to act upon their passion, in which films become slightly painful experiences, good ones at least: the ones you enjoy. You watch them and as much as you become enthralled by them you feel frustrated—you don't just want to be sitting comfortably in your living room or enveloped in the reassuring darkness of a cinema theatre, you want to be part of the process. This latent frustration becomes increasingly more difficult to ignore as time goes on, at least it did in my case, until something has to be done. So, you can say films have always been very important to me. Cinema definitely helped me a great deal during difficult and dark periods of my life, especially my teenage years. You know, there are two kinds of people: there are those who after having watched a film quickly label it with a five-word sentence and proceed with their life, and then there are "let's go and find a café, sit down and talk for an hour about what we've just watched" people. If I show you a film, you better be ready to talk about it later; you're not getting off the hook with an "I liked it". My adolescence was one big, bubbling, celluloid soup in which I immersed myself. I would watch anything. I would go to Videofobia, a local video rental in Rome as big as a phone booth but crammed with VHS tapes, floor to ceiling, and re-emerge from it an hour later with bags full of videocassettes. I would watch, indiscriminately, everything I could get my hands on during these expeditions. I would come back with some obscure eighties slasher, a film by Bela Tarr, a Mario Bava picture and a 1950s musical by Minelli or a previous one by Busby Berkeley. In the meantime, I would be reading constantly any book I could find, and in this sense, I have to be very thankful to my parents. I was brought up by two wonderful people that pushed and tried to give wings to any curiosity or passion I would manifest. Over time this apparently confused kaleidoscope started having clearer features. You start connecting filmic currents, directors, styles, overlapping trends, crossing genres, and not only do you start actually developing a palate but you also start seeing the grand design of things, the context films were born from.

Alberto De Martino and Sergio Leone.

Umberto Lenzi

It's a fascinating process and like every evolution it begins with a glorious chaos, a fascinating primordial soup. Snobbery, and the preconceived notions that it entails, are the worst enemies of personal growth. After a few experiences as a volunteer assistant I made my first concrete step in the right direction which meant signing up at that bootcamp called the London Film Academy. After that experience and four years in the United Kingdom I started doing a number of things. I've always had to recycle myself, towing along different roles in parallel. 1st AD was the first thing and something I actually still do, followed by a long stint as a senior editor for the monthly magazine Nocturno Cinema, which led to other collaborations and a series of gigs as a researcher and organizing events and retrospectives for the Italian National Film Registry. Then, about five years ago, I founded my company with which I started packaging special contents— featurettes, interviews, documentaries—for home-video labels such as 88 Films, X-Rated, Arrow Video, Xcess, Severin, Cineploit, Blue Underground, Turbine, Grindhouse Releasing, Cinestrange Extreme, and Capelight. In this mare magnum of booklets, short films, writings, screenings, articles, camera operating gigs, and hours on end of interviews, Darkening the Italian Screen popped out, a spontaneous germination. I had this idea of selecting and speaking with a number of diverse directors, over a number of topics, and basically using their words to tell the story of Italian genre and exploitation cinema: the rise and birth. One is free to think whatever they please about my book but it's a matter of fact that there is nothing else quite like it out there. I didn't want any repetitions. I wanted to give something new and fresh to people: directors that have never been interviewed, or at least never in English, or never this much in-depth; uncensored interviews, long detailed ones which put side by side create a tapestry. Even the essays that introduce the interviews, I didn't want them to have the usual monographic approach but to be more snapshots of a time and place.

Gregg Palmer, Tomas Milian and Alberto De Martino on the set of **Life is Tough, Eh Providence?**

Each chapter is a portrait of one director, their body of work, their time, and hopefully their personalities. Even though it has only just been published it wouldn't be possible now to put together a publication like it, simply because in the past few years so many of the book's protagonists have died—Umberto Lenzi, Giorgio Capitani, Franco Rossetti, just to mention a few. Darkening the Italian Screen *is a strange, bittersweet mix of ingredients but hopefully an entertaining one. Reality, as I wrote in the book's preface, is the result of multitudes, and its truth is never the fruit of a single point of view. It is only in the overlapping of perspectives, in the confusion of contradictions, in the ambiguous nature of opinions, in the proliferation of voices that we can hope to find the essence of what we are looking for and in the case of this book the points of view are often cynical, comical, sardonic, scandalous, and at times even malicious. But after all, not everything in the book is true, though you'll find no lies in it.*

M.H. Let us start by briefly talking about the peplum films. Although peplums and Italian Westerns may seem worlds apart, the two genres incorporate many of the same plot devices and character construction into their narratives.

E.E. Before continuing I think it's important to step backwards and talk briefly about the significance of the post-war years, which is the essential turning point to fully understand the evolution of Westerns, peplums, and their, let's say, inter-action. In 1948, 20th Century Fox decided to shoot The Prince of Foxes *by Henry King in the studios of Cinecittà, anticipating what, a few years later, would become a habit that gave rise to a unique period in Italian history which we all know as "Hollywood on the Tiber". The films in production were adventurous spectacles and romantic films, set among Roman ruins and narrow sunlit alleys, but most of all, they were what the industry called "sandaloni", of which the literal translation would be "big sandals", peplums, over the top, lavish and opulent mythological fantasies set in Ancient Rome.*

The Neorealist manifesto that forged or gave birth to the careers of auteurs like Rossellini, Vittorio De Sica, Pietro Germi, Giuseppe De Santis, and Alberto Lattuada, started fading, dying out completely in the mid-fifties. But by this time the success and invasion of American productions had introduced to the provincial and simple Italian and Roman society a new social phenomenon made up of an Olympus of divas and stars, parties, nightclubs, "paparazzi", and a jet-set lifestyle. The relationship between demand and offer whirls into an unprecedented frenzy and in 1954, 700 million tickets were sold to a public in need of candy-flavored Hollywood dreams and neon-lit stars. Italian cinema started building again, stronger and faster than ever: comedies, musical plays, cape-and-dagger, and period dramas were amongst the genres which producers were drawn to at the start of the fifties. But all this began attracting many, not only to the darkness of a film theatre but also towards the industry itself, now that the doors were wide open, and the demand was high. What can be described as a decade-long training period began for a great number of future directors. The possibility of creating a career in cinema was a difficult but concrete one and many took their first steps. So, the biggest connection between the two genres is the fact that many directors that would later make Westerns, and in some cases become bona fide specialists, started out directing mythological epics, or working on them as ADs, writers, or helming second units.

Let's not forget that two greats, Sergio Leone, who made his official directorial debut in peplums, and Sergio Corbucci, actually left quite a deep mark within the genre before passing onto Westerns, and as both of them declared in later years they were already dreaming about Western landscapes as they found themselves at work on their respective peplums. But to the two aforementioned heavyweights we can add also such pivotal figures as Alberto De Martino, Mario Caiano, Franco Rossetti, Ruggero Deodato, Vittorio Sindoni, Marcello Avallone, Umberto Lenzi, and Sergio Martino, all of whom have chapters dedicated to them in Darkening the Italian Screen *and all of whom owe a lot to those foam Corinthian columns and plasterboard temples. Needless to say, the list of names could go on but to answer your question more specifically, yes, we do find recurring narrative templates which become communicating bridges between the two genres.*

Lunch break on the set of **Tepepa** (1969)

De Martino, for example, in the early sixties wrote a film called The Seven Glad-
iators *which he intended to direct but was eventually made by Spanish Pedro
Lazaga, that was inspired—as the title easily suggests—by* The Magnificent Seven
*by John Sturges, which as we all know is a Western remake of Akira Kurosawa's
epic drama* Seven Samurai, *and this is such a wonderfully simple and easily grasp-
able testimony of the power of a solid narrative; a good story transcends genre.
So, in more than one case we can find attempts to create crossovers between the
two genres which show a certain awareness and willingness to experiment and
contaminate. For a question of physique du rôle, most actors active in peplums
were not able to make the jump to Westerns. Offhand, the only mildly successful
leading man to do so, that comes to mind at least, is Richard Harrison, but there is
one attempt worth mentioning. By 1968 peplums were dead and Steve Reeves, the
king of the genre, hadn't been working for at least three years, if not more. Well,
he was determined to make a comeback and of course tried to do so with a Western.* A Long Ride from Hell *by Camillo Bazzoni is Reeves' absolute last film and I
think it's a fitting image, or metaphor if you will, for what we are talking about:
the decade is dying out, a year before the film's release the Italian parliament is
discussing the new university reform which is one of the events that leads students
and protestors to flood the streets, the new is devouring the old—divorce, Vietnam,
the sexual revolution, and the terrorist-fueled Years of Lead waft at arm's length.*

Even Westerns have become increasingly more politicized and its heroes darker, more sexual, younger, and here we have this bulky epitome of a more naïve time and cinema trying to remain relevant—huge, bubbly, and muscly; strong and invincible, as we thought we were during the Italian economic boom.

Regarding Reeves and his last film, I want to give you a little present. Hopefully, this year the second volume of Darkening the Italian Screen *should be released and among the people I interviewed for it there is director/writer Francesco Barilli, who many will know as the man responsible for the 1974 horror–giallo* The Perfume of the Lady in Black. *Anyway, he worked on* A Long Ride from Hell *as an assistant director and this is a bit of what he had to say: "You could only feel a tremendous pity for Reeves. I have never laughed so much in my life as I did on that film. Just to give you an idea, I have roughly 120 pages written for what I was planning would become a book on the worst Western ever made. Let's start by saying that he was a dog, just terrible. A real dog of an actor. He didn't know how to hit a mark, how to move.*

On the first day of production it was raining, and I was sent to fetch Reeves. Keep in mind that he wouldn't speak to anybody from the production except me because he discovered I loved William Turner and Vivaldi—he also realized the producers were real swindlers, old school swindlers—so we would talk about Vivaldi and I would be the only one knocking at the door of his trailer. In reality, the madness began right from the beginning when we were selecting his outfit. One day he arrived in his costume... something incredible that he had gotten tailor-made in Mexico and sent to Italy: all black, with huge silver spurs, a silver band on this massive black hat, silver studded gun belt with a big star on the buckle. Basically a skin-tight Zorro outfit. We all looked at each other and I don't remember who said it first: "Your character is a fugitive from the law. He has just broken out of prison." "No, no, no this is my costume. I got this made in Mexico..." "But Steve... when can he wear this...?"

That was the beginning of the nightmare. Going back to the start of this anecdote: it was raining, I went to fetch him, and he comes out of the trailer and trips over his spurs, falling like a log, head-first in the mud. From that day, the crew retitled the film "tutti a casa" ("let's go home"). We never stopped laughing on that film. Reeves would be constantly doing stuff, hurting himself... like getting his spurs in his ass, falling off the horse... Once he went up to a well and started drinking. We all tried to stop him but he wouldn't listen. An hour later he started vomiting and shitting all over the set and had to stay in bed for a week."

M.H. The Italian Western genre was not born because of the success of Sergio Leone's **A Fistful of Dollars**; it was born out of wanting in Europe for Westerns that the United States no longer produced in abundance. Talk about the early years of the genre, the people involved, including those you interviewed for your book.

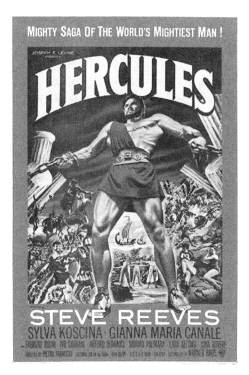

Left: Italian Poster for **A Long Ride to Hell** (1969)
Right: U.S. Poster **Hercules** (Le fatiche di Ercole, Italy, Spain, 1958)

E.E. Sergio Leone was the first that had a new and personal vision that, despite being moved by a deep love and knowledge of the great tradition of American Westerns, freed itself of its historical and most of all formal restrictions. That said we can find Westerns in Italian cinematography as far back as the silent era. In 1913 Roberto Roberti directs the Western drama Indian Vampire *starring Bice Valerian, but sticking to the post-war era we have to underline an essential difference between the birth of Westerns and that of peplums. The latter mentioned genre is the direct consequence of the presence of the American cinema machine on Italian soil. Americans, with many exceptions of course, came here mainly for mythological epics, cape-and-dagger, and adventure films, not Westerns. Starting from Hercules—I'm talking about the 1958* Le fatiche di Ercole *onwards—will use the anamorphic lens of Cinemascope, vivid colors, and a panoramic screen in the attempt to amplify the limits of the increasingly popular television monitor.*

The film, directed by Pietro Francisci, is not only one of the biggest and most successful examples of the genre—making the aforementioned Steve Reeves an international star and effectively characterizing and shaping dozens of peplums to come—but is also an important cornerstone for all Italian genre cinema. In fact, Reeves' epic emerges in that invisible borderline at the end of the "Hollywood on the Tiber" era and was the most ambitious Italian effort, both economically and visually, within the genre since the end of the war. This is just to explain that basically the biggest link to the Americans were peplums. In the subsequent years, among the bittersweet stories of the "commedia all'italiana", the rise of "musicarelli", and gothic horror this link was still strong. Just think that between 1960 and 1965 more than 100 peplums are put into production, representing 10% of the Italian film industry, and most of them did very well at the box office. Westerns, amongst this period of assessment, were still very much molded by the American perspective, and most of them are in the best of cases flat, with no identity. Films like Heroes of Fort Worth *by De Martino or* Gunfight at Red Sands *by Ricardo Blasco are exemplary of pre-Leone Westerns.*

The first is a quite laughable attempt at forgery and sees a band of Southerners after the Civil War become allies with an Indian tribe in the attempt to defeat a Union command, while trying to gain support from Emperor Maximillian. It treads territory in which Italians can't possibly win: the kind of historical events told require an authenticity in costumes, faces, and locations that is impossible to recreate, and in fact the result is naïf and innocent, awkward and clumsy, as De Martino himself admits. On the other hand, Blasco's film is definitely streaked with a more Latin touch but is still indecisive in freeing itself from the visual and narrative templates of the American approach. Although it's easy to shrug off films in this pre-Leone phase, which is populated but not excessively prolific, as forgettable sub-par products, actually one should look beyond the cringe educing cavalries and Native Americans and focus on other products Italians were doing in Spain. I mentioned Blasco's film before, Gunfight at Red Sands, *well the action scenes of that were actually directed by Mario Caiano, who is one of the most important figures, I feel, of the best kind of pre-Leone proto-Westerns. Caiano collaborated with writer Josè Mallorquì, who specialized in Westernish, Zorro-type stories.* Il segno del coyote *("The Sign of the Coyote"), made in 1963, is Caiano's first Western, not a pure one but still containing all the elements that characterize the genre: the village and gunfights, the dust, the over stylizations, horses, and villains. It is in Spain that Caiano, as well as other directors, starts learning the rules of Westerns, in a period that he describes as one of the most adventurous of his career, alongside American producer Harry Joe Brown who was attempting to recreate the great classics of the thirties, reimagining characters like Captain Blood and Zorro. Another interesting example of an Italian proto-Western of the early sixties would be* Duello nella Sila *("Duel of Fire") by Umberto Lenzi, released in Italy in 1962, which is set in the Risorgimento era, precisely in the Lucania of 1850. So, in a nutshell, if on one side the pure Westerns made in Italy, although maybe competently directed, were excessively derivative, on the other there were attempts to find different and original interpretations to the genre.*

M.H. Now let's talk about the first four directors you interviewed for your book starting out with Giorgio Capitani. In your book, Capitani acknowledges that his finest film is the classic Western **The Ruthless Four**. Why did he never direct another Italian Western? What were his thoughts on the Italian Westerns?

E.E. He definitely liked Westerns although I have a feeling it was more on a film-by-film basis as opposed to a love of the genre as a whole. Anyway, I'm very happy to have managed to get Capitani into the book. By the time I tried to get to him he had not only retired but was keeping away from everything: interviews, festivals, public appearances of any kind. I wanted a chapter on him because he was the last of a breed—he has passed away since—of director that doesn't exist and can't anymore. He wasn't the oldest director I interviewed for the book, but was the one that began the earliest and for the people he met, for all the turning points he witnessed, for the fact of having managed to survive since his debut as a director in 1952, all the crises the industry has gone through, he really had a gravitas, a weight to him that I felt the book needed, even if he isn't particularly well known abroad. The book had to have a character who could bridge the forties to the fifties and I consider myself lucky to have managed to get him. He indeed identifies his Western as being his best film, or the one he prefers at least; personally I don't know if I agree, appreciating most of his comedies from the seventies, especially the French–Italian co-productions starring Enrico Montesano, but that's neither here or there.

The reason he gave me for not having made more Westerns is that the film was not as successful in Italy as the producers were hoping. He adds to this the fact that by that time he was so heavily associated with comedies that the genre had trapped him and comedies were all they were offering. These motivations might well be true, but I would suspect they are incomplete. Regarding this there is one thing I would like to point out and that is that Italian film industry was pretty chaotic: we never had a layered, pyramidal industry like the Americans, where you've got the so called "studio system" where strategies are put in place and there is a certain communication between these giant film factories, where you've got independent cinema, the drive-in circuit… Of course I'm over-simplifying but undoubtedly in Italy there was one sticky, pulsating, overpopulated confused blob of an industry which somehow managed to function, and although in the long run its dysfunctionality is exactly what brought to its demise, for a long time this blob bounced away happily: sometimes it would slow down but then it would start up again, gleefully slapping its quavering jelly-like behind as fast as possible, bouncing its way towards the sunset. This makes it very difficult I think for foreign historians and film aficionados, especially Anglo-Saxons ones, to fully grasp the trappings and mechanics of the Italian film industry and in fact I often find a certain overly-romanticized perspective in English essays. Many years ago I was at the Venice Film Festival and an American film critic, a high-profile one, was talking about spaghetti Westerns as if it was a community of directors sharing notes and comparing points of views on the genre.

It's a very sweet and easy way to link things together but the fact of the matter is that there was no real awareness, let alone a community working hand in hand. De Martino, Petroni, and Corbucci smoking and drinking JB whisky in someone's living room, Castellari in a corner flexing his muscles as he ponders out loud on the use of slow-motion. Leone next door in his studio, knocking on the wall, warning them to keep their voices down because Valerii is trying to rest. Hardly any of these directors would even watch the films of their contemporaries. So, why didn't Capitani direct another Western? He directed The Ruthless Four *in 1967 and it was released in theatres the following year, the same year of another film of his, not surprisingly, a comedy. In 1969 he follows it with another comedy still starring a big name like Vittorio Gassman. Capitani couldn't afford to stop and those were pivotal years for him; he was building his reputation and was gaining increasing contractual power. As you know very well, by the early seventies Westerns were losing appeal with the general public and a selective and attentive director such as Capitani would not have bothered grappling with a dying genre. Those were also the years in which he was called to direct in the States, a failed opportunity as he details in my book… So, a lot was going on and it was a confused and frantic moment both for him and the industry itself. The "whys" and "hows" are difficult to pinpoint.*

M.H. Umberto Lenzi was a director who excelled in numerous genres. His entries in the Western spaghetti genre are odd examples. His first Western **Go For Broke** is a very competent film that gets bogged down by its endless use of the double-crosses. His second and last Western **A Pistol For a Hundred Coffins** is not without its issues, one being a rather odd introduction of some escaped lunatics into the narrative. In your book, Lenzi states that he hates Westerns and has a fear of horses. Was he offered any other Westerns? Lenzi Westerns to me are like Mario Bava's in whereas the question always arises, what if they would have had an interest in the genre, the results could have been amazing. *

E.E. In Lenzi's case, if on one side he is a narratively linear director, so perfect for Westerns, on the other hand he is also a kinetic director: his cinema is based on motion and dynamism and in fact he found his perfect place within police action films. He was also what many have defined as a perfect example of a journeyman filmmaker, which is a romanticized way of saying that he was at the service of the market's needs. He would do anything the industry would ask of him which has made his filmography rich and stimulating, and also historically significant because all the various passages and turning points are present within it but also fluctuating and convulsive. Not every so-called genre director was as available as Lenzi to tackle all genres. We were talking about Capitani, well he didn't like horror, and didn't approve of the genre's most violent strains. Other directors had political reasons not to get close to certain currents, like the so called "polizieschi", which some considered to contain inherent fascist overtones.

*Lenzi also directed the 1962 film **Duel of Fire** (Duello nella Sila, Italy, 1962), which is as Eugenio notes above is a proto-western. The action takes place in Italy instead of America. Duel of Fire is not technically an Italian western. M.H.

German VHS cover of Umberto Lenzi's 1968 western **Pistol for a Hundred Coffins**, which starred Peter Lee Lawrence and John Ireland   *MH collection

Your question though has quite a philosophical root to it. I'm serious: it opens up numerous questions. Does a genre contain a director, or can a director assimilate and contain a genre? What does it take to insert your poetics within the folds of tried and run-in genre? Do you have to love a genre to make it yours? How much dismantling is necessary and when does it become too much that you've betrayed the genre's spirit? Personally I don't think you have to love a genre but you definitely have to understand it enough to be able to find the interpretive key that works for you, and I think it's pretty evident that Lenzi was not able to find it. Now that I think about it, the only action film of his that takes a Western narrative template, Syndicate Sadists—*the connections between* The Cynic, the Rat and the Fist *are skin deep and really just stop at the film's title—is also his weakest effort, so I guess you could say Westerns have never brought him much luck, in any shape, way or form. All this brings me to another question still, a simple but essential one. What gives Italian Westerns their appeal? To be honest I've never really stopped and tried to find an answer to this question, and I imagine we could discuss it for hours, but the first thing that comes to mind is its lack of sacredness. The Italian West is not a physical place or a historical period but a parallel dimension which molds its imagery from popular culture, comic books, literature, and of course cinema itself. Italian Westerns bent and deformed reality, filled it with bold colors, sweeping ever-present musical scores and over-the-top violent parables. American Westerns, until the sixties, are part of the country's mythology, and in a way of its notorious utopic dream, the re-elaboration of their history and social consciousness. The heroes of the star-and-striped West were in many ways the idealization of the American spirit. Italy is not the US, so our genre is populated of survivors, slobs, frauds, tricksters, irreverent swindlers, ambiguous revolutionaries. So, simplifying, if the American landscape is one of a continuous moral struggle between good and evil, the need to build, and ultimately the shaping of a nation, the Italian one is a violent blood-soaked pastiche in which there is no room for values, where what counts is survival, mors tua vita mea, and if there are elements pertaining to American history they are only part of the scenography like the English on the "Wanted" signs: its force, its cadence, and its characters are profoundly Italian. I believe the best examples among our Westerns are exactly the ones that embrace their nationality. Lenzi's films, with a certain classical approach, seem to be fixed in a limbo, which as you pointed out doesn't quite work.*

M.H. Giulio Petroni is one of my favorite directors of Italian Westerns and one of its most underrated. Although he only helmed five Westerns, each is very good, with **Death Rides a Horse** and **Tepepa** being classics. His other three films, **A Sky Full of Stars for a Roof, Night of the Serpent**, and Life is Tough, **Eh Providence?** are lovely examples and highly entertaining. Tell us about Petroni's thoughts on Westerns in general. Similarities between **Death Rides a Horse** and Raoul Walsh's 1947 film **Pursued**, have been voiced before, what was Petroni's response when you asked him about this. Why did he not direct the sequel to **Life is Tough, Eh Providence, Here We Go Again, Eh Providence**? And what was Petroni's working relationship with Lee Van Cleef and Tomas Milian? And was John Phillip Law the choice of the director?

Giulio Petroni and John Phillip Law on the set of **Death Rides a Horse** (1967)

E.E. Giulio Petroni, like Capitani, was an actor's director which isn't as common as one might think, especially for directors of that generation. He loved the acting process and did everything he could to create a safe and comfortable environment for them. He always participated very closely in the casting process of his films.
"When I was approached to direct the film, the only name that was being bounced around was Van Cleef's one. Law was one of the various options we discussed. I remember Antonio De Teffè (Anthony Steffen) was one actor that was mentioned a couple of times. Terence Hill was another—remember that at that time he was doing serious, straight-up Westerns. There were quite a few in the mix. I ended up choosing Law because he was getting a lot of attention in the States, but I don't think he had done any Italian films before he was cast for mine. I remember an article, maybe in Variety, that kind of pointed him out as a newcomer to keep an eye on. But more importantly he had a certain quality I was looking for. De Teffè, Hill, Law…they all had a common trait.

They had a childish look, a certain purity. Clean faced, baby-eyed men. The story was about a traumatized child who grows up into a man thirsty for revenge, living in the past: reliving in his mind, in a continuous loop, those terrible moments of his past—watching his family being killed, his mother and sister raped. I wanted him to maintain the innocence of a child at least in his face, to contrast with the violence of his adult sentiments and actions. That said, Law isn't a great actor by any means, but I think he works well in the film. Sansone believed he had a new Clint Eastwood on his hands." Regarding his feeling towards the genre, what I can state without a sliver of doubt, because as much as I carefully avoid making mention of this in my book, Giulio was indeed my grandfather, is that not only didn't he nurture any particular love for the genre but he was also not a cinephile by any means. He understood the genre and more importantly understood straight away it could work as a container of ideas and ideologies. His roots though were firmly gripped in literature and in fact he states in my interview, as well as in others, that the written page was where the inspiration, and structure, for his Westerns came from. "It was a chance to go back to the kind of spirit that animated the adventure novels I would read as a kid," is how he puts it. I think this answers the first of your questions. In 1961, two years after Giulio makes his debut as a film director—I specify film because he came from a decade as a very successful documentarian—his first novel is published. He will go back to writing, and documentaries actually, once he abandons cinema. A Sky Full of Stars for a Roof moves from Steinbeck's Of Mice and Men for example. He was made very much aware of the similarities between Death Rides a Horse and Pursued but he's always insisted on saying that he has never seen Walsh's film. On this specific matter I would believe, it would surprise me a great deal if I discovered he was lying. Keep in mind that the story is the work of Luciano Vincenzoni; Petroni was called in with a first treatment already in place, which he retouched and sewed to fit his needs but the main plot is not his. I think it's safe to write off this whole parallelism as a coincidence, which film history is riddled with. So anyway, literature has always had a very important role in his life and most of his films, whatever the genre or result, have a strong narrative structure. It shouldn't surprise then that he found himself penning his Westerns with very high-profile screenwriters such as Bernardino Zapponi, Franco Solinas, and Vincenzoni. Even because Petroni had reliable production support and consequentially budgets supporting him that say Umberto Lenzi, who we've just finished talking about, didn't have—definitely not for his westerns. Petroni, unlike other directors such as De Martino or Enzo G. Castellari, was not raised in the trenches of the filmmaking world. Sure, he had to pay his dues, go through the channels of the industry—he worked as an AD, extensively as a documentary maker as I mentioned previously—but he was just as much forged in the living rooms of the Roman intelligentsia. He was considered within certain circles an intellectual; he brushed elbows with people like Campanile, Franciosa, Pasolini. Petroni had authorial ambitions which mind you don't make him better than his contemporaries mentioned in the book and this interview, but compared to a few, definitely more coherent conceptually. The genres, the tones, and even the themes which are recurrent give his filmography a tight coherency.

Despite the fact that his Westerns are so different from each other, there is a very strong thematic unity, the torque as the polarizing element around which the story rotates: revenge and stolen innocence. Interesting, in this respect, is the role of children: the opening sequence of Death Rides a Horse, *in which the child, who will later become John Philip Law, witnesses the cruel extermination of his family or* Nest of Vipers, *in which Askew is forced to live with the remorse of having killed his own son while drunk, and then of course Tepepa, where the last one to dirty his hands with blood is little Paquito. Even Adorf and Palmer, in their respective films, are, perhaps, nothing more than children too grown-up for their context. The figure of the child is always surrounded by violence or contaminated by it. Trauma and the emotional aftermath is also a recurrent theme within Petroni's later films, in the seventies. Add to this also the anti-Christian/Catholic element which is ever present in all the films he has directed. I define, in* Darkening the Italian Screen, Night of the Serpent/Nest of Vipers *as an openly atheist Western because of the "anti-evangelical", as Petroni phrases it, sentiments manifested by Luke Askew, the lead. There is a tendency to stuff all these directors into one big cauldron but actually if you stop and focus on background, choices, and production support, you realize that many all have in common the fact of doing commercial films, and by that I mean films literally aimed at making money. In Italy, the word "commercial" is an insult; it relegates whatever product into a sub-category which is very difficult to crawl out of. This backward thinking is something I hope emerges in the book because I tried to underline it as much as possible. Going back to Petroni, the fact he grew up in a financially rich and healthy film industry and he was used to being supported by money and time made it so that he was one of those directors that struggled the most with the crises in the late seventies. I think the words of Romolo Guerrieri really condense what happened to many directors like himself or Petroni: "I was one of those directors who got hurt the most by the crisis. Those who survived were people who were able to direct films with increasingly smaller budgets and in less time. Plus, I had the possibility of choosing the films I wanted to work on.*

Of course, always with a margin of compromise but generally I had the luxury of being selective. Something you just can't be during a crisis, so I attempted to make a few films for…money. By the late seventies and early eighties directors were asked to become mercenaries. They were given a budget and a time frame: if you didn't like it you were replaced like that, a snap of finger, maybe by a DOP, or some 1st AD willing to accept anything just for a shot at directing. I decided to retire; it was simply more dignified." This brings me to your second question; he didn't direct the Providence sequel for the same reason he was adamant at the idea of helming the first one. By the early years of the seventies Giulio managed to emancipate himself from producers, with whom he had always had a bad rapport, and opened his own company Azalea. A big mistake: he had ideas and ambition but not a financial mind. His first film, which he also directed, Non commettere atti impuri *("Do Not Commit Impure Acts") in 1971 with Barbara Bouchet, did fairly well but he needed to pump money into his company which is when Providence came into play.*

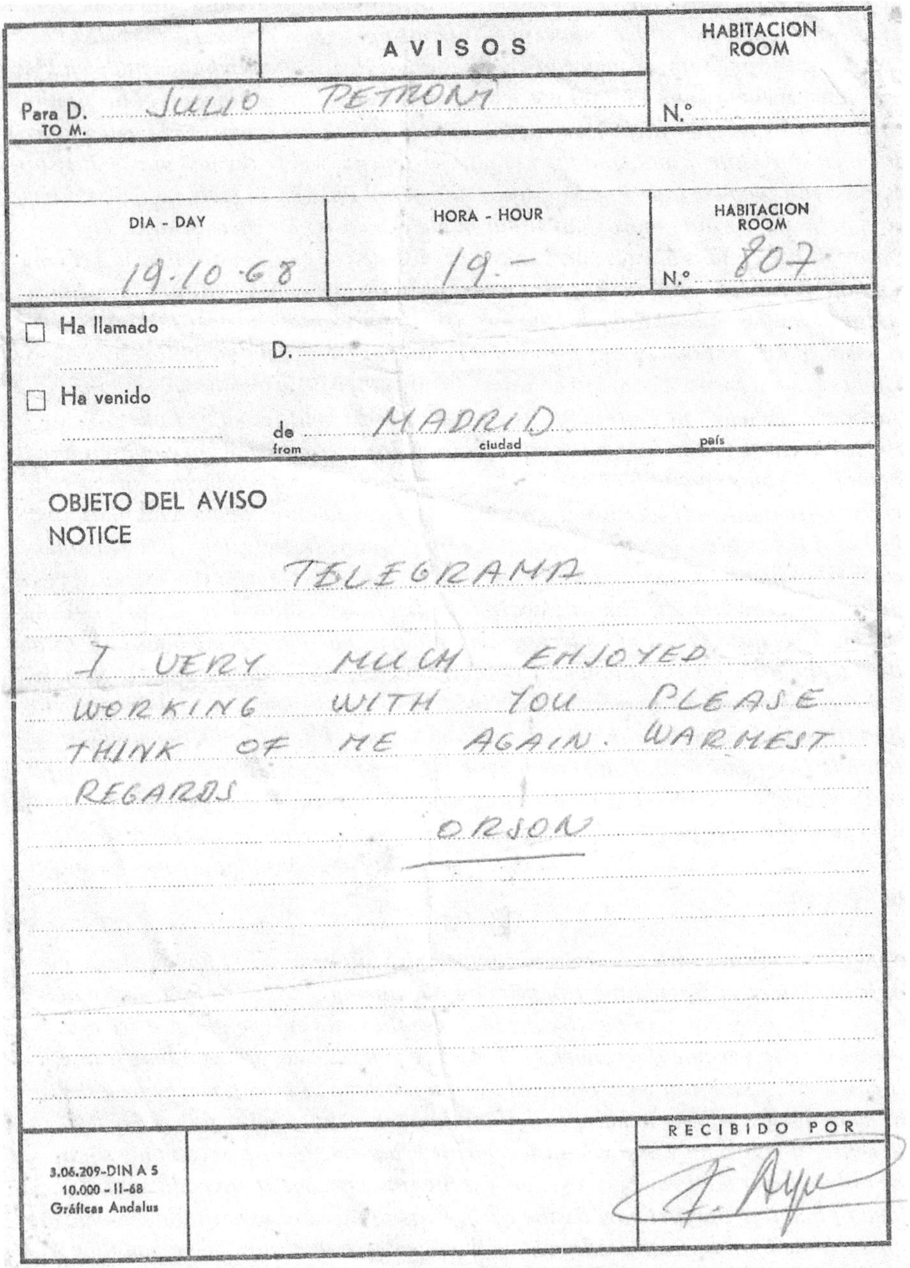

AVISOS

HABITACION
ROOM

Para D. JULIO PETRONI
TO M.

N.º

DIA - DAY: 19.10.68

HORA - HOUR: 19.–

HABITACION
ROOM
N.º 807

☐ Ha llamado

D.

☐ Ha venido

de MADRID
from ciudad país

OBJETO DEL AVISO
NOTICE

TELEGRAMA

I VERY MUCH ENJOYED WORKING WITH YOU PLEASE THINK OF ME AGAIN. WARMEST REGARDS

ORSON

3.06.209-DIN A 5
10.000 - II-68
Gráficas Andalus

RECIBIDO POR

Original Telegram from Orson Welles to Giulio Petroni concerning the 1969 film **Tepepa**, which Petroni directed

Although, as much as by 1972 the Western genre was gasping for air and the farcical was devouring the mythos which had been created up until then, Providence was still a reasonable compromise, production-wise. You had a strong cast, a strong crew—you know of course Mario Bava is responsible for some of the optical effects and gags—and he was able to bring on board people like Ennio Morricone who signs the score. That said you can tell quite easily we are talking about a foreign body within his filmography. It wasn't his kind of humor; it contains very few of his visual traits and it's the first and only Western of his that was not shot in Spain, in Almeria. "Apart from my personal aspirations, it must be said that the genre had started to decline and I didn't want to find myself involved in the vulgarization that was taking place. I felt guilty enough, having directed Providence. So, I immediately made it clear that I wasn't interested. You can't make more than one film of that kind, plus I felt the need to move on to something new. Westerns were dead, and in fact the sequel made half the money my one made."

M.H. Alberto De Martino directed four Westerns. His first one, **Assault on Fort Texan**, is average at best with the reliable Edmund Purdom in the lead. His second film, **One Hundred Thousand Dollars for Ringo**, is a brilliant film with an excellent performance by Richard Harrison and brilliantly directed. **One Hundred Thousand Dollars for Ringo** was very successful financially, but De Martino only directed two more Westerns, the effective **Django Shoots First** in 1966 and 1972's **Here We Go Again, Eh Providence?** Why did De Martino direct only two more Westerns? What was the inspiration for **One Hundred Thousand Dollars for Ringo**?

E.E. Ah Alberto, he was a very funny man. He had this massive office at his home in Rome with walls covered with posters of each and every one of his films and furniture just delivered straight from the mid-seventies—it was like a time capsule and I would sit there knowing sooner or later I would have to gulp down half a glass of Amaro Petrus he insisted I accept, a tonic liquor you could use to kill cockroaches or drain the kitchen sink. But he was a delight to be around; he just had that twinkle in his eye, the twinkle of a man that had fun, enjoyed every minute of the ride. He encompasses so much of what we've been dwelling on in this interview: he started working during the "Hollywood on the Tiber" years, learnt his craft on peplums and adventure flicks, both Italian and American productions, made his debut within the genre, and directed a purely imitational pre-Leone Western, but went on to evolve and find his voice, was a self-proclaimed genre director, happy to satisfy the markets demands, but channeled himself through quite a strong production system, tried to be selective with his work, bit off more than he could chew towards the end of the seventies and after a few more years hiding under the pseudonym "Martin Herbert" retired in the mid-eighties. He has one of those blueprint filmographies, if you know what I mean. Regarding the origins of his Ringo he would often complain about the fact very few people got the subtext of the film. The kid in One Hundred Thousand Dollars for Ringo *is called Shane.*

He is the protagonist of Shane, *the 1953 George Stevens classic. What he had in mind was to tell the story of that character's childhood. De Martino's film was what allowed the character to live the experiences in the picture with Alan Ladd. Also, Ringo isn't a reference, De Martino states, to Tessari's films starring Giuliano Gemma, but to John Wayne's character in* Stagecoach.

M.H. What was the opinion of the Italian westerns overall from the directors you interviewed in your book?

E.E. It's difficult to answer this question because each and every one of the directors interviewed had such a different approach to, feeling, and general interpretation of the genre. What can definitely be said is that they all owe something to it. Out of the twelve directors interviewed for the book, eleven have had something to do with the genre, most as directors, but some as ADs or on second units. Point of arrival or crucial stepping-stone, it doesn't matter, all of them should be and are grateful to have had an opportunity with Westerns. Some loved the genre deeply, like Castellari and Caiano, others were more detached but managed to find their place like Petroni, De Martino, or Guerrieri, others despised the genre like Lenzi and others just skimmed the surface like Deodato. I will tell you a story. In the mid-eighties, Giulio Petroni, who had retired for some time from cinema and was working solely as a novelist and documentarian tried to make a last attempt with a film, Il rivale, *which translated is "The Rival", based on a book by the same title he had written a few years previously. A novel, like many by the author, intimately personal in which it is difficult to distinguish literary fiction and personal experience. We find New York in it, where Petroni lived for many years; tormented loves, and of those the director of* Death Rides a Horse *and* Tepepa *had many; the scent of oriental lands; and the ghosts of a complex childhood. All the features of the literary Petroni are present, but also the films of the last phase of his career: the morbid, erotic dramas. The Petroni writer begins in 1961 with the controversial* La città calda *(translation: "The Hot City"), published by Feltrinelli, and will continue over the years with heavily autobiographical works, so-much-so that they can be considered something close to "diaries of the soul". 'The Rival" hits bookstores in March 1980. Then, roughly seven years after the well-received publication, in a time in which Petroni had finally digested the brutish disappointment of having seen his* Labbra di lurido blu *("Lips of Lurid Blue", 1975) massacred by critics and the financial disaster of* L'osceno desiderio—Le pene nel ventre *("Obscene Desire", 1978), he tried to put together a new film. Petroni's attempt to reconcile with the seventh art will be covered by the newspapers of the time. Paese Sera, Libertà, and Il Lavoro will devote a lot of space to the news, while Avvenire even titled the article: "Giulio Petroni finally returns on a set". It was time to break the exile he had chosen for himself but needless to say what the result of this effort turned out to be. "I never would have imagined it, but I actually missed making Westerns. As much as I had digested and probably expressed everything I could with that genre, the freedom and professionalism I had experienced in that phase of my career seemed long gone."*

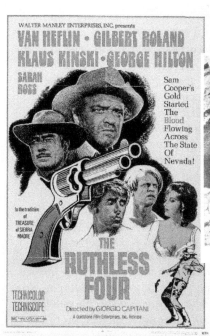

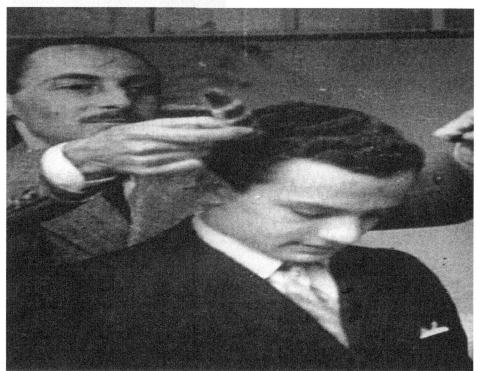

Above: U.S. Poster and Lobby card of Capitani's The Ruthless Four
Below: Vittorio Cottafavi and Giorgio Capitani

123

By the time Petroni attempts to place himself once more in the directing chair, the cinematic West was long dead, dead and buried. Those few films that had been made in the first half of the eighties and the catastrophic flop of what was to be the rebirth of the genre, Tex e il signore degli abissi ("Tex and Lord of Deep", 1985) by Duccio Tessari, had knocked the last nail into the coffin of spaghetti Westerns. It was no coincidence that when it came to producing Django 2—il grande ritorno ("Django Strikes Back", 1987), a project initiated at the same time as Tessari's film, producer Spartaco Pizzi together with director Nello Rosati, who took over after Corbucci had rejected the script, chose a setting and approach that had little to do with the genre that had given birth to the 1966 cornerstone. Franco Rossetti, the main writer of the original film, who also has a chapter dedicated to him in Darkening the Italian Screen, was contacted by Corbucci for the sequel: "By the late eighties, my relationship with cinema in general was feeble let alone the one with Westerns. Since the late sixties I hadn't worked with Sergio, but I would sometimes run into him or maybe call him once in a while. It was with a phone call, if I remember correctly, that he told me about the idea of a sequel. A proper sequel I mean, not another…you know… Westerns with the name Django thrown in or used in the title just to capitalize on the success of the original film. The idea of a sequel sounded like science fiction to me, especially at that specific moment. The only Italian Westerns that you could see at the time were cut versions of old films shown on private broadcasting channels. Sergio sounded quite excited about the idea and although he never said so explicitly, I had the impression he wanted to involve me in the project. I'm not the kind of man that says no, and I would have done it, but I was cautious. He never called back. Initially I thought that maybe I was wrong, maybe he didn't want to work with me again but then I met him coincidentally and asked him about it…this was a couple of years later. His answer was, 'Forget about it…. I'll never learn.' He looked sad as he smiled."

Our hero (Franco Nero) retired for fifteen years in a convent in South America. One day news comes to him that his only daughter, Marisol, has been kidnapped by the notorious Orlowsky (Christopher Connelly in his last appearance), a Hungarian prince devoted to prostitution and slavery, known as El Diablo. Django goes looking for his daughter with the help of Professor Gunn (Donald Pleasence) and a handful of Indios. Rosati signed the film with the pseudonym Ted Archer. He had directed comedies and erotic films for the most part and here he directs action of which, truth be told, there is an abundance but with no verve or personality. Although technically a Western, there is a methodical removal of the genre on an iconographic level. Nero's attire and appearance, ponytail and belts of bullets crossed over his chest and the geographical context (the film is shot entirely in Colombia), seem to look much more towards Rambo than to the black-dressed mercenary that has become an ultra-violent icon of a cinema long gone. Django's first and only official sequel is in fact this, the glass container of a distant echo. Corbucci dies two years later in 1990 while Giulio Petroni will no longer be able to approach cinema and soon afterwards will write a book entitled Il rancore (translation: "The Rancor", 1989). For a moment just before the final and definitive blow to the Italian film industry there was a naive dream in the air to go back to those glorious years of the spaghetti West…

Enzo Castellari and Franco Nero on the set of **Keoma** (1976)

M.H. One name that pops up quite frequently in your book is Tomas Milian. Can you paint a picture of the enigmatic Milian for our readers?

E.E. Yes, and I'm glad you asked me this question, because what I was hoping would happen with the book is that people that I couldn't get for it or that had already died would still be present. Key figures like Ennio Morricone, Lucio Fulci, Riccardo Freda, Italo Zingarelli, Mario Bava, and Milian. Each personal consideration of the protagonists interviewed for the book, who have intertwined careers with theirs, each slice of gossip and indiscretion, every anecdote slides in, adding, sometimes clashing, always enriching the previous one, creating pungent portraits, somewhere along the road, dowels find place in the structure and maybe something not too dissimilar to the truth starts seeping through. Specifically regarding Milian, he's particularly present throughout because so many of the directors worked with him: Umberto Lenzi, Giulio Petroni, Romolo Guerrieri, Alberto De Martino, Sergio Martino, and even George Hilton mentions him a few times, because the book doesn't contain only interviews with directors, let's not forget. All of them have strong opinions about him, nobody just shrugged him off and what is incredible is that they all say the same things, the brush strokes are pretty much the same, each one adds a little detail, a little nuance.

Of course, the stories and anecdotes differ but ultimately, they all seem to have met the same identical man. OK, talent, they all describe a very big talent, a force to be reckoned with—although many add that he had to be restrained at times—a histrion that would tend to overdo things, maybe even ham them up. An insightful, uncompromising, method actor—he did form at the Actor' Studio and really held actors like Montgomery Clift and Marlon Brando in great consideration, he was part of that American movement. He was also very much aware of the star power and prestige he brought to the films he would act in. Keep in mind that by the mid-sixties Milian was a big deal, a box office draw, an actor people were interested in. He would often be presented in gossip magazines; a film with Milian was going to be covered by the media. This though we all know, what really comes out and which people aren't likely aware of are the insecurities, the self-loathing, the perception he had of himself, the drug use, the childhood traumas, his bisexuality. Milian was such a fragile man who would compare himself to other actors, his co-stars, and would feel threatened by the ones that were considered good-looking: Franco Nero, Luc Merenda, Maurizio Merli. He would ask for special attention from his directors. I think Petroni summarizes pretty well: "He especially had problems with his physical appearance. He felt ugly and would constantly be comparing himself to other men. This is one of the reasons he felt the need to seduce everybody. Tomas hated, in a pathological way, the idea of being unnoticed or unappreciated." There is a lot of juicy gossip on Milian in the book but once all the pieces of the mosaic are put together the image that emerges is that of a tormented man which was hurting much more than his outward and outrageous persona would lead you to believe.

M.H. Tells us what you are currently working on?

E.E. In a few months another book of mine is going to be released, written with German university professor Marcus Stiglegger. It's a publication entirely dedicated to William Friedkin's controversial Cruising. I am continuing to work on extras for various labels. One package I'm particularly happy with is the one for Arrow Video's release of Ovidio G. Assonitis' exorcist rip-off Beyond the Door. One of the discs will contain a feature-length documentary on the Italian demonic-possession trend of the seventies. Also, I hope to give wings to the second volume of Darkening the Italian Screen. It will concentrate on directors that debuted behind the camera in the seventies and eighties; among the people I interviewed I would like to mention Lamberto Bava, Aldo Lado, Assonitis, Luigi Cozzi, Antonio Bido, Luigi Montefiori, also known as George Eastman, and many others. It's all done, finished, but to be honest it all depends on how this volume we've been talking about fares sales-wise. Hopefully enough people will buy the book for McFarland to green light part two. Besides this I'm also writing a children's book and a script for a feature-length film, which I'm very excited about. All this as I try to survive, because we all sound cool when we are giving an interview but at the end of the day I'm just a dreamer moving around trying to do as much as possible hoping something will stick.

Spanish pressbook ad for **Wrath of God** (1968)
Variety ad for **Today it's Me... Tomorrow You!** (1968)

ROY COLT SHOOTS HIS MOUTH OFF!

A 1995 Interview with American Actor Brett Halsey About the 5-Film Spaghetti Western "Phase" of his Euro Movie Career (c.1966-1970)

By Steve Fenton(e) & Dennis Capicik; with Special Thanks to Michael "Ferg" Ferguson. *[Asterisked annotations in italics and square brackets by SF]*

Introduction:

This now-quarter-century-old interview, carefully transcribed 100% word-for-word from an audio microcassette tape by Yours Truly within days after it was first record-ed, was conducted at Mr. Halsey's then-residence in Toronto, Ontario by Fenton(e) and Capicik on April 30th, 1995. While the following quite substantial excerpt, which gathers together everything that BH revealed to us about his quintet of SW gigs, has heretofore never been published—yes, it's an exclusive to The Spaghetti Western Digest!—the lion's share of this interview originally ran in John Martin's "Eurocentric" British fanzine *Giallo Pages* (Procrustes Press, 1999), and was more recently reprinted in its entirety (minus what's hereunder, needless to say) in Troy Howarth's book *Splintered Visions: Lucio Fulci and His Films* (Midnight Marquee Press, 2015). Appropriately enough, Dennis and I first met Brett Halsey in Toron-to at the North American premiere of his friend Dario Argento's much-maligned slasher flick Trauma (1993). The initial—unfortunately rather-too-perfunctory, for our liking—interview which sprang from that chance meeting in the lobby of TO's Bloor Cinema in September '93 was originally published in issue #12 of long, tall Texan Craig Ledbetter's crucial zine *European Trash Cinema* (ETC). Following that, the better part of a year-and-a-half later, BH granted us a second, much longer and more in-depth interview session, from which sprang both the long excerpt that ran in **Giallo Pages** as well as the following shorter section; the latter being "outtakes", if you will, that we intended to utilize later in a proposed-but-aborted Spaghetti Western-themed project. And now, almost exactly 25 years later, its time has finally arrived! Barring the odd sentence here and there, once again, we repeat, the section that follows below has never been published before in any form, and hopefully it contains material of interest to fans of the genre. So... enjoy! |- SF

TSWD: So, is it true in your opinion that, as some believe, the Spaghetti Western was a logical offshoot of the peplum (or "sword-and-sandal") film, even though we believe the two genres don't really share that much in common at all?

BH: Yeah, they were, but they didn't follow the Spaghetti Western directly, though. After the sword-and-sandal came the James Bond imitations. There were two types of "sword-and-sandal" films: there were the strongman pictures with Hercules, Maciste and so on. Then there were also the swashbucklers.

[NB. Mr. Halsey's contributions to that latter subgenre of the Euro "historical costume spectacle" genre include future one-time-only SW director Riccardo Freda's The Seventh Sword a.k.a. Seven Swords for the King (Le sette spade del vendicatore, 1962) and the same director's The Magnificent Adventurer a.k.a. The Burning of Rome (Il magnifico avventurie-ro, 1963).]

Brett Halsey as Bill Kiowa in **Today it's Me... Tomorrow You!** (1968)

TSWD: Archetypically and culturally speaking, we believe the Italo brand of western has much more in common with the rural bandit movies made in Italy during the 1950s and early 1960s, which often had vendetta plotlines similar to those in SW's. *[NB. "Pre-spaghetti" examples of the Italian bandit genre include SW genre influencer Pietro Germi's **The Bandit of Tacca del Lupo** (Il brigante di Tacca del Lupo, 1952) and future SW director Umberto Lenzi's **Duel of Fire** (Duello nella Sila, 1962).]*

*BH: They probably were the same plots. Even American films such as *[Clint Eastwood's]* Unforgiven *[1992]* also deal with revenge; most of these films deal with revenge of some sort.*

TSWD: Basically, they were all influenced by each other, then?

BH: The actors, especially the Americans, would bring some "knowledge" to the genre that the Italians just didn't have at the time. Generally, the Italians that I worked with regarded the Western as just another form of adventure film. They didn't get too involved with making them correct. They made mistakes with costumes, signs... The "Indians" were pathetic; they just dressed-up gypsies! I'm talking about the authenticity of the costumes. They would have things like a revolver before revolvers were invented.

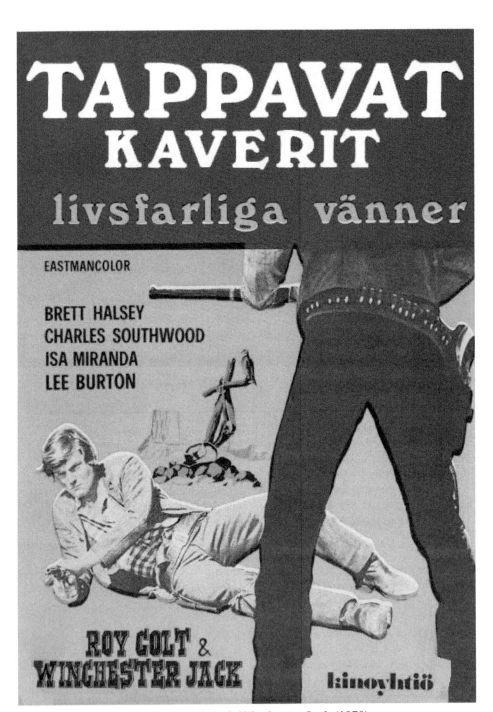

Finnish poster for **Roy Colt & Winchester Jack** (1970)

Some of them *[i.e., the actors]* even tried to wear spurs. Soon enough you would get rid of those, because it's hard to work in spurs. It's even relatively hard to walk in them, not to mention fighting, because you always get caught in them.

TSWD: Westerns were merely that month's "bread-and-butter", so to speak?

BH: Yeah.

TSWD: Was "everybody" in Almería, Spain during the late-'60s?

BH: We used to stay at the Grand Hotel Almería, and there were always other film companies there. The hotel we stayed at was right downtown, but the luxury hotel where a lot of the Americans stayed was the Aguadulce [named after a municipality in Seville, Spain]; but it was forty minutes out of town. It was a beautiful place, but totally impractical to stay there.

TSWD: The little desert there *[i.e., in Almería]* was shot by cinematographers in such a way that they made it appear much larger, when in fact it was really only a few sand-dunes...

BH: Yeah. It's gone now. It was only a couple of acres. They shot part of *[David Lean's]* Lawrence of Arabia there *[incidentally, said '62 Brit historical epic just happened to feature soon-to-be spaghetti superstar Fernando Sancho in an uncredited bit-part as a brutal Turkish gaoler. Sancho, whose thesping services were in big demand at the height of the SW craze, would go on to appear in two out of BH's five genre outings]*. There wasn't much to do in Almería, actually outside of the hotel; and you weren't supposed to go into town, because the gypsies came down from the hills and hung out at the plaza at night to have knife-fights!

TSWD: You should have showed-up with your sixgun blazing! *[Laughter]* So Almería was basically the rural asshole of Spain?

BH: Well, they had beaches, but they were really dirty. There was a lot of tar everywhere, which I suppose came from the ships.

TSWD: On a different note, you had helped to produce **Kill Johnny Ringo** *[Uccidete Johnny Ringo, 1966; BH's first Italoater]*, but got ripped off...?

BH: Oh yeah, seriously! They came to me with a script which was terrible, but they wanted me to do the picture. I said, "Look, I'll do the picture on one condition: I own the rights to the entire English-speaking world, and I can bring in some of my own people to fix the script." So we did it. We completely revamped the script. I remember the director coming up to me in the morning and saying, "What are we going to shoot today?" When the picture finally came out, there was some sort of Mafia financing, there was a bankruptcy, and my rights got lost. I got nothing. I didn't even get the money to pay the people that I hired!

131

Spanish Pressbook for **Kidnapping** (1969)

The whole end of that picture, all the shootout, where I go through town killing everybody, none of that was in the original script. Well, the last half-hour of the script was in a courtroom. Who the hell wants to watch a courtroom?! After we made the deal, I said, "Okay, now the first thing we're gonna do is we're gonna throw the courtroom out." He said, "That's the whole picture!" In westerns you wanna see people shooting guns, and blood! Any psychological-type film needs really good writing. Westerns are formula. I have to confess, I don't remember seeing any Italian Westerns when I was there, except the Eastwood pictures. I never saw any of the Trinity pictures—any of them. Because, when I'd go to the movies there, I'd go to see the American movies! One time, I remember I was talking to someone at the embassy, and he told me that there were 50,000 Americans living in the Rome area. I don't think there are 10,000 now [i.e., circa the mid-'90s]. But there was a culture, so you'd go to the English-language movie theatres, and they would be full.

TSWD: Edd "Kookie" Byrnes *[1932-2020]* believed that making movies in Europe was just a "game." *[Byrnes was a three-time "name-value" Yank co-star of such fine SW's as "E.G. Rowland"/Enzo G. Castellari's **Payment in Blood** a.k.a. Renegade Riders (7 Winchester per un massacro, 1967) and the same director's **Any Gun Can Play** a.k.a. Go Kill and Come Back (Vado... l'ammazzo e torno, 1967). His third and final genre appearance came in Nando Cicero's **Red Blood, Yellow Gold** a.k.a. Professionals for a Massacre (Professionisti per un massacro, 1967).]*

BH: Edd Byrnes was not very well-liked. The famous story about Eddie Byrnes was that he was pitching a tantrum, and he took out his passport: "I'm an American! You can't talk to me like that! I'm an American! Blah-blah-blah..." Who gives a shit if he's an American?! I don't want to talk about him though, because it's all bad. *[On that note, since Mr. Byrnes only just passed-away on January 8th of this current year, perhaps it's for the better that BH tactfully refrained from saying any more about him. R.I.P., Edd!]*

TSWD: Frank Wolff *[1928-1971]* was over on the Continent for a long time. He was a great actor! You worked with him. Do you have any memories? His suicide was very tragic, very horrific...

BH: He was extremely bitter that he hadn't done more with his career. He also had a very crude mouth. Some people were afraid of him, but he was a good actor, and I didn't mind him at all. Yeah, he was obviously troubled, but everybody liked Frank.

[Having been an early draft casting choice to star in no less than Sergio Leone's prototypical A Fistful of Dollars (Per un pugno di dollari, 1964), while Mr. Wolff ultimately appeared in a grand total of eleven Euro-shot oaters, his highest-profile genre appearances can be seen in Leone's sprawling epic Once Upon a Time in the West (C'era una volta il West, 1968) and Sergio Corbucci's snowbound ode to man's inhumanity to man, The Great Silence (Il grande silenzio, 1968). That same year, Wolff also served as one of the narrators of Patrick Morin's American-made TV documentary Western, Italian Style, which amounts to a truly priceless time-capsule indeed for SW enthusiasts/completists (for those interested, an upload of this fascinating 38m program can be viewed on YouTube at the URL addy https://www.youtube.com/watch?v=X-VaxLqLPYI).]

BH: Not only did he *[Frank Wolff]* *emasculate himself, he did it with Schick injector blades! I mean, it wasn't just a clean cut. He sat there on the toilet while he was alive and slashed at himself! I got the story from Amy De Sica, Vittorio's daughter, who was an agent at the time. It was either his wife or girlfriend who called Amy, because she was his agent. So Amy went over, she was pregnant at the time, and she was the one who opened the door. She had a miscarriage.*

TSWD: How about Nakadai Tatsuya *[仲代 達矢 (1932-)]*, the great Japanese samurai actor?

BH: There's a funny story involving Tatsuya Nakadai on *[Tonino Cervi's Dario Argento-co-scripted]* *Today We Kill, Tomorrow We Die!* *[Oggi a me... domani a te!, 1968]*. *He had never ridden a horse before, but he had this samurai determination. I remember the last scene when I'm chasing him through the forest, there were all these roots sticking out of the ground, but he wouldn't look down. So he would trip and fall, trip and fall... You can even see it in the film. He fell off his horse a few times. The scene when he's chasing the stagecoach, he fell off his horse while all those other horses were behind him!*

*[Among other iconic roles, Nakadai, of course, was the great rōnin antihero played by Mifune Toshirō's (三船 敏郎 {1920-1997}) main opponent in Kurosawa Akira's (黑澤明 {1910-1998}) chanbara classic **Yojimbo** (用心棒 / Yōjinbō, 1961), which—unofficially!—served as the inspiration/basis for Leone's **A Fistful of Dollars**. Neatly prefiguring his later appearance in a single SW of his own (i.e., the Cervi/Halsey film), in the Kurosawa film, Nakadai is seen toting—and shooting—a US-made 5-shot Cavalry revolver as well as his lightning-swift samurai sword.]*

TSWD: Nakadai wouldn't use a stand-in?

BH: He had a stand-in at some point, but most of the time he would do it himself. He got there a week before the picture, and that's all he knew about riding horses. He had a translator (I think it was his wife). We probably would've communicated more, had he spoken English. But he spoke no English, and didn't know how ta ride a horse. He was amazing to work with! It was a real learning experience working with him. You have this contrast: like, with William Berger, who was in trouble with drugs.

TSWD: Tell us about working with William Berger *[1928-1993]*...

BH: I remember one story. In Today We Kill, Tomorrow We Die!—*the scene where we were all lined-up talking and I'm looking over at Bill, and he is slowly falling off his horse! It was really strange to watch him, because it was so slow. He had a real big problem with drugs and the police. The police had told him that they were going to bust him, and they got him. He was in a summer house or something, I'm not sure.*

Bill had this "intellectual" persona he sometimes tried. Wayde *[Preston (1929-1992)]* and I were always laughing. When Bill wasn't working, he would go off and read his book, but half the time the book would be upside-down! I think he just got into the drug culture. I wasn't a part of that group. In fact, most of the action actors weren't, because it is too easy to get hurt. You have to stay alert. We were always very careful... I saw Bill Berger about four years ago *[i.e., circa '91; he died in '93]* with his daughter, and he seemed really straight.

The Spaniards used to think that all Americans were alcoholics. Because, after work, we'd congregate at the bar and drink whisky. But the Spaniards were much worse than we were, because first thing in the morning when you go to work there's this coffee truck... only they have brandy. So the Spaniards would start drinking coffee and brandy in the morning, and they'd drink brandy all day long! The coffee is—WOW! You think espresso is strong?—try Spanish coffee...!

TSWD: What was your **Today We Kill, Tomorrow We Die!** co-star Bud Spencer *[r.n. Carlo Pedersoli (1929-2016)]* like?

BH: Nice man. He lived in this big villa. He had a lot of money! He was an Olympic swimmer, I believe *[He was indeed!]*. I think he competed in the butterfly stroke. *[A two-time European freestyle swimming champion, Spencer went on to represent Italy in the Olympics at both Helsinki, Finland (1952)—where he won a silver medal—and in Melbourne, Australia (1956). A real man of action, as befitting his powerhouse screen persona, Spencer was also a boxer, as well as a rugby and polo player.]* Well, he got fat later. A real gentleman, though. He speaks English very well.

TSWD: How about stunt arranger / stuntman / actor Romano Puppo *[1933-1994]**?

BH: He speaks English perfectly. He doubled *[Lee]* Van Cleef *[1925-1989]* and worked with Van Cleef right to the end. As a matter of fact, he lived with him in Hollywood for quite some time. I remember Van Cleef from The Commander **[Der Commander, Italy/West Germany, 1988, directed by Anthony M. Dawson"/Antonio Margheriti, in which BH played the McPherson character]*, and we were shooting in the Southern part of Italy. When we weren't shooting, he was telling my wife how happy he was because he was a recovered alcoholic. He would go on and on all the while he was drinking beers! Beers first thing in the morning, and drinking all day! By the end of the day, he was completely loaded! He was very nice, though. He couldn't have been nicer.*

*[A charismatic performer in his own right, the grizzled, tough-looking Romano Puppo's SW appearances are legion. By our rough count, he appeared onscreen in close to two-dozen—often top-flight—spaghettis, plus undoubtedly had his hand in any number others, both in front of cameras (if often going uncredited) and also behind-the-scenes as a stunt coordinator. Some of Puppo's highest-profile roles are to be found in Leone's **The Good, the Bad and the Ugly** (Il buono, il brutto, il cattivo, 1966),

Sergio Sollima's **The Big Gundown** (La resa dei conti, 1966), Lucio Fulci's **Massacre Time** (Le colt cantarono la morte e fu... tempo di massacro, 1966), Tonino Valerii's **Day of Anger** (I giorni dell'ira, 1967), Giulio Petroni's **Death Rides a Horse** (Da uomo a uomo, 1967), "Frank Kramer"/Gianfranco Parolini's **Sabata** (Ehi amico... c'è Sabata. Hai chiuso!, 1969) and Michele Lupo's **California Goodbye** (California, 1977). Puppo also became a major player in the '70s Italocrime movie genre too, as well as contributing to other actioners of all types.]*

TSWD: You used to carry your Colt .45 revolver around Spain. We read that Giuliano Gemma *[(1938-2013) often billed as "Montgomery Wood" on his SW's; shades of BH's own "Montgomery Ford" handle]* was considered one of the quickest draws out of all the Western stars, Americans included.

BH: Well, that was probably a publicity stunt. If you're walking around all day with a gun strapped to your waist, you play with it. The fast-drawing, the twirling... I had my own rig, because the balance has to be right to do that sort of stuff. You wanna look good, too! You never wanna look at the holster when you put the gun away. You want to flip it around and not break your concentration.

There was a thing that happened with this actor named Freddy Quinn, who was a big singing star in Germany *[r.n. Franz Eugen Helmuth Manfred Nidl-Petz, Quinn was the Austrian-born star of usual Hollywood director Sobey Martin's shot-in-Yugoslavia musical sauerkraut oater The Sheriff Was a Lady a.k.a. In the Wild West (Freddy und das Lied der Prärie, 1965), guest-starring US va-va-voom vixen Mamie Van Doren.]* *A recent issue of Bravo* *[a long-running Berlin-based entertainment media magazine]* *had just come out, and there was this full-page ad with Freddy demonstrating fast-draw. I was at this restaurant with some people, including a journalist, and said: "This is bullshit! I'll bet Freddy any day a 100 dollars that I'll draw and fire before he shoots himself in the foot!" Well, to my astonishment, they printed it! I was kind of concerned that he would get offended, because he has this sort of husky tough-guy image in Germany. So, I saw him about a year later, and he said, "You're right! Would you teach me? So he brought out his guns and holsters, and he wasn't offended at all. He figured if he wasn't doing it right that I could show him, and I admired him for that*

TSWD: Did you do a lot of Method-acting on the set to try and get into that "antihero" frame of mind?

BH: No, not at all. It wasn't that romantic. I mean, you do get into the mindset, but you have to spend time at it just like any other job. You have to be prepared, but that doesn't mean you take it home with you. It's easy to walk around posing like a tough guy; it's the other side that's hard!

Brett Halsey and Tatsuya Nakadai in **Today it's Me... Tomorrorw You!** (1968)

People were not as involved as you would like to think. You get into the mindset, and you do your job. Even at lunchtime, you take your guns off. A lot of actors used to take their guns home. For example, the fast-draw. I still have a holster at my house. It's a special fast-draw holster made in California, because they didn't know how to make them in Italy. I even had my own boots, spurs... I still have all that stuff.

TSWD: So there wasn't anybody you knew who thought he was a real cowboy...?

BH: *The closest thing I can remember is Mickey Hargitay putting on his cowboy gear and riding down Via Veneto for a promo.* *[Famed muscleman Hargitay's (1926-2006) five-film-strong SW résumé includes José Luis Monter's Spanish-majority co-production **The Sheriff Won't Shoot** (Lo sceriffo che non spara, 1965) and Emimmo Salvi's **3 Bullets for Ring**o a.k.a. Three Graves for a Winchester (3 colpi di Winchester per Ringo, 1966), the latter co-starring equally-ripped peplum/SW star Gordon Mitchell.]* ***That's about the closest thing I remember. You have to remember that this was merely a job for most people. When I did those sword-fighting pictures with Riccardo Freda, I didn't take my sword home. (Well... sometimes I would!) *[Laughter.]****

TSWD: You did a lot of your own stunts. Did you ever get hurt badly?

BH: Every picture! The worst accident I had was on Kill Johnny Ringo, when I had my head split open from here to here *[motions from the front of his forehead to the top of his pate (OUCH!)]*. We had this actor from a school; when you do these types of film, you have to take people from this institute *[presumably he is referring to Rome's renowned film school, the Centro Sperimentale di Cinematografia?]*. He was the one who at one point during the film gets my gun and hits me over the head with it. I knew he wasn't holding the pistol right, so I showed him how to do it. So before we shot the scene, I grabbed the guy and said, "Listen you son-of-a-bitch, if you hit me with that gun, I'm going to kill you. I'm going to kill you right here!" *[laughter]*. During the scene, I just knew it wasn't going to work, and turned around, and knew he was going to hit me. WHACK! He just opened my head right up. I went down, and he started to cry because he thought I was going to kill him. I couldn't get up, though, and they took me to the hospital. I couldn't believe he started to cry! I said, "Jesus, you could have at least waited until we got the shot!" Then the hospital said they wanted to keep me for ten days! I had to sign myself out of the hospital, because we had to finish the picture. So we went home and had to write the next day's script! I had to do the rest of the picture with my hat on, because they shaved part of my head!

TSWD: What do you remember about shooting **Roy Colt & Winchester Jack** *[1970, BH's final SW, directed by Mario Bava]*?

BH: Bava tried to make it a comedy, and some of the comedy just didn't work. Unless you have a budget and have a lot of time, it's hard to do a comedy western. It was raining a lot when we shot that. There was an actor, Charles Southwood *[(1937-2009) "Winchester Jack"]*. He was American. It wasn't a question of not liking, I liked him. We didn't get along; we didn't "mesh." There was no antagonism, but we weren't pals... If there's any kinda personality conflict between actors, I think you just tend to act by yourself. It gets into a competition. I think what happened was he started doing some competitive things and I had a lot more experience, so I knew how to counter. He did some other Westerns, didn't he?

*[Yes, he did. Southwood's only eleven-film-long filmography contains no less than five SW's; coincidentally, the same total as BH's. Besides RC&WJ, Southwood's SW CV also includes "Irving Jacobs"/Mario Amendola's **I Protect Myself Against My Enemies!** (Dai nemici mi guardo io!, 1968), "Miles Deem"/Demofilo Fidani's **Stranger... Make the Sign of the Cross** (Straniero... fatti il segno della croce!, 1968), **Sartana's Here... Trade Your Pistol for a Coffin** (C'è Sartana... vendi la pistola e comprati la bara!, 1970) and "Antony Ascott"/Giuliano Carnimeo's **Guns for Dollars** a.k.a. They Call Me Hallelujah (Testa t'ammazzo, croce... sei morto – Mi chiamano Alleluja, 1971); as with BH's own five-pack, all are, to varying degrees, enjoyable examples of the SW form. Incidentally, Guns for Dollars' page at the *Internet Movie Database* mistakenly claims that one of its alternate titles is **Deep West**

(which is actually the name of its '72 sequel, that was likewise directed by "Ascott"/ Carnimeo and co-starred George Hilton, Agata Flori and Roberto Camardiel).]*

BH: Today *We Kill, Tomorrow We Die!* **was *[Tonino]* Cervi. Then I did** *Kidnapping* **for *[Alberto]* Cardone** *[this lesser-seen film (a.k.a. Kidnapping! Paga o uccidiamo tuo figlio / "Kidnapping! Pay Up, or Your Son Dies", 1969) is incorrectly listed on the IMDb as Twenty Thousand Dollars for Seven, which is actually an alternate Anglo title for The Wrath of God, a film that shares the same director and much of the same principal cast as Kidnapping]*. **They wanted me to use the name "Montgomery Ford" again on the Bava picture,** *Roy Colt.* **I didn't wanna do it, and then I agreed to do it under another name. Well, it became a big success; I torpedoed myself, it was so successful. So, in the contract they used it for the next picture, but not the next one. They couldn't use it for the Bava picture. It was all the same company.**

TSWD: As you mentioned to us once before *[unfortunately, not while the tape recorder was running!]*, you're of the opinion that the late Alberto Cardone *[a.k.a. "Albert Cardiff" (1920-1977)]* was an underrated director. What are your memories of working with him?

BH: Always cheerful, always ready. Good, fast. I remember once on *To the Last Drop of Blood,* **we had a fight with a famous Italian stuntman** *[namely Franco Fantasia. The film BH is referring to is now more commonly known as **The Wrath of God** (L'ira di Dio, 1968), but its original Spanish title is Hasta la última gota de sangre ("To the Last Drop of Blood"), hence BH's use of its English translation, which was also the film's shooting/unsold Anglo export title. Its TTLDOB title is not be confused with "John Byrd"/Paolo Moffa's **Bury Them Deep** (All'ultimo sangue, 1968), starring Craig Hill, which had also been announced in some tradepapers as the similarly-titled To the Last Drops of Blood.]* **We had this fight at the end of the picture, and Cardone wanted a crane-shot, and the producer wouldn't give him the money. So he went to the fire department and got them to bring their ladder truck up; run the ladder up, got up there with the cameraman, shot down on the fight in the sand at Almería.**

[Contrary to BH's recollection, in actuality his and Fantasia's energetic brawl—an unfairly one-sided knife fight on desert terrain, during which Halsey's revenge-bent, all-black-clad Mike Barnett character goes bare-handed against his opponent's glinting cuchillo—occurs, not at its end, but just over a third of the way into the movie (@ around the 34m mark). Director "Cardiff"/Cardone's inventive improvised utilization of the firetruck's ladder in place of renting a costly crane results in several stylish "bird's eye-view" shots of the action, with his elevated camera peering down on the struggling combatants from about 50ft overhead.]

139

TSWD: What about Gianfranco Baldanello *[a.k.a. "Frank G. Carrol" (or "Carroll")]*, who directed you in your '66 SW debut, **Kill Johnny Ringo**?

*BH: I found him kind of nice, but ineffectual. He wasn't very inventive. He was okay. I would never put him in the class of any of the other people we were talking about. Nice person, but I just didn't find that he had any original ideas. Mediocre's a good word. I was surprised when I saw his name later; it just surprised me that he continued. *[Baldanello is best-remembered as a director of tongue-in-cheek/slapstick actioners, including a number of SW "spoofs".]* I was surprised that he ever worked again after our picture, because he just didn't... *[BH's sentence peters-out to dead air for some moments.]* He'd come to work empty-handed.*

TSWD: Do you have any other general remembrances of shooting your Spaghetti Westerns?

BH: There was a funny incident while I was shooting a film with Wayde Preston *[i.e., the above-discussed **Today We Kill, Tomorrow We Die!**]*. *It was winter and it was icy, and we're supposed to be riding out of the shot. And people were coming around to see these cowboys, because we rode a lot different than the Italians. So all these people are waiting for us to come around this mountain, and we show up walking, leading our horses. And everybody is, like, "What's going on?!" We look at them and say, "There's ice all over the place. We'll slip and fall. What, are you crazy?!"*

We used to have a lot of fun with the horses. You had to know how to shoot off of horses. You have to shoot over their ear, but most importantly you have to know that the horse has been doing it. Because there were charges to set off the blast from the gun. It's like someone coming up to you and shooting a gun next to your head. It would scare the hell out of you! So, one of the first things we would ask when dealing with a new horse is if he's "gun-broke". "Oh, yeah, yeah." So us Americans would step up next to the horse and shoot our gun off and see how he reacts before we get on him.

Did you ever hear the story about the bridge from The Good, the Bad and the Ugly? *They had set the charges and they got ready to shoot, and the bridge just slumped. Nothing blew up! Of course, they had to rebuild it. Then they got some people from the Army to reset the charges. Days go by until they are finally ready to shoot again. Again nothing happened! Then the General in charge of ordnance for the Spanish Army came down from Madrid to personally set the charges... and then somebody had set it off accidentally! The whole bridge went. The General simply got in his car and drove back to Madrid, because he was so embarrassed.*

Let me tell ya a story about Audie Murphy's The Texican *[**Texas Kid**, 1966, an American-produced-but-shot-in-Spain oater directed by seasoned Hollywood B-western specialist Lesley Selander, in which BH did not appear]*: *there was a producer—his name isn't important—an American. Anyway, this particular producer used to come on the set late in the morning—ten or eleven o'clock—and look around and find all kinds of things that he didn't like, and start complaining about this and complaining about that. So one day he walks on the set and he starts bitchin' about something, and Audie *[1924-1971]* walked over to him; didn't say a word, just walked over to him—popped 'im, knocked him on the ground. He stood over him and looked down, and said, "You wanna complain about things around here, you get here in the morning when the rest of us do. Otherwise, shut-up!" And that was the end of that. He was quite a guy; I liked Audie *[legendarily known as the most-decorated American serviceman of World War 2]*. *It was a real fascinating experience making *[Jesse Hibbs']* To Hell and Back *[USA, 1955]* with him.*

****

Conclusion:

In the early '60s, Brett Halsey went to Italy and back. But not before he'd spent more than a solid decade working in Europe, during which time he appeared in the five Spaghetti/Paella Westerns he discusses above, plus many other highly entertaining movies of all genres besides!

French Lobby Card: **Today We Kill, Tomorrow we Die**

BRETT HALSEY BIO

By Steve Fenton(e)

Billed early in his career sans one 't' as "Bret" Halsey, real name Charles Oliver Hand, born in Santa Ana, California, U.S.A. on June 20th, 1933; a nephew of celebrated U.S. Admiral William F. "Bull" Halsey (1882-1959), commander of Allied Forces in the Pacific theatre during World War II (on film, Admiral Halsey's character has been played by the likes of Robert Mitchum and James Whitmore). The future Brett Halsey—a stagename partly inspired by his famous military uncle—himself served in the U.S. Navy for a term prior to getting into movies. He also worked as a radio disc jockey, as a page at CBS-TV, then as a freelance actor. According to a promotional piece entitled "Comic's Wife Discovers Star," contained in the domestic pressbook for the JD's-'n'-jalopies teen flick **Speed Crazy** (USA, 1959, D: William J. Hole, Jr.):

Brett Halsey... was a Columbia Broadcasting System page boy when he was discovered as a potential screen actor... His discoverer was Mary Livingston, wife of comic Jack Benny. Upon seeing Halsey, then only 19 years of age, she contacted William Goetz, studio executive, and arranged for Halsey to be interviewed... Two days later, Halsey had a Universal-International contract in his pocket and during the next two years had appeared in 14 motion pictures...

The youthful Halsey's pro film career proper began with uncredited bit-parts at Universal Pictures in the early-'50s, where his first credited role came in the zany series hickcom **Ma and Pa Kettle At Home** (USA, 1954, D: Charles Lamont), in which he played the eponymous comic hillbillies' teenage hayseed son, Elwin. Further uncredited bits followed while Halsey spent two more years in Universal-International's new talent program; during which time he filled a supporting part as a young U.S. soldier in the action-packed Audie Murphy autobiopic **To Hell and Back** (USA, 1955, D: Jesse Hibbs). Halsey also bit-parted anonymously in Jack Arnold's gillman thriller **Revenge of the Creature** (USA, 1955); as did his fellow U-I contract player and long-time friend Clint Eastwood, interestingly enough.

On television that same year, a gangling, baby-faced Halsey appeared in an episode, directed by George Blair, of the short-lived western teleseries **Brave Eagle** (USA, 1955-56). That series was highly unusual for its time in that it not only featured a heroic lead character of Native American origin (albeit played by paleface Keith Larsen), but also included a number of true aboriginal actors in supporting roles. . As Winchester-packin' novice homesteader Bill Hardy ("You listen to me now, or hear my *gun* speak!"), guest 'star' Halsey was not only a horsethief but a sneering Indian hater to boot ("I *know* Indians are treacherous! I learned that in the Cavalry when I found my best friend with his *scalp* gone!"). Needless to say, in keeping with the show's wholesomely moral tone—it was produced by apple pie oater role model Roy Rogers' company, after all—Halsey's ornery character ultimately becomes reformed and learns to live in peace with his more tolerant aboriginal neighbours. In a pair of subsequent episodes ("The Gentle Warrior" and "The Spirit of the Hidden Valley"), Halsey even got promoted to playing a native buck named Swift Otter. The following year he appeared in an early episode of **Gunsmoke** (USA, 1955-75). His homegrown TV work in this same general period included guest stints or bit-parts on a number of other western teleseries, including **The Adventures of Jim Bowie** (1956-58), **Bat Masterson** (1958-61), **Death Valley Days** (1952-70) and **Mackenzie's Raiders** (1958-59).

The later-1950s brought Halsey—even though he was by then in his mid-twenties, but didn't look it—roles as 'teenage' rebels in a number of post-rock'n'roll JD ("juvenile delinquent") theatrical dramas, including schlock/trash specialist Edward L. Bernds' irresistibly-titled 'tough chick' flick **High School Hellcats** (USA, 1958), in which he played a 'good guy' who wisely chose to pursue his post-secondary education rather than get mixed-up with the wrong crowd. Another archetypical example of the JD genre—boasting still another catchy title—was **Hot Rod Rumble** (USA, 1957, D: Leslie H. Martinson). This high-speed humdinger cast Halsey as Jim, a preppy rich kid college boy who not only takes offence at the hepcat hero's cooler dress sense ("Look at that *bum*!") but envies his superior driving prowess too, so sneakily slips some grinding compound into his road-racing rival's crankshaft in order to sabotage his heap. In the final reel, Halsey and the hero go car-to-car to decide who is the better man. Guess who wins? (Hint: not Halsey!)

He was billed fourth on Allied Artists (AA)'s **The Cry Baby Killer** (USA, 1958, D: Justus Addiss), for which second-billed Jack Nicholson made his screen debut in the title role. Executive-produced by Roger Corman and penned by actor-screenwriter and frequent western 'baddie' performer Leo Gordon ([1922-2000], whose one-and-only SW appearance came in Sergio Leone's and Tonino Valerii's **My Name Is Nobody** [1973]), **The Cry Baby Killer's** main catalyst who brings about the title character's ultimate run-in with the law and inglorious downfall was played by none other than Halsey, as yet another handsome heel. Dressed for success in a dark blazer and snazzy print tie as a conceitedly dapper womanizing 'pimp' named Manny Cole ("He's a *punk*, baby!"), in an early scene intended to establish his troublemaking character, the actor is shown spiking his 16-year-old bobbysoxer girlfriend's Coke with hard liquor (a.k.a. 'panty-remover'). He subsequently collaborates in the cowardly group-beating of Nicholson as the otherwise 'wholesome,' misunderstood hero. In another scene, Halsey—who repeatedly utters the word "punk"!—baits Nicholson by saying, "Are you lookin' for action, or ya gonna stand there flappin' ya yap all night?" Standing an easy half-a-foot taller than Nicholson, during a late-night parking lot rumble Halsey gets gutshot with a gat wrestled from one of his flunkies by Nicholson, following which Halsey as the not-at-all-manly Manny—still alive, but critically wounded and thus hospitalized—is not seen again for the duration. His shooting precipitates wayward 'nice boy' Nicholson's fatal comeuppance with the law during a tense hostage-taking standoff.

That same year ('58), Halsey had filled an uncredited bit-part in Phil Karlson's above-par apple pie western **Gunman's Walk**, starring Van Heflin and Tab Hunter. Also in Hollywood the same year, Halsey filled yet another anonymous bit in Robert Wise's acclaimed crime/courtroom drama **I Want To Live!** During a single less-than-minute-long scene at a drunken party attended by U.S. Navy seamen and hookers, the actor played a youthful, neatly-uniformed gob who propositions 'good-time girl' Susan Hayward to spend a wild weekend with him down Mexico way, an offer which she politely declines due to his being "too young." Mostly seen in profile, Halsey delivered his half-dozen lines in confident style, and even got to briefly lock lips with star Hayward before vanishing for the remainder of the narrative.

It wasn't until the following year that Halsey first achieved stardom of sorts, albeit via still another JD-type entry geared towards the teenaged drive-in set. Top-billed on the aforementioned **Speed Crazy** (USA, 1959), the actor—further described in the film's above-quoted pressbook as "a handsome screen newcomer" and "one of Hollywood's most promising young stars"—was cast as yet another joyriding road-hog ("a top flight sports car racing driver") named Nick Barrow, who was colorfully described by the film's trailer narrator as "a thrill-jockey, roaring his way from town to town, from girl to girl... Around every curve of a road or a gal!" By no means averse to pulling a knife on a dame, as well as trashing a malt shop during a fistfight, Halsey's motorized megalomaniac proudly proclaims, "When I get behind the wheel, *I'm* the boss! If somebody crowds ya, ya push 'em back like a guy swats flies!" For all his bravado, however, in the final reel he winds up dying in a fiery wreck after his tires are shot out by police and his car plummets off a cliff. The film was distributed by Allied Artists (a viable competitor of American-International Pictures [AIP]), who released a good many similar entries and for whom Halsey had already worked more than once by this point in his then-still-fledgling career. Additionally in '59, Halsey co-starred in his one-and-only Hollywood theatrical B-western from the period as an actual credited performer, namely same director William Hole, Jr.'s **Four Fast Guns** (USA, 1959).

In yet another major career boost, the actor went on to play a lead role second only to Vincent Price—as Halsey's onscreen uncle—in Edward L. Bernds's nonsensical-if-entertaining B&W horror sequel, **The Return of the Fly** (USA, 1959). Essentially playing at "Son of the Fly," Halsey co-starred as Philippe Delambre, inheritor of his late father's seemingly-genetically-encoded obsession with developing a foolproof matter-transmitter capable of safely disintegrating a human being at Point A then reintegrating it in one piece and in its original order at Point B. Accidentally on purpose thanks to a sneaky saboteur, Halsey's experiments go horribly—and at times *hilariously!*—awry, resulting in his atoms becoming all-mixed-up with those of the titular insect. In what undoubtedly amounts to one of the more outrageous images of his entire career (barring perhaps his Lucio Fulci phase), for one shot courtesy of the not-so-special effects department the actor's living head ("*Help me!*") was crudely optically grafted atop the body of a common housefly! Add to this the double indignity of Halsey being obliged to spend much of the running time encased inside a monstrous, bulbous-headed 'human fly' costume, and you can easily understand why Halsey—like much of the rest of the cast—spent the duration of the action with his tongue planted firmly in his cheek. On the upside, while hidden away out of sight inside that gigantic flyman mask, he could presumably laugh as much as he liked without anyone ever being any the wiser.

For Charles R. Rondeau's youth-oriented romantic melodrama **The Girl in Lovers' Lane** (USA, 1960), Halsey starred as cowlick-curled, smooth-talking Bix Dugan, a directionless drifter jumping freights from nowhere to anywhere ("Wherever this train's headed: I ain't particular") who winds up serving as grudging 'mother' to a younger greenhorn vagrant whom he meets while they are hitching a free ride in a boxcar and thereafter takes under his wing. Essentially playing a classically westernesque loner character (decribed as "some stranger") transposed into a more modern milieu, while he has an instinctive aversion to commitment or responsibilty of any kind, the older, wiser, taller Halsey character tutors his junior companion in the ins-'n'-outs and ups-'n'-downs of the drifting life (e.g., "The idea is to keep your face *away* from his fist!"). During a nocturnal back-alley rumble with shit-disturbing poolhall punks, the quick-witted, two-fisted Halsey improvises defensively by using a garbage can lid as a handy shield. After Halsey's character hits on a girl at a small-town diner somewhere in the ass-end of beyond, she subsequently winds up murdered, and, predictably enough, the rap is pinned on the misunderstood antihero (it comes as absolutely no surprise at all that slobbering, lop-eyed , leering co-star Jack Elam—one of the American brand-name actors to be found in this issue's unsung SW mini-classic **Three Gun Showdown** [1968], as well as making several other spaghetti appearances—proves to be the actual culprit). However, before it ultimately comes to light who the real killer is and Halsey our wrongly-accused star is duly vindicated, his intermittently melancholic Bix character suffers being beaten unconscious by the victim's distraught father and, not only that, but he is very nearly lynched by incensed vigilantes to boot.

The year following toplining **The Girl in Lovers' Lane,** together with future SW ten-timer Mark Damon and SW no-timer Michael Callan, Halsey won a Golden Globe Award as Most Promising Male Newcomer of 1961. After playing an Italian named Giovanni Guasconti—a Neapolitan living in Padua—in the "Rappaccini's Daughter" segment of Sidney Salkow's Nathaniel Hawthorne-based horror triumvirate **Twice Told Tales** (USA, 1962), the brown-haired, green-eyed Halsey received an offer to travel to Italy for real to appear in a pair of lavish costumed swashbucklers helmed by one-timer SW director Riccardo Freda: **The Seventh Sword** a.k.a. **Seven Swords for the King** (*Le sette spade del vendicatore*, Italy/France, 1962), starring BH as a swordslinging aristocratic Spaniard named Don Carlos de Bazan; and

The Magnificent Adventurer a.k.a. **The Burning of Rome** (*Il magnifico aventu-riero*, Italy/France/Spain, 1963), which was shot on authentic Venetian locations and starred BH as local historical hero Benvenuto Cellini. Made just prior to the impending Spaghetti Western boom on the European Continent, these two films were multinational co-productions, as were many other commercial movies produced in Europe during the 1960s.

Capitalizing on the once-lucrative economic climate in the Italian film industry, from March 1962 until sometime in 1971, Brett Halsey took up more-or-less permanent residence in Mamma Roma, where he continued furthering his acting career in period costume epics and pseudo-007 espionage flicks (e.g., **Spy in Your Eye** [*Berlino, appuntamento per un spie* / "Berlin: Appointment for a Spy", Italy, 1965, D: Vittorio Sala], co-starring Dana Andrews [1909-1992], future name-value guest star of a single SW, "Anthony M. Dawson"/Antonio Margheriti's lively **Take a Hard Ride** [*La parola di un fuorilegge... è legge!*, Italy/Spain/USA, 1975]). In the mid-'60s, Halsey also began frequenting various other commercial Italian film genres, including eventually starring in no less than five (5) Spaghetti Westerns, all of which are of some note (and to various degrees stand as quintessential examples of the distinctive cinematic form that readers of *The Spaghetti Western Digest* know and love). During this particular phase of his career—evidently in a bid by producers to cash-in on the bankable Anglo alias of Giuliano Gemma (a.k.a. "Montgomery Wood")—Halsey was billed under the pseudonym "Montgomery Ford" twice (once without his consent). In the midst of his SW 'phase,' Halsey also starred in Mario Bava's silly-if-amusing Rashômon-inspired (!) sex comedy, **Four Times That Night** (*Quante volte... quella*, Italy, 1968). Playing swinging, uh, metrosexual Gianni Prada ("An actor out of a western?" asks one character of him), Halsey therein understandably lusts after hot mod dollybird Daniela Giordano (whose known SW credits include at least ten titles, including "Anthony Ascott"/Giuliano Carnimeo's great fun Gianni "Sartana" Garko starrer **Have a Nice Funeral, My Friend** [*Buon funerale amigos!... paga Sartana*, Italy/Spain, 1970]). Elsewhere in **Four Times That Night**, BH gets himself entangled in various shenanigans, usually of a mildly racy (okay, saucy) sexual nature, including getting 'mistaken' for a homosexual, and the uninhibited star not only strips down to his ultra-brief hipsters but does an (almost!) nude shower scene too. Presumably, it being the so-called Swinging 'Sixties and all, the actor took it all in his stride in the proper spirit.

Upon his return to the USA, during the '70s Halsey did more television, including episodes of the lightweight 'buddy-buddy' western series **Alias Smith and Jones** (1971-73), starring the ill-fated Pete Duel, who died young under tragic circumstances in 1972 (Duel's sole experience on a quasi-Euroater came in **Cannon for Cordoba** [1970, D: Paul Wendkos], an American 'tourist' production shot on locations in both Spain and Mexico). Also during the early '70s, Halsey appeared as Dr. Adam Streeter on the popular—and evidently never-ending!—daytime soap opera **General Hospital** (1963-).

Italian locandina for the 1966 Brett Halsey film **Kill Johnny Ringo**

The actor later turned his hand to writing fiction, publishing a novel entitled *The Magnificent Strangers* (Bantam Books: New York, 1978), which the author has compared to Federico Fellini's acclaimed film **La Dolce Vita** ("The Sweet Life", Italy, 1959). Halsey's novel is a 'fictionalized' account of American actors living, loving, having sex, working and self-destructing amidst the bustling Roman film industry at the height of the '60s co-production boom. Within the book's text, a fictional character known as "Dusty Miles" is accredited with launching the entire spaghetti western craze; while writer Nancy Holmes is accredited with allegedly coining the former put-down / future term of endearment "Spaghetti Westerns" for an article in *Town and Country* magazine (might there actually be some truth to this?). Following excerpt from *The Magnificent Strangers*—which took its name from an early shooting title for Sergio Leone's **A Fistful of Dollars** (*Per un pugno di dollari*, Italy/Spain, 1964)—name-drops a number of real-life Euroater alumni, including "Monty Ford" (!), an informal form of Halsey's own briefly-utilized SW alias:

"...they're all here. Gordon Scott's doing Buffalo Bill; Richard Harris [i.e., Harrison] is playing Johnny Ringo; Clint Eastwood just came over to do one for Sergio Leone; Craig Hill is doing one; Steve Reeves is producing one; Lex Barker is starting another in Yugoslavia; Monty Ford, Wayde Preston, Mark Damon, Lang Jeffries; even that wild Hungarian, Micky [sic] Hargitay, is playing an American cowboy."

Halsey subsequently also authored another novel, *Yesterday's Children* (Knightsbridge: New York/Los Angeles, 1990). Sometime in the late-1980s, Halsey had relocated to Toronto, Ontario, Canada, where he found regular work in "Hollywood North" (and elsewhere) while frequently commuting back and forth between TO, Los Angeles and Rome.

Uncredited under his more familiar name (and evidently billed as "Alan Collins" [no, not the Alan Collins—a.k.a. Luciano Pigozzi, many-time spaghetti character actor—who is not in the film!]), Halsey appeared as desk jockey/talking head General Morris in "Bob Hunter"/Bruno Mattei's zilch-budget stock footage free-for-all **Cop Game** (Giochi di poliziotto, Italy, 1988), mostly in one-on-one expository dialogue exchanges with slumming Italo stunting ace Romano Puppo. Very much a gimme-my-damn-paycheque-and-lemme-outta-here kind of affair, judging from the looks of things, Halsey quite likely polished-off his few sparingly-spaced scenes in a single day—two, tops—then got the hell outta Dodge. And who could blame him, given such a seedy and cheesy context?!

Without a doubt one of the most outrageous roles of Halsey's entire career can be found in Italo splattermeister Lucio Fulci's **Touch of Death** (Quando alice ruppe lo specchio / "When Alice Broke the Mirror", Italy, 1988). For this luridly endearing gorefest, the actor toplined as aging gigolo Lester Parson, a mild-mannered, bearded, bespectacled and outwardly respectable character behind whose easygoing façade lurks a thoroughly demented psychopathic killer. First seen eating a very rare steak—which just happens to have been freshly-carved from the thigh of a nude dead girl stashed in his basement!—Halsey then takes a chainsaw to carve up her remainder, then stuffs it into a meat grinder and feeds the minced leftovers to his in-house hogs... all without getting even so much as a speck of blood on his pale-blue yuppie golf shirt in the process, yet! Despite his fancy home and white Mercedes, due to a compulsive gambling habit Halsey's character runs-up astronomical debts with his bookie, so hits upon the idea of financially exploiting 'eligible' unattached females, then offing them and misappropriating their valuables as a way to make ends meet (...and *meat*!). Having answered a 'Lonely Hearts' classified ad, he grudgingly has sex with a rich 'bearded' lady, then shortly bludgeons her to death in highly brutal fashion... only she isn't quite as 'dead' as she seems, so he is obliged to shove her head into a microwave oven in order to do a proper job of it (amounting to the film's most gratuitous and disgustingly drawn-out splatter setpiece!). In a subsequent scene, after a homeless man spies him in the commission of one of his crimes, Halsey runs him over in his Merc—not just once but fully *eight* times (ludicrously enough, the victim actually survives his injuries)! Having been duly if generically tagged "The Maniac" by the press, Halsey's Lester character thereafter shaves off his beard, dyes his hair fair and dons oversized oval-lensed glasses so as to alter his identity (in this mode the actor strongly resembles SW three-timer Joseph Cotten!). Lester's victims also include a millionaire's widow with a disfigured upper lip—much tasteless 'comedy' is here derived from Halsey's aversion to kissing her—as well as a soprano operatic chanteuse, latter of whom he garrottes with a whip during some kinky S/M sex games that get too rough. As if his life wasn't more than complicated enough already, it becomes still more so when a copycat killer—who may (or may *not*) only be a figment of his deranged imagination—begins tormenting him via telephone and commits murders for which Halsey is blamed (he monitors news reports of the crimes on the radio of his ghetto-blaster). In the final reel, when the narrative veers into psychological would-be Hitchcockian territory, Halsey's addled character sees a vision of his 'shadow' alter-ego (i.e., his guilty conscience) as he expires from a gunshot wound. An uneasy combination of the quaintly whimsical and hideously ugly (despite the fact that Fulci tactfully kept the gruesome gore murders to a minimum), in another of the film's succession of poor-taste scenes, the star kicks Lester's onscreen pet kitty-cat Reginald... for *real.*

Also for Fulci and also in a highly lurid context—albeit a far-less-gruesome one—Halsey starred in that director's kitschy softcore erotic drama **The Devil's Honey** a.k.a. **Dangerous Obsession** (*Il miele del diavolo*, Italy/Spain/France, 1986). Cast therein as a surgeon named Wendell Simpson, the impotent hubby of brunette French sex-bomb Corinne Cléry, because he can only get it up via kinky means, in one typically gratuitous scene Halsey's character is titillated by a hooker while she for some reason paints the crotch of her see-thru pantyhose with red nail polish (!). Elsewhere, one of the working girls whose services he pays for complains, "It's worse than fucking a *monster*! You're a *freak*!"

Shortly after wrapping a garish low-budget nunsploitation horror movie (**Demonia** a.k.a. **Liza** [Italy, 1990]) for Fulci, Halsey was contacted with an offer to appear in perennial critics' darling Francis Ford Coppola's megabudget Mafia drama **The Godfather, Part III** (USA, 1990)—talk about going from one extreme to another! While he receives generous screentime therein, Halsey's part as a New Hampshire judge—which, according to BH, had originally included ample dialogue—ultimately became a non-speaking one thanks to Coppola's fondness for shooting (then not using) miles of extra footage that would have severely over-extended the finished cut's total running time. *Circa* the early-'90s, two disparate icons of Spaghetti Cinema came together when Halsey introduced none other than splatter maestro Lucio Fulci to none other than Clint Eastwood!

Halsey's first wife (from 1954-59) was a former "Miss Universe," Renate Hoy, who gave him two children: a son, Charles (born 1956), and a daughter, Tracy (b. 1957), the latter of whom went on to become a psychiatric nurse. His second wife was an Italian actress, the luscious Luciana Paluzzi (whose sole SW is Ferdinando Baldi's well-above-average **The Forgotten Pistolero** a.k.a. **Gunman of Ave Maria** [*Il pistolero dell'Ave Maria*, Italy/Spain, 1969]), whom Halsey married on February 12th, 1960 (they were divorced in 1962, ironically enough the same year that Halsey first worked in Italy). Paluzzi gave him a son, Christian (b. 1961), who *circa* 1985 was working as director of international sales at Wolf Schmidt's Hollywood-based Kodiak Films (as of 1995, Christian Halsey was employed as President of the motion picture division of Solomon Entertainment Enterprises in LA). Brett Halsey's third wife was beauteous Bavarian singer-actress Heidi Brühl (1942-1991), whom he married on December 28th, 1964 (though she never appeared in a cinematic Euroater, Brühl did star as rootin'-tootin'-shootin' Wild West heroine Annie Oakley in a 1963 Berlin stage production of the musical "*Annie Get Your Gun*". Stateside, the actress is likely most familiar to psychotronic cinema buffs as Princess Jana, the fresh-faced heroine of Byron Haskin's sword-and-sorcery Arabian Nights fantasy adventure **Captain Sindbad** [West Germany/USA, 1963]). With Brühl (they were divorced in 1976, and she died of cancer in 1991), Halsey fathered a son, Clayton, who went on to become an established Hollywood film editor; and a daughter, Nicole, a future Munich-based singer-writer. While the IMDb doesn't even mention her, his fourth wife (as of 1993, estranged) was Farideh Halsey, an Iranian princess living in Toronto. His fifth and current wife is Victoria Korda.

In amusing TV spots for the locally-well-known Leon's furniture outlet (in Toronto), Halsey got his pant-leg humped by an over-amorous (out-of-frame) pooch. These priceless ads—which aired in 1996—were even funnier still when viewed dubbed into Cantonese on the local multilingual ethnic cable station! The unseen mutt's unseemly behavior was implied by no more than a rhythmic flapping motion of Halsey's trousers, and his droll reaction as he looks down and realizes the cause of this is utterly priceless to behold (guess you had to be there!). As of 1997, Halsey was living and teaching a film acting course in Costa Rica, where he had previously produced and

irected a series for local television. He also appeared in televised public information spots regarding taxation on behalf of the 'beloved' (!) governmental agency

Revenue Canada (our version of the IRS). In 2000, Halsey appeared in TV commercials for Canada's coffee-and-donuts megamagnate, Tim Hortons. In July of 2007, he was a guest at the Western Film Fair in Charlotte, North Carolina (the roster also included non-SW U.S. actor Robert Dix). In more recent years, besides being a regular fixture at various fan conventions, Brett Halsey has made intermittent appearances in indie movies, including guest-starring in Michael Fredianelli's low-budget, offbeat, spaghetti-influenced 'neo'-western **The Scarlet Worm** (USA, 2011). Just for old times' sake, BH is billed under his old "Montgomery Ford" handle, and the film's cast also includes SW alumni Dan van Husen, Michael Forest and the voice of long-time Rome-based dubber Ted Rusoff. Halsey's final (American) film credit (thus far) dates from 2015.

BH'S SW FILMOGRAPHY (IN ROUGHLY CHRONOLOGICAL ORDER):

1. **Kill Johnny Ringo** (*Uccidete Johnny Ringo* [It]; Matad a Johnny Ringo [Sp], Italy/Spain, 1966. D: "Frank G. Carroll"/Gianfranco Baldanello)
2. **Today We Kill, Tomorrow We Die!** (*Oggi a me... domani a te!*, Italy, 1968. D: Tonino Cervi)
3. **The Wrath of God** (L'ira di Dio [It]; *Hasta la última gota de sangre* [Sp], Italy/Spain, 1968. D: "Albert Cardiff"/Alberto Cardone)
4. **Kidnapping** (*Kidnapping! Paga o uccidiamo tuo figlio* [It]; *Forajidos implacables* [Sp], Italy/Spain, 1969. D: "Albert Cardiff"/Alberto Cardone)
5. **Roy Colt & Winchester Jac**k (*Roy Colt e Winchester Jack, Italy*, 1970, D: Mario Bava)

[Below follow three proposed productions from the height of the SW genre's popularity, all of which were hoped to star BH. Unfortunately, none of the movies ever got made.]

¡Salud**os Gringo!** (Italy, 1966) |– This title—Spanish for "Greetings, Gringo!"—was proposed by Selecta Film to star BH. It may feasibly have developed into his completed western **Kill Johnny Ringo** (from the same year). But don't quote us on that.

Far From Texas (Italy, 1968) |– To have been shot *real* far from Texas (try outside Rome!) starting in May of '68. Alfio Contini, long-time cinematographer, here hoped to trade hats and direct a western for Clodio Cinematografica's Genovese producer Leopoldo Pescarolo. Hoped to star was "Montgomery Ford," alias you-know-who.

Zorro (Italy, 1969) |– Beginning that September, Panda Film producers Ermanno Donati and Luigi Carpentieri planned to do a talkie remake of Douglas Fairbanks' original silent version of **The Mark of Zorro** (USA, 1920). BH was approached to play the title role and apparently even went so far as reading the script, but the project never materialized.

[With Special Thanks to Michael "Ferg" Ferguson |- SF]

** All photos used in this review courtesy of Steve Fenton.**

German vhs of **Hudson River Massacre**

Hudson River Massacre: MVD Classics

MVD Classics' recent release of **Hudson River Massacre** (*I tre del Colorado*, Italy, Spain, 1965), aka **Canadian Wilderness**, is a cause for celebration. The film, as far as I can ascertain, has never had a DVD or Blu-Ray release; only a fistful of VHS releases, but none with English subs or dubs. Therefore, when this release was announced a few months back, I was hesitant to preorder it as a film as obscure as this one, surely the print used would be of inferior quality. And I had seen the film years back, which was the cut German VHS release of the film with fan-made subtitles, and the quality was in a word, *awful!*

Now, this film is not your average Spaghetti Western! No, not even close. I would put in the same category as the *Winnetou* films and their related Sour Kraut cousins. Not that **Hudson River Massacre** involves Indians and pale faces, but it rivals those other films in the scope and breadth that the film encompasses. A broad sweeping film that takes place in Canada and the issues between the British and the French residents. The British are trying to control the French-Canadian populations destinies, trying to rob them of their freedoms and rights, and forcing them to live under the rules of the British monarchy. So, yeah, there is no iconic 'stranger' out for revenge or to make a few dollars. It is a film with some depth, some emotion, and even romance. And we do have a character out for revenge, that being the George Martin character Victor DeFrois, who is out to avenge the death of his brother. In scope and content Hudson River Massacre reminds one of the 1966 film **Django Does not Forgive** (*Mestizo*, Spain, 1966).

George Martin and Franco Fantasia

James Sullivan (Santiago Rivero), who runs the Hudson Bay Company, has some trumped-up charges brought against Charles DeFrois and two other men, saying that they were part of Leo Limoux's (Franco Fantasia) gang. Limoux and his fellow French-Canadians are violently rebelling against Britain's oppression. But Charles is not aligned with Limoux but is executed because of lies brought forth by two of Sullivan's flunkies. After Victor arrives and witnesses his brother's execution, he decides to join up with Limoux and exact his revenge against Sullivan. After leaving his jealous girlfriend, Nela (Diana Lorys), at the saloon where they live, Victor must pass a series of manly test conducted by Limoux to prove his prowess with various weapons. Sullivan wants all the trappers to sell their pelts to the Hudson Bay Company only and will do whatever he can to make sure that happens.

153

Limoux concocts a plan to kidnap Sullivan, but when they storm Sullivan's house, they find he is out and kidnap his daughter Ann (Giulia Rubini) instead. After making it back to camp, Leo, who plans to take many pelts through the frontier, sends Victor to a cabin to guard Ann. Leo wants to get through the frontier so he can trade the pelts for guns and ammo and help the rebellion. Limoux offers Sullivan a deal, safe passage for the return of Ann, and if the English do not accept the deal, allowing Leo and his gang to escape through the frontier than Victor is to kill Ann, therefore getting his revenge for his brother's death. On the way to the cabin, Ann alerts two trappers, and they follow the pair to the cabin, but they do not plan to liberate her and to take her back to her father but have rapist designs. Victor saves Ann from the men, and in the resulting dispute, takes a bullet in the shoulder. Ann must decide whether to flee or try and save Victor; she chooses to help Victor, who she realizes is not such a bad guy after all. A romantic angle develops between Ann and Victor. But when Nela finds out that Victor and Ann are in the cabin together, she spells the beans to Sullivan (including the secret code to kill Ann or bring her back to her father), that after she's tied to a post and whipped. The military, along with Sullivan, devises a plan to trap Limoux and his men in the frontier and eliminate the whole lot.

First off, the sound and picture quality of this release is outstanding. MVD Classics release of this film starts with a tacked-on French credit, which notates it an Eurocine release before the full Spanish credits are presented after the execution of Victor DeFrois' brother Charles. I can honestly say that this viewing has changed my mind about this film considerably. While it's not great, it deserves more praise and easily fits into the above-average category. Not an average Italian western, and to me that is not such a bad thing as anything new or different is always welcome. The film also has three females who are a vital part of the narrative, and that adds another layer to it. While there is the romantic angle between Victor and Ann, there is the jealous Nela and Limoux's woman Swa. Now Swa is, without a doubt, one of the most atypical female characters in an Italian western and has a sadistic twinkle in her eye and is totally devoted to Limoux and his cause. Swa is vocal and an integral part of the freedom fighters and shows her intensity in an excellent barroom fight with Nela that results in Nela's death. It's Swa who rides out to warn Victor about Sullivan and his men approaching and sacrifices her life for Victor so that he can cross the border for help. Victor heads out for the U.S.-Canadian border with Ann his English woman by his side, all the while being pursued by Sullivan and the British Red Coats. Amando de Ossorio who is best known for his horror series of the "*Blind Dead*" films, here directs his second and last western, the first being The **Tomb of the Pistolero** in 1964. Amando de Ossorio does not disappoint here and while the action is a bit clunky at times, the direction overall is outstanding. The cinematography by Fausto Zuccoli must be singled out here for praise for both its scope and clarity, which this release bathes within. The score by Carlo Savina is competent and has a more traditional western feel to it, but solid. The story was written by Amando de Ossorio, from an idea from Bob Sirens and the additional dialogue supplied by Jesus Navarro Carrion and H.S. Valdes. Filmed at the Fort/Dehesa de Navalvillar (Colmenar Viejo) and Rio Alberche (Aldea del Fresno)- provincial di Segovia. [1]

Upper: Mounties ready to attack Leo Limoux and his gang!
Bottom: The dastardly James Sullivan (Santigo Rivero) whips some information out of Nela (Diana Lorys)

Amando de Ossorio's first western 1964's **Tomb of the Pistolero** also stars George Martin and is strictly a Hollywood clone, but does have an adequate script. However, its scope is limited, as are some of the character constructions. Martin was born Francisco Martinez Celeiro in Barcelona, Spain, in 1937. Leon Klimovsky's 1964 western **Billy the Kid** (Fuera de la ley, Spain, 1964) was Martin's first western and co-starred the American Jack Taylor, who also appeared along with Martin in **Tomb of the Pistolero** (La tumba del pistolero, Spain, 1964). Martin would appear in many westerns, sometimes in lead roles, others in character or secondary parts. After accumulating forty acting credits, Martin retired from acting in the mid-'70s and moved to the United States, where he became a very successful real estate developer.

The rest of the cast is outstanding, including Giulia Rubini, as Ann Sullivan, who was a regular in spaghetti westerns. Rubini would follow this film up with three consecutive westerns, including her last acting credit in the Anthony Steffen oater **A Stranger in Paso Bravo** (Uno straniero a Paso Bravo, Italy, Spain, 1968). Diana Lorys appears as Victor's jealous girlfriend and accrued many western credits, including appearing alongside Lee Van Cleef in **Bad Man's River** (El hombre de Río Malo, Spain, Italy, France, 1971). Pamela Tudor turn as the masculine Swa is one of the highlights of the film, Tudor starred in six westerns, with **Last of the Badmen** (Il tempo degli avvoltoi, Italy, 1967) being her most recognizable western. The celebrated and prolific Santiago Rivero appearing here as James Sullivan gives the film a most fitting antagonist and helps give the hero of the piece a worthy advisory. Rivero worked in many genres, including quite frequently in spaghetti westerns, including in the above-mentioned **Django Does Not Forgive**.

While the release from MVD Classics is barebones, thats more than acceptable when considering the scarceness of the movie and the stellar print and audio provided- let's hope that MVD Classic can release more of these obscure spaghetti westerns!

[1]. IL Vincino WEST, Carlo Gaberscek, ribis, 2007.

Diana Lorys and Pamala Tudor, **Hudson River Massacre**

A FEW REVIEWS MORE!
-STEVE FENTON

My Name Is Pecos (*Due once di piombo a.k.a. Il mio nome è Pecos*, Italy, 1967)

Plot Synopsis: (*ATTN: THIS PARAGRAPH CONTAINS SPOILERS!*) The man called Pecos Martínez (Robert Woods) is out for revenge after the brutal Joe Clane ("Norman Clark"/Pier Paolo Capponi) masterminds the massacre of his entire family. Now boss of a ruthless cutthroat gang, Clane terrorizes the Mexican-Texican frontier, especially the town of Huston [sic], where sheriffs never live long and terrified residents eagerly await their salvation by the Texas Rangers. Local businessmen have learned too late that, even by siding with Clane in the interests of personal gain, their fate is ultimately the same as those who oppose his domination. Brack, one of Clane's men, has relieved the gang of its ill-gotten gains ($80,000) from a recent bank haul in Laredo. After first hiding the loot in a cask of rum and delivering it to his silent partner, Eddy Tedder the bartender ("Louis Cassel"/Luigi Castellato), Brack is caught by his former accomplices. Before he can reveal the loot's location, one of Clane's flunkies jumps the gun, killing Brack. Following this, a gang-member shoots down the telegraph wire—the town's sole lifeline to civilization—effectively cutting Huston off from all outside help.

Clane subsequently swears vengeance against Pecos after he dares kill two of his men. Elsewhere, Clane gang-members Emerson, Mudd and Blackie (Piero Morgia) attempt to rape Nina ("Christine Josani"/Cristina Iosani), the waitress at Tedder's saloon. Pecos kills all three men, but is soon captured by the gang. Feigning knowledge of the stolen loot's location is all that saves Pecos from an instant death. Upon escaping from the gang's grasp, Pecos is taken under the wings of Nina, Miss Mary Burton (Lucia Modugno) and her father, Dr. Burton ("Julian Rafferty"/Giuliano Raffaelli), whose surgeon's hands have long since been crippled by Clane. Tedder's brother Ned ("Morris Boone"/Maurizio Bonuglia) is murdered by Clane's thugs when he tries to ride for help from the Texas Rangers. Eddy Tedder—who has long kowtowed to Clane—now rebels against the gangleader. Dr. Burton also offers resistance by refusing to hand over the contested rum barrel. His daughter Mary is interrogated cruelly as to Pecos' whereabouts. When Burton attempts to defend her, he is shot dead by one of Clane's men. Coming out into the open for the final faceoff, Pecos calls the gang out. He delivers the loot-barrel into their hands using late undertaker Morton (Umberto Raho)'s mule. After Clane confesses to having murdered the Martínez family, Pecos blows-up the keg, which has been packed with dynamite hidden beneath a decoy layer of paper money. Pecos then kills-off all his remaining men and strangles Clane, thus freeing Huston from their hated criminal influence.

Theme song lyrics: "*Behold a man called Pecos / The meanest gun in the West / He lives to kill / He won't give up until / Assassins [are?] laid to rest...*"

Pier Paolo Capponi as Joe Clane: "*You idiot! You killed him off too fast. You can't deal with a corpse. How're we gonna find that money now...?*"

Umberto Raho as mortician Morton deals the death card: "*Ace o' Spades, Queen o' Spades... Pecos Martínez is gonna kill you!*"

"*Apart from the makeup...they were both a lot of fun and frivolity, Mike... The original Pecos was the best of the two, because of the story-line ..but the second one was also a good action film!*" -Robert Woods star of **My Name is Pecos** and **Pecos Cleans Up**

Star Robert Woods and future director Demofilo Fidani (who worked in the present film's wardrobe department, as well as serving as its production designer) presumably met for the first time here and reteamed on the sequel, **Pecos Cleans Up** (also reviewed below, following this one). The two would later re-collaborate on the highly-decent "spaghetti-zapata" **Pray to God and Dig Your Grave** a.k.a. **Say Your Prayers and Dig Your Grave** (*Prega Dio... e scavati la fossa!*, Italy, 1968), for which Fidani served as co-producer.

Despite playing a Mexican in supersnazzy bellbottoms with 12-inch-wide cuffs, Woods opens **My Name Is Pecos**—directed by future Italocrime top gun Maurizio Lucidi, credited hereon as "Maurice A. Bright"—looking much like Giuliano Gemma (who never actually played a Hispanic in any of his spaghetti westerns, surprisingly enough). During the rather odd prologue, our hero is accosted by a poor man's Lee Van Cleef / Black Bart at a drinking well; who without invitation trades Woods an empty pistol for a $20 bill. The scene appears to be a variation of the real Cleef's intro to Sergio Sollima's fabulous **The Big Gundown** (*La resa dei conti*, Italy/Spain, 1966); except here the tables are turned on the fake Cleef. When Woods turns his back and secretly fills the gun with bullets from his hatband, the bad guy draws on him while demanding to know his name. As the bad guy bites the dust, Woods strategically mouths the film's English title (he repeats it twice more later). Sung by one Bob Smart, "The Ballad of Pecos" sounds too much like Eric Burdon & The Animals' 1964 Britpop hit "House of the Rising Sun." Its instrumental refrain repeats when Woods bursts through the swingin' doors and he and Dante Posani's polecats take an instant dislikin' to one another. When the Mexican requests tequila at the bar, the outlaws warn him that *mexicanos* ain't allowed to down liquor in them parts ("Man like you's much better off drinkin' *mule's milk*!"). *Mexicanos* also ain't allowed to carry guns... so, in compliance with that local bigots' by-law, Woods shoots it instead, leaving both hecklers horizontal. This disturbance kick-starts a gramophone, which belts-out a lopsided *mariachi* tune. ("*Tequila... por favor*," Woods politely asks again.) A slight variation of this entire scene was replayed in the sequel.

The so-called "Norman Clark" a.k.a. Pier Paolo Capponi's Clane character is a redneck in more ways than one: Not only does his throat bear a scarlet scar from where the hangman's noose unfortunately once failed to do its job properly, but he's also a complete-and-utter bigot besides (e.g., "There are too many Mexicans—even in Mexico!"). As the cleverly-named Morton, Umberto "Umi" Raho ("'Ye shalt bury the dead'") is the way-overbooked Huston [sic] undertaker ("I've never seen a gravedigger lookin' more like a gravedigger!"), who tows corpses to Hades behind a silver-belled mule named Lucifer ("They *all* come to me, one day or another!"). Morton can read a poker deck like tarot cards and much prefers the sweet smell of money to the sickly reek of embalming fluid. . The underhanded undertaker is willing to sell more than just an honest funeral for a golden dollar ("You *vulture*! Go back to your cemetery and feed on the dead"). When his two-ply personality is exposed by Pecos, Morton begs for forgiveness while hiding behind a Bible (whose hollow text sneakily hides a derringer).). Just one among several blond gunmen herein, German-born future producer Peter Carsten utters more than one surreal line (case in point,

ROBERT WOODS
PETER CARSTEN
LUCIA MODUGNO

REGIE
MAURICE A. BRIGHT

Produktion
Italcine TV Rom

Technicolor°
Techniscope

MEIN NAME IST PECOS

MY NAME IS PECOS

WELTVERTRIEB
WORLD SALES / VENTE A L'ETRANGER
UFA-INTERNATIONAL
Export, Import, Co-Produktion
8 München 15, Sonnenstraße 19 / Germany
Telephone: 55 79 26 / Telex: 05 / 23 265
Cables: UFAINTER MÜNCHEN

Above: My Name is Pecos... German Press-Sheet.
Opposite page: Top: Italian Poster. Bottom: Italian Locadina.

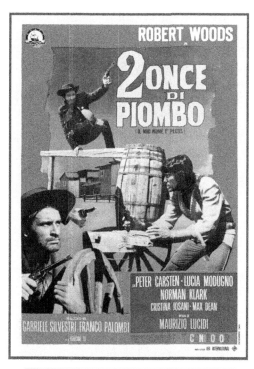

"Those two boys could do anythin' with their pistols... except *eat* 'em!" and "You could shoot out his brains... and still leave his *mouth*!"). And it takes fully four (count 'em!) shots from a long gun to bring feisty Sal Borgese (playing an hombre of decidedly slender morals nicknamed "Slim") to a complete standstill... albeit horizontally.

As in many a spaghetti western, **My Name Is Pecos**' scurrilous criminal element exploit human frailty and even outright physical handicap, which it sometimes inflicts. Playing a grinning thug in a hat almost as broad as his shoulders, the towering "George Eastman" a.k.a. Luigi Montefiori's exceedingly-not-nice character ("The only thing we'll ever find around here is *vultures*!") drags a lame man by his one good leg. Years before in the town of Bandera, Giuliano Raffaelli's sympathetic Doc Burton character had had every bone in both hands cracked by Clane's gunbutt (hints of Corbucci's **Django** [Italy/Spain, 1966]). Woods is pulverized stupid by Clane's whole pack (hints of Clint the Squint in both Leone's **A Fistful of Dollars** [*Per un pugno di dollari*, Italy/Spain/West Germany, 1964] and **For a Few Dollars More** [*Per qualche dollaro in più*, Italy/Spain/West Germany, 1965]).

Perhaps as a result of his double-beating and still other indignities being heaped upon him, Woods is far more sullen here than he would be in **Pecos Cleans Up**, but is not above making straight-faced cracks regarding his enemies' sluggish senses ("Dead men can't hear... and you, my friends, are *dead!*"). Another character—the outlaw played by above-cited unbilled bit-player Dante Posani—subsequently keeps the motif alive ("You have two sharp eyes, *mexicano*. And I know a good way to *close* 'em fer good!"). Surplus 'sight' gags runneth over into the sequel. Even with all its snappy dialogue, however, the forerunner is far more gleefully sadistic. (*SPOILER ALERT!*) As 80-grand's worth of fluttering paper smackers sprinkle down all around them, Woods finishes the job left undone by that sloppy hangman when he wrings "Clark"/Capponi as Clane's neck but good with his own bandanna. Better late than never!

Closing lyrics: *"The blood ran deep / The blood ran high / The blood was deep / In pain he heals their cry... Revenge, thy name is 'Pecos.'"*

Half as colourful as its follow-up but twice as serious, as Italoaters go, **My Name Is Pecos** is solid enough, if thoroughly derivative (by no means always a bad thing!). [*With some input from Michael "Ferg" Ferguson.*]

Notes: On German releases of the Pecos duology, Woods' title character was re-named "Jonny Madoc". Costumers on both productions were "Miles Deem"/ Demofilo Fidani and Mila Vitelli/"Valenza," who also worked with Woods on the cheapo-but-great-fun **Savage Guns** a.k.a. **His Name Was Sam Wallash, But They Call Him Amen** (*Era Sam Wallash!... lo chiamavano... E Così Sia*, Italy, 1971). Camera assistant on **MNIP** was Aristide Massaccesi, later to become better-known to Eurotrash cinema geeks as gazillion-aliased sleazemeister "Joe D'Amato". European Video Corp (EVC)'s erstwhile videocassette of **MNIP** from the Netherlands—a copy of which served as basis for this review—came letterboxed and dubbed into English (with native Dutch subtitles). The Texan town of Huston [sic] was presumably named after director John rather than Texican patriot and hero of the Alamo Sam Houston!

Pecos Cleans Up (*Pecos è qui: prega e muori*, Italy, 1967)

Plot Synopsis: (*ATTN: THIS PARAGRAPH AND THE NEXT CONTAIN SPOIL-ERS!*) Paco, Pinto and Pepé, a trio of transient Mexican *mariachis* (respectively played by "Peter Vidal"/Piero Vida, Umberto Raho and "Louis Cassel"/Luigi Castellato), witness an attack by El Supremo's bandits—led by El Rayo (Simon Lafitte)—upon a peaceful homestead. At the scene, a dying *padre*'s last gasps make mention of the fabled Treasure of Montezuma. According to the Indians, this is hidden inside the Golden Barque ("the Boat of Gold"), a ship now kept in dry dock at the Temple of Tescoco. The map leading to the treasure had been hidden in the farm's pigeon-house. The three musicians quickly locate it, but are disappointed to learn that the temple stands on Barangos Mountain: smack-dab in the domain of El Supremo (Erno Crisa), who is reputedly none other than a direct descendant of Emperor Mon-tezuma himself. While the common peons believe the legendary hoard—a fabulous sum weighing some 40,000 pounds—shall someday finance a people's revolution, Supremo seeks to use it only to overthrow the *status quo* and start his own oppressive feudal regime.

Pecos Cleans Up, French 120 cm x 160 cm Poster.

Pecos Martínez, a youthful Mexican and once close friend of legendary revolution-ary hero Emiliano Zapata, is renowned for his proficiency as a *pistolero*. Upon being impressed by Pecos' pistola precision during an altercation with some loutish *grin-gos*, los musicians three seek his involvement in the treasure hunt. Don Alfonsino informs them that their map is next-to-worthless and that the genuine parchment is hidden somewhere within the treasure cave. Elsewhere, Supremo's men have kid-napped Ramona (Luciana Gilli), daughter of Don Gonsalvo Altamura, the Governor of Matamuros. Having placed the 20,000-peso ransom at Rio Canco, two *federales* from Mexico City rendezvous with El Rayo to arrange the exchange at the Tienda del Sol, only to have El Rayo abruptly murder the soldiers in cold blood. Along with Dago and Frenchie Thonville ("Pedro Sánchez"/Ignazio Spalla and "Charles Gate"/Carlo Gaddi), Rayo agrees to steal the ransom from Supremo. Aided by Pinto, Pepé and Paco, who pose as *regolare* deserters from the regiment of Francisco Pérez, Pecos kills Dago and his *muchachos*. After first introducing themselves by playing "*The Song of the Gold*," the three musicians win an audience with Supremo himself. Pecos subsequently wins the chief's trust by concocting an elaborate ruse and presenting him with both Dago's corpse and the missing ransom money. He then points the way to a spurious map. An expedition is planned to a nearby cavern at Nuestra Cruz, the grotto of San Guadalupe, where Pecos' decoy map claims the treasure awaits them for easy picking. Meanwhile, with the invaluable assistance of an Indian maiden named Eliza ("Brigitte Winter"/ Brigitte Wentzel), Pecos' three singin' sidekicks liberate Ramona. On their way to the grotto, Pecos uses guile to separate Supremo from his two remaining disreputable lieu-tenants, Thonville and "El Rayo". Cunningly, Pecos brings about the demise of each, exploiting their respective individual vices: sexual lust (for *doña* Ramona) and greed (for gold). Earlier, Dago had died because of his gluttony (for food). Upon confronting Supremo, the self-proclaimed libertador ("liberator") of Mexico, Pecos strangles the wouldbe dominator with his own whip just as a dynamite charge is about to blow the entire mountain to pieces. Rejoined by Ramona, Eliza, Paco, Pepé and Pinto, Pecos at last reveals the whereabouts of the gold.

Robert Woods as Pecos gets apolitical: "*If the Devil was living in Mexico and needed a partner, his first choice would be El Supremo... a blood-sucking animal, feeding at the heart of Mexico! A foul weed choking the life from our country!... He's a worm!*"

Don Alfonsino, the priest: "*I believe México could use a good revolution.*"

Simon Lafitte's character toots his own horn: "*They call me 'El Rayo'...it means Lightning!*"

Playful sequel to the above-discussed **My Name Is Pecos**, again directed by the effi-cient Maurizio Lucidi under his "Maurice A. Bright" alias, that is lent an unusual feel and appearance by both the script and set designers. Many of the props and dressings were apparently left-over from the preceding peplum period of Continental cinema, some of them possibly even reused from Osvaldo Civirani's South American-set **Hercules Against the Sons of the Sun** (*Ercole contro i figli del sole*, Italy/Spain, 1964), co-starring Mark Forest and impending SW superstar Giuliano Gemma. **PCU**'s Temple of Texcoco (presumably designed by Demofilo Fidani and Mila Valenti, who handled both art direction and costumes here) is a modest four-tiered, twenty-foot 'Aztec' pyramid built of adobe against a rockface. Like its Egyptian equivalent (or perhaps something challenged by Indiana Jones!), a complex system of counterweights and boobytraps leads to the fabled treasure stashed at its centre. Much of the exterior action unfolds amidst the russet Roman dirtpits later favoured by Fidani after he became 'better-known' as director "Miles Deem" and occasionally re-employed Woods 'for old times' sake'.

As our main heavy of the piece El Supremo, self-proclaimed last heir to the noble Aztec monarchy, Erno Crisa is so full of himself that he sits on a throne, carries a coiled bullwhip as his 'royal sceptre' and forces a drunken Roman Catholic priest named Josélito to grovel at his feet and hail him as "the Almighty, the All-Powerful" ("The imbecile is still loyal to his ridiculous God!"). *Padre* Alfonsino meanwhile pauses to take a bracing slug of sacramental vino in the interests of deriving some liquid courage when the holy spirit alone isn't enough to inspire him. Ironical considering his unrepentant anticlericalism, with his unshorn locks, round-roofed black sombrero and evil black cape lined with red silk, Crisa resembles *Saturday Night Live*'s satirical RC clericomic Father Guido Sarducci ("You should *pray*," he later advises star Robert Woods).

Decadent-looking, lustful gunman Carlo Gaddi (dubbed into English by a Frenchman) plays it in an Eastwoodian poncho. When Gaddi's moment to die inevitably arrives, Woods commands his *mariachis* to strike-up a cheerful French can-can number to provide appropriate (quote) "background music". Even in a dowdy patchwork serape, Luciana Gilli makes a heroine worth sacrificing even 40,000 pounds of solid gold for. Teutonic-looking cool, pale blonde Brigitte Wentzel/"Winter"—at least according to press materials, anyhow—plays an "Indian" maiden. Meanwhile, Woods' normally paler complexion is for the occasion darkened with coffee-coloured greasepaint, and he is also dubbed with a Gallic-sounding accent (e.g., "The only thing that's waiting for you is the *undertaker*... and a deep *hole*!"). El Supremo's unfriendly, uncultured louts fail to appreciate the rich musical heritage of Woods' home country ("Hey, you greasers... Play something else besides that filthy Mexicano music!"). Intent on teaching the mariachis to dance to a different tune, a henchman perforates the floorboards at their feet with his lead 'flute', and he ain't just whistling Dixie, neither.

Cue heroic intervention by Woods, who doesn't take kindly to gringo redneck peckerwoods (he would soon play another lusty Mexican libertador in Edoardo Mulargia's excellent if budget-conscious oater, the above-cited **Pray to God and Dig Your Grave** a.k.a. **Say Your Prayers and Dig Your Grave** [Italy, 1968], co-produced by Fidani and also featuring familiar supporting player Gaddi). With justified rudeness, Woods unplugs the surly Frank character's cee-gar from his big mouth and takes an irreverent drag before countering the other's dissing of his beloved homeland with a recommendation of México that a travel brochure couldn't put forth any better ("It's a beautiful place. You just have to understand it"). Realizing the boorish *gringos* are too stupid to ever comprehend, Woods opts to further their education with six smart, shiny bullets, hot off the hammer ("Let the *coyotes* have them!").

165

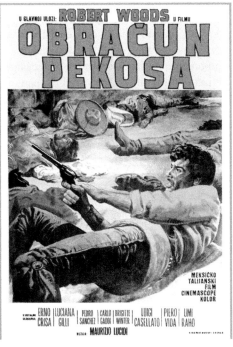

Left: German Press-Sheet: **Pecos Cleans Up**.
Right: Serbia- Yugoslavian Poster

While Pecos is all for national pride, when it comes to money matters he doesn't even trust his own countrymen, though. And while he justifiably despises the caste system which is wielded like a spiked whip by El Supremo, Pecos evidently sees no personal ethical discrepancy in riding his horse while his three musical buddies tag along on foot like loyal dogs ("Our way is his *way*," admits Umi Raho with the blind obeisance of a serf).

Upon witnessing El Rayo's cowardly cold-blooded killings of the Mexican troopers, Woods instinctively masturbates his Winchester barrel in anticipation of avenging this heinous crime (ironically, in the aforementioned **Pray to God / Say Your Prayers**, he thinks nothing of eliminating the faceless representatives of authority with extreme prejudice and zero regard for such niceties as mercy). Pecos later informs "Pedro Sánchez" a.k.a. Ignazio Spalla as Dago (tactfully pronounced "Daggo", just so's you know!), who casts aspersions on his optical prowess, that his eyes work fine. Just prior to having his own closed permanently by Woods, Dago brags, "I can open another one in the middle of your forehead, *amigo!*" The encounter closes along with fully fourteen other orbs—totaling precisely siete *bandidos*—joining with Dago on the neverending blink. Just for realism's sake, Woods actually pauses for a fast reload between kill #6 and kill #7 (he is only using a *six*-shooter, after all, you see. That said, many another SW didn't bother to keep count of such things as how many bullets a particular firearm might be capable of firing before needing to be reloaded).

166

Keeping the sardonic metaphors a-comin', Gaddi subsequently remarks, "They must have given Dago something very difficult to digest... and he *choked* on it." To which, Woods affirms, "Uh-huh: two ounces of lead under his heart!" When his tricorn of underprivileged sidekicks prepare to loot Dago's fresh corpse—having himself only just broken the Fifth Big No-No no less than seven times—Woods piously cautions, "You mustn't *steal*. It's against the Seventh Commandment." Woods injects further theological philosophy ("Money is the Devil's pastime—that's why he made the coins round, so they would roll and people would have to run after them"). Adding further irony, Woods at times here bears a quite strong facial resemblance to late, uh, 'well-armed' American porno stud John C. Holmes! That said, Pecos performs such sleight-of-gun-hand as aiming and shooting without even drawing his pistol from its holster (no mean feat, even for a cool-as-a-cigarillo SW antihero!).

Weakest link in **PCU** is, sad to say, Coriolano "Lallo" Gori's somewhat emaciated score which, rather than complementing/enhancing the action by blending symbiotically with it, mostly just lays flat either behind or on top of it like a damp horse blanket. Nonetheless, **Pecos Cleans Up** amounts to an enjoyable, if fancifully-plotted, hybrid that is well worth a SpagWester's time. Both **PCU** and its forerunner **MNIP** recently became made available in what are without doubt their optimal video releases to date by Wild East Productions, as a BD/DVD combo (Volume 50 of WE's ongoing series entitled The Spaghetti Western Collection). [*With some input from Michael "Ferg" Ferguson.*]

Notes: Scriptwriter Adriano Bolzoni had previously penned a character named "El Rayo" into one of Robert Woods' earliest Euroaters, Alfonso Balcázar's **The Man from Canyon City** (*L'uomo che viene da Canyon City*, Spain/Italy, 1964); while an unrelated "El Supremo" popped-up in the sub-supreme **The Great Treasure Hunt** (reviewed elsewhere this ish). *PCU* was formerly available in Holland on pre-recorded Beta/VHS (PAL format) videocassette from both the Cannon and Expert labels, presented letterboxed and dubbed into English (with Dutch subtitles, natch). Assistant director was Aldo Lado. Halfway across the world that same year, celebrated masked wrestler "Santo, El Enmascarado de Plata" (a.k.a. Rodolfo Guzmán Huerta) hunted the fabulous legendary hoard in René Cardona's **El tesoro de Moctezuma** / "Montezuma's Treasure," co-starring frequent western alumnus Jorge Rivero and actually lensed in the real México against authentic pre-Hispanic ruins rather than a jerrybuilt, cost-conscious simulacrum thereof.

The Greatest Robbery in the West (*La più grande rapina del west*, Italy, 1967)

Plot Synopsis: (*ATTN: THIS PARAGRAPH AND THE NEXT CONTAIN SPOILERS!*) Monroe County, near Fort Adams, Texas, 1880. Middletown's prosperity rests on its cattle industry. Knowing full-well that the coffers of the town bank are overflowing with lucre, David Phaylard (Jack Betts a.k.a. "Hunt Powers") plots a spectacular caper along with the Jarret Gang to relieve the West Bank—hopefully without any bloodshed—of $500,000 in gold coins. On the day of the robbery, Phaylard disguises himself as a monk, placing the wooden effigy of the non-existent "Saint Abelard" upon his wagon, which he parks outside the bank so that the statue stands beside one of its windows. One of the gang-members creates a fiery diversion, while inside the bank Jarret (Walter Barnes) and his boys immobilize the staff and grab the gold, which is then placed inside the Saint's effigy via the nearby window. The citizens are not terrorized and the alarm is not sounded until the culprits are long-gone. The gang makes short work of a pursuing posse, and the bank-robbers then split up. Taking the statue, Phaylard heads for a golden rendezvous with his accomplices in the aptly-named Poorlands. Nowever, neither Phaylard nor Jarret intend to split the loot with their accomplices. A $3000 reward is offered by the county judge.

French Poster: **The Great Robbery in the West**

Eccentric—and boozy!—town layabout Billy "Rum" Cooney (George Hilton) intervenes, seeking retribution against Jarret's lookout man for the murder of his brother Martin, the former Poorlands sheriff (Enzo Fiermonte). Jarret's gang occupies Poorlands awaiting a native guide to lead them to Pueblo Rojo, Mexico. Meanwhile, Phaylard becomes increasingly disenchanted with the brutal tactics of Jarret, who plans to raze the town before lighting-out toward Mexico. Phaylard, Rum and Mark ("Jeff Cameron"/Goffredo Scarciofolo) join forces with the mutual goal of eliminating the Jarret Gang. Sheriff Norman (Tom Felleghy) and his 30-man posse from El Paso approach Poorlands, where Jarret stages a mock funeral to throw-off their suspicions. Forced to pose as his late brother for the deception, Rum 'volunteers' a number of Jarret's men to join the posse. Having long since gotten wise to the gold coins, Rum decides he wants to hang onto the pecuniary delights for himself, so he stuffs the storage statue with worthless gravel instead. Unbeknownst to his rivals Phaylard and Jarret, Rum has stashed the golden goodies amongst a cache of explosives. When the trio confront each other and finally consider an amicable three-way split of the loot, the explosives are accidentally detonated, killing Jarret and showering a Heavenly downpour of gold coins into the grateful hands of local poor folk, in fitting recompense for their suffering at the bloodthirsty bandits' hands.

"Hunt Powers"/Jack Betts as the bogus Brother gets self-righteous: "*Brethren! The wrath of the Lord has been visited upon your city of sin!*"

Walter "Piggy" Barnes as Jarret hurls a porcine insult: "*You pig!*"

As with the Pecos two-pack discussed this same ish, **The Greatest Robbery in the West** was likewise directed by Maurizio Lucidi, an above-average filmmaker who makes the best he can of the present material, resulting in an entertaining if lightweight SW time-killer. **TGRITW**'s very first image shows a macrophotographic downpour of shiny coins, which is immediately followed by an unusual minute-long sequence of actors' dialogue laid atop primary-hued stylized portraits of various cast members seen in frozen action scenes from the film. Credits proper then commence, with an even-more-elaborate animated montage that includes multi-colored silver dollars with bulletholes plugged dead-center. Evidenced by this elaborate intro and the apex year of its origin (when every new Italoater must have seemed like another potential B.O. gold mine to dollar-eyed producers), **The Greatest Robbery in the West**—more inappropriately and nondescriptly a.k.a. **Halleluja for Django** (an Anglo translation of its German title, *Ein Halleluja für Django*)—was afforded a budget generous enough for such extravagant creative flourishes as these.

As a flippant, buck-scrounging drunkard (as per his onscreen nickname of "Rum"), Hilton basically plays a more comedic variation of his lush character from Lucio Fulci's **Massacre Time** a.k.a. **The Brute and the Beast** (*Le colt cantarono la morte e fu... tempo di massacro*, Italy, 1966) combined with his acrobatic antihero from Enzo G. Castellari's **Any Gun Can Play** a.k.a. **Go Kill and Come Back** (*Vado... l'ammazzo e torno*, 1967). Incidentally, according to original Italian production records, that Castellari film had commenced shooting in April of '67, while **TGRITW** began a mere month later in May. If these dates are correct (or even just roughly so),

169

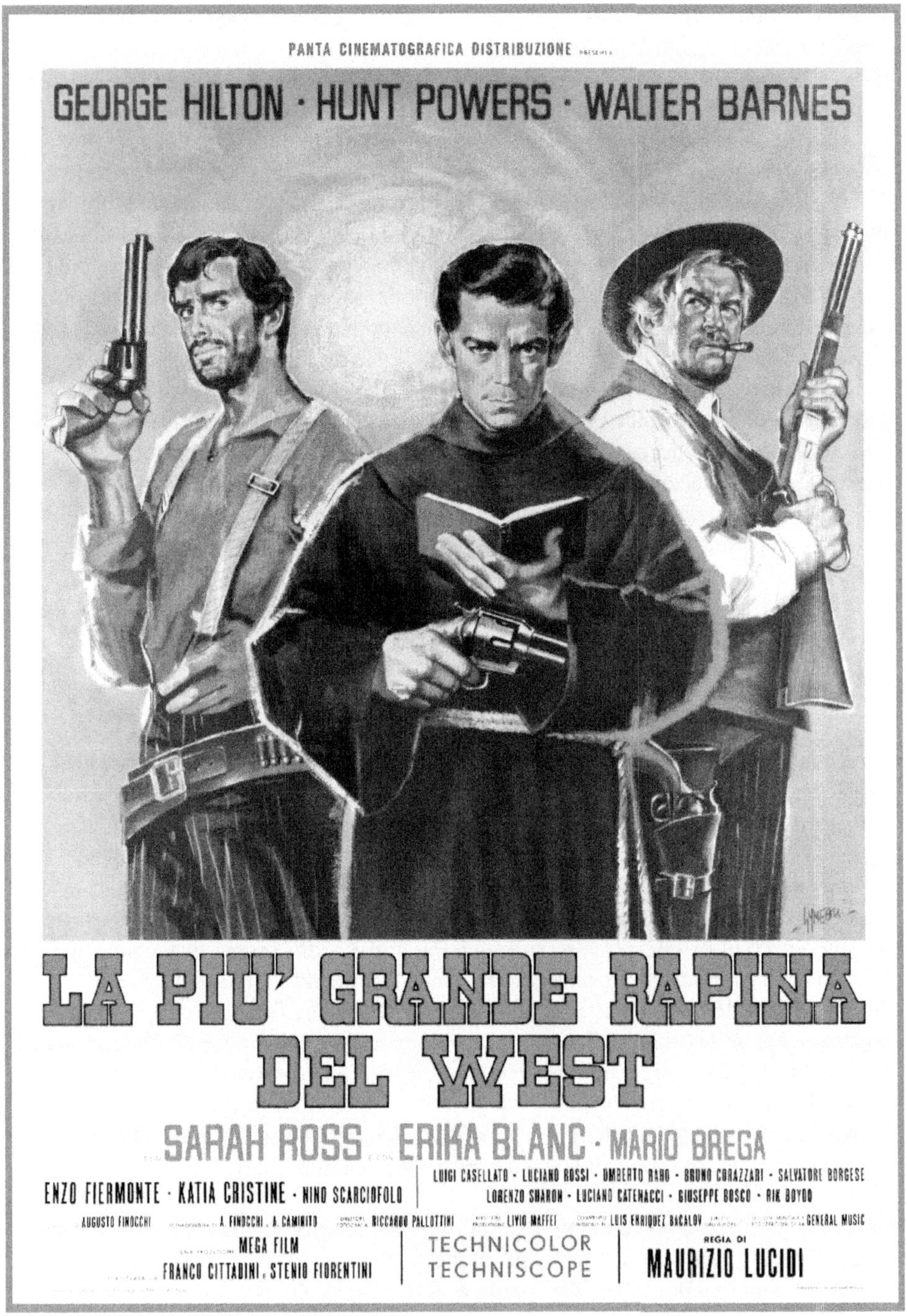

The Greatest Robbery in the West: Italian Poster

this attests to the lightning speed at which movies were being churned-out in the Euro industry at the height of the production boom back in those days. Each made by a different production company, *Any Gun Can Play* saw its domestic Italian release late that September, while **TGRITW** premiered in Italian theaters come October of that same year; spaced precisely a month apart. While **AGCP** was entirely shot in Italy, **TGRITW**, although wholly Italian in origin rather than a co-production with Spain, was (as with scores of other Italo-input movies of the time) at least in-part shot on some Spanish locations, in this case at the Desierto de Tabernas western town backlot in Almería, Andalucía, shooting site of a great many other SW's.

In **TGRITW**, our present film under discussion, enjoying the taste of his namesake waaay too much, Billy Rum's such an alcoholic he risks a possible pig-stickin' from antsy cellmate Bruno Corazzari rather than part with his precious canteen of booze. In typically effortless Hiltonian fashion, our hero de-knifes Corazzari then twangs the blade safely out of its owner's reach amidst the jailhouse ceiling beams. Hilton soon escapes captivity through a secret trapdoor to give his onscreen murdered big brother (Fiermonte) a good Christian burial after his corpse has been left to 'ripen' on Poorlands' downtown drag, serving as a grim warning to other wannabe law-abiding citizens. He thereafter runs smack (read: *SMACK!*) into a four-fisted beating from by-then-already-well-seasoned stuntmen/actors "Rick Boyd"/Federico Boido and Salvatore "Sal" Borgese. Hilton spends much of the running time locked in a cell, causing Powers to ponder just how he constantly keeps on escaping to muss-up the gang's plans. When buffalo-gutted Mario Brega gets all tanked-up and attempts to ravish Rum's lissome girlfriend (Erika Blanc), Hilton obliges Powers by slipping out of captivity once again to rush to her rescue. To force Hilton's cooperation after he hides the gang's loot on them, Powers nails-up his getaway chute, thus sealing him in the clink.

Here foreshadowing Italo future action star Fabio Testi (another badass performer who started out as a stuntman), Hunt Powers' stint as a phony *padre* might easily fit into one of his co-star George Hilton's '70s "Anthony Ascott"/Giuliano Carnimeo oatcoms. No sooner has Powers given a belligerent Indian guide a bellyful of bullethole than he piously resumes his Bible and clerical cassock (albeit worn with cowboy boots and spurs; for after all, the Devil is an unruly mount!).

Powers' and Hilton's co-star, blocky American ex-NFL footballer Walter Barnes (of the Philadelphia Eagles), seems to really relish his casting against type as the arrogant, hot-tempered outlaw chief who places Poorlands—which lives up to its name in more ways than one—under the jackboot of pseudo-Nazi tyranny. After his henchman Paolo Magalotti is lynched by Hilton, Barnes as Jarret orders the rounding-up of all town citizens. Recognizing his big chance at the brass ring, boyish guest star Jeff Cameron (here billed under his other alternate name of Giovanni [actual Christian name Goffredo] Scarciotolo) gives a spirited performance, especially during his barroom roundhouse with Hilton and when he gets roped-and-horse-dragged by Corazzari and criminal cohort Luciano Catenacci. For opposing the bank-robbers, Cameron is noosed to a bellringing rope that shortly becomes the final resting place of aforementioned minor bankrobber Magalotti.

And now for some backstory on the production... In a rare turn of events indeed for a 'B'-grade spaghetti western, **The Greatest Robbery in the West**—surprisingly enough—became subject of an "exclusive" on-the-set newspaper report in the U.S. of A., written by journalist William Price Fox for New York's *Saturday Evening Post* (circa May-June 1967) and entitled "Wild Westerns, Italian Style" . While visiting the set overseas over a two-day period, Fox met various cast and crewmembers and observed up-close and first-hand the behind-the-scenes firing mechanism of a bona fide Spaghetti Western-in-progress.

Over the course of the article, a native lighting technician explained one of the main reasons for shooting without direct sound: "No one can keep an Italian quiet... You've *got* to shoot with no sound." Hunt Powers described a scene they had shot—(quote) "an Italian first"—wherein he was to have sex with actress Sonia/Sonja Romanoff (a.k.a. "Sara Ross") upon a monk's cassock spread-out beneath a church altar, of all places. Upon subsequently reconsidering this decision, the director then shot an alternate version of the scene—this time minus all the Roman Catholic trappings—to hopefully avoid Vatican censors (what remains of this scene evidently occurs between the pair of actors at an isolated shack following the robbery). Two versions of another scene were also photographed: a surgeon treats a man for a gunshot wound to the stomach, inflicted by a golden bullet, during which the doc gouges-out the precious projectile with an exclamation of glee... whereupon a stampede of men excitedly leap upon the suffering patient in hopes of striking more gold! Possibly on account of its poor taste, the scene was cut for potential export (if it was ever shot at all?). Upon witnessing the English-dubbed export print reviewed here, it's difficult to ascertain just where this sequence might fit in (two men are shown being shot in the belly, in-cluding Brega, but nary a 'golden bullet' is mentioned. So go figure!). Either way, any of this potential missing footage—assuming it even actually made it onto celluloid in the first place—would make an ideal 'special feature' for inclusion in a deluxe Blu-ray or DVD edition of the movie someday.

As was further reported in that *Saturday Evening Post* article, during production Powers and Walter Barnes, Americans both, delivered their dialogue in their native English. George Hilton, a Uruguayan by birth who became a long-time resident of It-aly, spoke Spanish. Brescian-born Erika Blanc (r.n. Enrica Bianchi Colombatto) spoke her native Italian, while blonde burgeoning starlet Katia Christine, from Holland (who plays Katy O'Brien in the film), spoke French (she only has a couple of tiny scenes in the final product). In Germany, where he was a popular draw due to his appearances in the hugely-profitable *Winnetou* series, Barnes would receive star billing. In Italy and Spain, Hilton. For America—where, incidentally, he was virtually unknown, even under his real name of Jack Betts—Hunt Powers would topline.

The title makes this appear to be a 'perfect caper' flick, *à la* Dino Risi's popular con-temporary crime comedy **The Treasure of San Gennaro** (Operazione San Gennaro, Italy/France/West Germany, 1966) and Giuliano Montaldo's bank heist drama **Grand Slam** (*Ad ogni costo*, Italy/Spain/West Germany, 1967). That said, the actual robbery in **TGRITW** is dispensed with in most perfunctory fashion, and the plot overall has more in common with subsequent 'town-held-hostage' spaghettis like the Andrea Giordana star vehicle **Taste of Death** (*Quanto costa morire*, Italy/France, 1968; directed by one of the *least*-known Sergios in the Spaghetti West, genre one-timer Sergio Merolle), which gave **TGRITW** support player Corazzari a much-more-substantial role as Barnes' equally-fascistic counterpart. Much of Luis Enríquez Bacalov's rather unmemorable score rearranges that hoary apple pie western standard "The Yellow Rose of Texas". There are far too many characters written-in for the screenplay to comfortably accommodate them all, meaning inevitable loose ends are left trailing. Much like Cameron, the ladyfolk are given little to do, but a spirited catfight does break out between Ross and Blanc.

The ironic 'meek shall inherit the wealth' ending was used in a number of other westerns (e.g., "Newman Rostel"/Bianco Manini's **Hallelujah to Vera Cruz** [*Partirono preti, tornarono... curati*, Italy, 1973], for one). Of course, our assembled antiheroes of **TGRITW** merely laugh at this cruel card the Lord has dealt them... straight from the bottom of the deck.

Despite all its enviable advance American press—which many a bigger-budgeted and/or better Italoater would have *killed* for!—**The Greatest Robbery in the West**, as with its shot-back-to-back companion-piece **Sugar Colt** (Italy/Spain, 1966. D: Franco Giraldi), never received any official theatrical or TV (and in **TGRITW**'s case, to date even video, so far as we know as of this writing) release stateside, despite all its producers' high hopes (i.e., pipe dreams).

And to think they were actually entertaining notions of a spinoff teleseries at one point, too! If they'd at least been able to fire-off a pilot episode for posterity, that'd be something, but the proposed project—assuming it had ever even been a serious proposition at all, and wasn't merely overconfident bravado for the benefit of that on-set NY reporter—never made it off the drawing-board, we're sorry to say. Having said that, **TGRITW** itself, while far from atrocious, is only an at-best middling example of the SW form, although the fact that it 'triple-barrels' together three such Euroater luminaries as Powers, Hilton and Barnes makes it required viewing for serious followers of the genre. [*With some input from Michael "Ferg" Ferguson.*]

Notes: Despite there being no known current physical media release of this film available domestically (?), under its **Halleluja for Django** title, an upload—evidently taken from a German source, but dubbed into English—was formerly available to stream VOD on Amazon Prime (@ *https://www.amazon.com/Halleluja-Django-George-Hilton/dp/B01MRNUIE7*), but has since been made unavailable in that format (at least in Canada, where I live!). Master-at-arms on the film was Sal Borgese. Its assistant director was Aldo Lado. Powers and Cameron had first worked together on **Sugar Colt**, and would meet again during the early '70s on the lovably off-the-wall 'improv'-oaters of "Miles Deem" a.k.a. Demofilo Fidani.

REPOKER DE BRIBONES

MARK **DAMON** · ROSALBA **NERI** · ALFREDO **MAYO** · DIRECTOR TONINO **RICCI**

The Great Treasure Hunt: Spanish Pressbook

The Great Treasure Hunt (*Monta in sella figlio di...!! / "Saddle-Up, You Son-of-a...!!"*, Italy/Spain/USA, 1971)

Plot Synopsis: (*ATTN: THIS PARAGRAPH CONTAINS SPOILERS!*) The 1880s. Sam Madison ("Stan Cooper"/Stelvio Rosi) is arrested while trying to rob the Denver Bank. Elsewhere, his brother Dean (Mark Damon) defuses a potentially ugly saloon standoff involving a middle-aged card-cheat named André, "The Frenchman" (Alfredo Mayo) and his pretend "niece" Agnes (Rosalba Neri), the best two cottonpickin' safecrackers-cum-confidence tricksters in them there parts. After André and Agnes steal his horses and vamoose, Dean follows them to convince the pair to assist him in knocking-over the maximum-security Denver Bank. . As Agnes and André prepare for the stickup, Sam Madison is readied for a-hangin'. During the chaos caused by the bank heist, Dean springs Sam from the noose's tightening embrace, and all four escape to their hideout. At the cabin they find "Blind" Felipé (Luis Marín), who reels-off a tale about dictator General El Supremo in Chihuahua, Mexico, whose wealth of gold, pirated from the downtrodden *pueblo*, is jealously guarded in an impenetrable fortress vault.

Spanish Pressbook. **The Great Treasure Hunt**

Demanding a $1-million share, Felipé leads the motley crew across the Rio Grande, eliminating an inquisitive Federale border patrol along the way. Felipe is soon tossed in jail by Supremo, who takes a fancy to Agnes. The general keeps the only key to the gold vault on a chain around his neck, which must be acquired via seduction by Agnes, who knocks the amorous Supremo out cold with his pistol butt. Simultaneously, Dean and Sam engineer the release of Felipé, creating a diversionary explosion, only to be thwarted upon realization that the safe has, not just one lock, bu*t three*. To save time, the adept André blasts it open with TNT, thus alerting Supremo's soldiers. Holed-up in the fortress strongroom, the gringo gang bowls-over the charging general with a point-blank cannon shot, before bringing the roof down around their ears by exploding the powder magazine. Outside the fortress walls, an unforeseen doublecross awaits the four gringos, however: Felipé, revealing that he is *far* from blind (no kidding!) and representing the best interests of the Mexican people, claims the booty in their name. Thus, the opportunistic *gringos* are, ironically enough, exploited in turn, but are at least permitted to leave in peace.

Italian ad: *"FURTI... RAPINE... RICATTI... in un western che non vi dara' un attimo di tregua..."* ("THEFT... ROBBERIES... BLACKMAIL... in a western that won't give you a moment's respite...")

Giancarlo Badessi as El Supremo: *"Good pistoleros are worth their weight in gold."*

1987 Trans-World Entertainment videotape blurb: *"He Killed For a Fortune in Gold... Now He May Die For It!"*

Eccentric cartoon credits and an *awful* comedic 'hillbilly' theme tune indicate right off the bat that this is a lightweight Euro western, which tries hard to amuse but, apart from a few enjoyable action set-pieces, ultimately fails in its primary objective. Although it's listed at the IMDb only as a joint Italian/Spanish co-production, according to tradepapers of the day **The Great Treasure Hunt** was actually co-financed—presumably in a strictly minority capacity?—by an American company (namely Sidney Balkin & Associates) and, thematically speaking, the film is quite reminiscent of other, much costlier US-backed 'fortress of gold' westerns shot in Spain during the same period, including John Guillermin's **El Condor** (1970), co-starring Jim Brown and Lee Van Cleef, and Sam Wanamaker's **Catlow** (1971), co-starring Yul Brynner and Richard Crenna.Directed by Tonino Ricci, **TGTH** was intended as a loose follow-up to Mark Damon's and Rosalba Neri's vastly-superior **Johnny Yuma** (Italy, 1966. D: Romolo Guerrieri), and should have been far, far better. Damon seems most uncomfortable throughout, getting to dress in both complete white and then black wardrobes (when seen innocuously riding-in at the outset, he wears white; later changing into black for the criminal business). With his mod post-'60s bangs and sideburns here, he is simply too much of a prettyboy, it must be said. Neri, often a.k.a. "Sara Bay" at that time, is quite fetching in her butchy duds, but is far from convincing as a "Frenchwoman" (further belied by comments like "Whut're we waitin' fer!" spoken in a pseudo Southern twang). Other than this, Neri delivers her usual devious *femme fatale* schtick, and is quite fetching for sure in her flared black leather pants.

She tickles El Supremo's hot Latin loins by offering herself up as collateral on the dictator's high poker bet. As predicted, good-natured triangular rivalry blossoms between screen brothers Damon and Cooper, each vying for Neri's fickle affections, telegraphing the obligatory inter-fraternal punchup (set to boisterous ragtime trumpet). Redford, Newman and Katharine Ross' tomfoolery in **Butch Cassidy and The Sundance Kid** (USA, 1969. D: George Roy Hill) is here mimicked to lesser effect on about a thousandth of the budget.

Damon, Cooper, Neri and Mayo make for the *stupidest* bunch of outlaws, as they fail to spot Luis Marín's phony-baloney 'blindman' routine from a mile off (they are *gormless* gringos, after all!). The actor delivers one of the absolute *least*-convincing 'sightless' acting jobs ever seen (pun intended); strictly of the stare-straight-ahead-and-don't-blink variety (even Tony Anthony as **Blindman** [Italy/USA, 1971. D: Ferdinando Baldi] does a more convincing job, and that's sure saying something. The costumers might just as well have slapped a pair of opaque black glasses on him and had done with it!). Marín makes absolutely zero acting attempt to convince us he possesses anything less than crystal-clear 20/20 vision, and is constantly shown openly observing onscreen goings-on. Bringing to mind William "Banjo" Berger's musical mayhem in **Sabata** (*Ehi amico... c'è Sabata. Hai chiuso!*, Italy, 1969. D: "Frank Kramer"/Gianfranco Parolini), Marín holsters his firearm inside his guitar. Ricci's largely unimaginitive direction fails to use the blind bandit angle to its best advantage, such as, say, having Felipé pretend to *smell* the gold rather than seeing it; which might have helped add some much-needed conviction to his mindless blindness act. Yet, despite his alleged visual handicap, no one seems at all curious as to how Marín handles a gun and gets around so well. Damon & Co. never once question his blindness, even after hearing surprising confessions like "I am blind, but I shoot very well in the dark!" When the cat is finally outta the bag, a stupefied (or perhaps half-blind?) Damon none-too-swiftly realizes "You ain't never bin *blind*, have you?!" Gee, no kidding, neighbor! Open yer eyes an' smell the coffee!

Equally as unbelievable, be it by night or in broad daylight, Damon's gang goes about its moneygrubbin' machinations right under the very noses of their 'hosts', who are apparently more blind than they are, and never notice anything's amiss. Even more clued-out is Giancarlo Badessi as the horny General, who thinks way more with his little head than his big one and falls for Neri's flirty manipulation like a frustrated virgin schoolboy on his first date while the boys use this distraction to crack open the jail. Badessi shows-off his pendulous moobs during a bubblebath with Neri ("She's a woman, but she *ain't* no lady!"). At another point, even after he's revealed he can see her feminine pulchritude all-too-clearly, fake blind guy Marín's not interested in Neri's blatant attempt to desert Damon's sinking ship and join the Mexican cause (i.e., share in the money).

REPOKER DE BRIBONES
MARK DAMON·ROSALBA NERI·ALFREDO MAYO
Director: TONINO RICCI   technicolor

It is our 'heroes' who emerge as the ultimate scumbags of the piece for openly coveting wealth obtained via the suffering and subjugation of the Mexicans: thus, are just as reprehensible as Supremo himself is for trying to exploit their misery. But such is the superficial nature of the script that these peripheral ethical concerns barely seem relevant, and are ultimately justifiable simply because **The Great Treasure Hunt** is a 'comedy,' and you can get away with anything so long as you have a smile on your face (although we the viewers more often find ourselves laughing at it rather than *with* it). Finally, after Marín's band of patriots have left the picture, Damon's side rolls one of their number (i.e., Mayo) who's been holding-out, ending up with a sizeable share of the ill-gotten profits anyway.

Daft dubbed dialogue is punctuated by double negatives (="I am not to be disturbed for no reason in the world!"), and even *triple* negatives (="Ain't nobody nowhere!"). Respected Spanish Buñuelian thespian Alfredo Mayo—who quotes Alexandre Dumas, just to prove he's really "French"—fills a role tailor-made for Antonio Casas; who must've been on vacation at the time and who specialized in this type of 'cultivated, upper crust' role. Another of the few plusses to be had has background Mexicans conversing in Spanish rather than merely dubbed English or getting no dialogue at all. Composer Luis Enríquez Bacalov's annoying original theme music (no apparent soundtrack album was released contemporaneously) sees mercifully minimal usage; he slums it further by reusing key pieces from his score for Corbucci's **Django**, such as the "coffin" theme and the Federales' trumpet piece. Swooping violins and harpsichord add extra texture. It is during the action centerpiece that the score becomes least-effective: generic and melodramatic. But for the most part, Bacalov's often smooth, easy-rollin' Hispanic compositions add class to this farcical (im)perfect caper flick disguised as a western.

What is easily the most-original scene is when El Supremo gives thumbs-down on peons convicted of stealing food. Perched atop grain sacks with nooses looped about their throats, the starving men are gradually hanged when a firing squad shoots the sacks full of holes and the grain leaks out from under their feet, leaving them without a leg to stand on (so to speak). Other than his condonation of such contemptible behaviour, Badessi's little tin Caligula is way too goofball to be in the slightest bit threatening, and **TGTH** ultimately amounts to nothing more than inoffensive fluff for the easily-amused, of interest primarily because of its principal cast. [*With some input from Michael "Ferg" Ferguson.*]

Notes: As usual, the US (Trans World) video box 'plot description' gets it all wrong!

His Name was Holy Ghost: Yugoslovian Poster

His Name Was Holy Ghost (*Uomo avvisato mezzo ammazzato... parola di Spirito Santo / "Forewarned, Half-Dead... The Word of Holy Ghost"*, Italy/Spain, 1971)

Plot Synopsis: (*ATTN: THIS PARAGRAPH CONTAINS SPOILERS!*) México, 1918. General Ubarte (Poldo Bendandi)'s Federal troopers burst into a sleepy peasant border village, putting it under the heavy boot of martial law. Murdering and ransacking, the troopers interrogate peons as to the whereabouts of the town patriarch, Don Fermin Mendoza (Georges/Jorge Rigaud)—the rightful President—who is dragged before General Ubarte, the self-styled Presidential interloper. Holy Ghost (Gianni Garko), the famous gambling bounty-hunter, who has recently won a goldmine in a high-stakes poker game, visits Ubarte to stake his claim. However, the greedy General has taken possession of the mine, located in the Sierra Madre, and refuses to surrender it. Fugitive Don Fermin goes into hiding from Ubarte's patrols, but he is eventually recaptured along with his daughter, Juana (Pilar Velázquez), to be rescued by Holy Ghost, who then interrogates the lawless four-man Crowe gang regarding the whereabouts of the gold. Allied with Juana and Carezza Lee (Cris Huerta), a lunk-headed, ham-fisted prizefighter and rogue, Holy Ghost determines to overthrow Ubarte, save the townsfolk and in the process acquire the much-contested yellow stuff. Samuel Crowe ("Paul Stevens"/Paolo Gozlino), whom Don Fermin mistakenly believes to be his ally, is in actuality working on General Ubarte's side. For this, Don Fermin makes a formal declaration of war against the General. Infiltrating Ubarte's fort by hiding inside a 'complimentary' wagonload of prostitutes deployed to tempt the soldiers, Holy Ghost and Carezza cause a ruckus. During the confusion, Ubarte turns the tables on his own men, and Holy Ghost pursues the treacherous "President" through subterranean catacombs beneath the fort. Upon realizing their leader is a traitor, Ubarte's troops mutiny, joining with their rebellious countrymen against him. Holy Ghost makes the discovery that the "treasure" is actually nothing but next-to-worthless nuggets of gold-painted lead! The real gold has been snagged by Crowe, to whom Holy Ghost pays a visit. Eventually realizing that his own partner Carezza has attempted to bilk him, Holy Ghost keeps both their shares for himself and rides off, leaving Carezza trapped in a deep pit.

"Italcowtowner" (a cumbersome in-house term coined by some wag in *Variety* way back when), made by "Anthony Ascott" a.k.a. Giuliano Carnimeo following yet another "Sartana" starrer, **Gunman in Town** a.k.a. **Light the Fuse... Sartana Is Coming** *(Una nuvola di polvere... un grido di morte... arriva Sartana*, Italy/Spain, 1970). Incidentally, the film that first introduced Gianni Garko as a character called Sartana was "Albert Cardiff"/Alberto Cardone's **Blood at Sundown** a.k.a. **$1,000 on the Black** (*1000 dollari sul nero*, Italy/West Germany, 1966).

Garko here plays yet another thinly-veiled variant of his most profitable and memorable SW creation, Sartana. For one of his more spectacular entrances herein, Holy Ghost descends via bellringer's rope from the belfry of the Elios Studios western town backlot church, with his pet dove—presumably named Pax?—perched upon his left shoulder like an albino pirate's parrot (much was made of this motif in international promotional materials for the film). While long universally-recognized as a symbol of peace—as in its 'ironic' usage here as the familiar of a seasoned gunslinger—according to noted animal behaviourist Konrad Z. Lorenz in his celebrated book of zoology *King Solomon's Ring* (Berlin: Verlag Dr. G. Borotha-Schoeler, 1949 [first English translation New York: Crowell, 1952]), in its instinctual habits the dove is actually one of the most comparatively 'vicious' members of the avian family. It is perhaps fitting then that in the present context such a creature accompanies the quick-to-kill Garko; who—illustrating the old adage that birds of a feather do indeed flock together—totes this decidedly un-gunshy avian sidekick around with him in a wicker basket. Holy Ghost, who lends new meaning to the biblical term "thy Divine bounty," appears and disappears at the most opportune and/or inopportune moments (all depending on whichever end of his gun you happen to find yourself!). First appearing in a bushier drop-handlebar mustache, black ribbon tie and beige frock coat, Holy Ghost's weapon of choice is a futuristic full-auto repeating carbine (more like '*assault rifle*'!). While crossing the Rio Grande, Holy Ghost opens-up with his reapin' repeater on what are apparently Mexican peons, whereupon Pilar Velásquez as the patriotic Juana accuses him of being an "evil gringo bastard!" for committing the despicable deed. It is only upon closer inspection that we realize the supposed dead 'peons' are in actuality hated Federales hiding beneath decoy *sombreros* and ponchos. As ever, masquerades are vital to the story, with Garko dressing-up as the effeminate hippy 'mister madam' (w/ exploding tophat!) to a chicken-cart full of hookers.

The 'whore-wagon' idea is pure Ascott (albeit pinched from Sergio Corbucci's **Compañeros!** [*Vamos a matar, compañeros*, Italy/Spain/West Germany, 1970]), described as "a modern version of the Trojan Horse" in one Anglo export pressbook synopsis. The scene wherein Garko tortures a Federale captain by letting his pet dove peck birdseed from the man's bare abdomen is a kinder, gentler reminder of yet another scene in **Compañeros!** (i.e., the old starving-rodent-on-the-belly trick).

In keeping with the filmmakers' predominantly RC origins, the 'angelic' Holy Ghost at one point bribes a stingy priest. Precisely twelve of Ubarte's soldiers enjoy their "Last Supper" along one side of a long banquet table beneath a crucifix (this scene was cut from Spanish prints due to its overtly blasphemous connotations). Georges/ Jorge Rigaud gets tied to a cross, while his loyal peons are forced to file past and spit upon their beloved patriarch. A man is shot then strung-up as a warning/deterrent to other would-be "patriots". When condemned to face his own firing squad, Garko as the picky Sartana insists on rearranging the riflemen to suit himself so that the sun is not in his eyes. He then abruptly unfurls his ever-present cape, dazzling the tactically-repositioned soldiers with sunbeams glaring off its silver tinfoil lining so as to spoil their aim, then—again in classic Sartanian fashion—producing twin snubnose .38s and 'firing' the firing squad. Further demonstrating his imperturbable nature in classic SW antihero style, Garko nonchalantly lights his cigar after striking a match on the boot-sole of a hanged corpse.

'Full-figured' Spanish actor Cris Huerta disguises himself as—of *all* things!—a nursing mother who downs enemy troopers with an 'exploding infant' (i.e., dynamite swaddled-up in a baby blanket). This is followed by the spectacle of big-boned

Titanus

GIANNI GARKO in

UOMO AVVISATO MEZZO AMMAZZATO...
PAROLA DI SPIRITO SANTO

con PILAR VELASQUEZ · PAUL STEVENS · CHRIS HUERTA

rega di ANTHONY ASCOTT un produzione italo spagnola LEA FILM (Roma) - C.C. ASTRO (Madrid) realizzata da LUCIANO MARTINO

EASTMANCOLOR · sviluppo e stampa LV di LUCIANO VITTORI

Italian Fotobusta: His Name was Holy Ghost

'women'—actually male rebels in drag—wearing low-cut bodices beating-up hapless soldiers. Hiding his telltale ursine facial growth behind a dainty lady's fan, hefty he-man Huerta also appears as a portly prostitute, and would cross-dress yet again in same director "Ascott"/Carnimeo's even zanier **Once Upon a Time in the West There Was a Man Called Invincible** a.k.a. **They Called Him the Player with the Dead** (*Lo chiamavano Tresette... giocava sempre col mort*o, Italy, 1973), in that case opposite George Hilton. Next-to-plotless but fun nonetheless, **His Name Was Holy Ghost** was made with a far more generous budget than that later, spoofier effort. Comedy here is less soft-centered than that in Ascott's *Tresette* and *Hallelujah* films, though all the other slap-happy Ascottisms are here: epitomized when Holy Ghost's followers blast the Federales' garrison/guardhouse using nitro-filled hens' eggs as hand grenades! A spaghetti tradition ever since Franco Nero first wrapped his mitts 'round a Gatling as you-know-who in you-know-what, Garko uses a rather fake-looking 'water-cooled', Vickers-type prop machinegun to chop down the opposition wholesale. A boxer pitches apples with unerring accuracy like baseballs (Garko had himself lobbed a steel-cored baseball as an anti-personnel projectile in "Frank Kramer"/Gianfranco Parolini's tongue-in-cheek WW2 action romp **Five for Hell** [*Cinque per l'inferno*, Italy, 1969], whose rudimentary plotline might easily have been derived from a repurposed SW script). In **HNWHG**, troopers' guns are spiked with… pea soup! Frypans and water-dippers are used as improv blunt instruments. Playing Ubarte's colonel/attack dog in his usual bastardly manner, the great Giovanni "Nello" Pazzafini gets 'crowned' with a world globe like Atlas.

German Lobby Card: His Name Was Holy Ghost

Playing a Mormon moron, Huerta (described in the pressbook as "a real mountain of muscles") does his oft-repeated Bud Spencer strongarm routine, holding a card-cheat upside down and shaking him, then smacking a cohort in the kisser with the card table, causing him to spit teeth. Huerta takes a chair smashed over his head without blinking, clocks four men with a soup ladle and dunks another man facefirst in a scalding cauldron of baked beans (this movie was made at the height of 'Trinitymania', after all). He kisses the Book of Mormon before deploying it as a projectile to KO a gunman. When he stops a horse dead in its tracks by yanking back on its tail, the rider somersaults clear out of his saddle! Huerta goes bare-knuckles during a slapstick prizefight with another pudgy pugilist: a match he can only win when enraged to the point of losing by Garko's taunts. He indents his opponent in a wall. Keeping the pugilism flowing, Ascott then immediately segues into a barn-trashing spectator riot.

As General Ubarte, as much modelled after an 007 supervillain as Holy Ghost is after 007, brawny, pockmarked character actor Poldo Bendandi also plays at Eduardo **"Django"** Fajardo in tinted oval glasses with fat stogie and swagger-stick. Franco Pesce (the lovable "Dusty" from Garko's **Sartana** a.k.a. **If You Meet Sartana... Pray for Your Death** [*Se incontri Sartana prega per la tua morte*, Italy/West Germany, 1968]) fills a bit part as an aged town official beneath a Colonel Sanders wig and goatee. The neanderthal features of Salvatore Boccaro (the future "Sal Boris" a.k.a. "Boris Lugosi") can be glimpsed amongst background revolutionaries here and there. Gildo de Marco as a bungling, cross-eyed Mexican lugs a bellbottom-barrelled blunderbuss. Endearingly, even the most inept and comedic peon is shown to be a fierce, fearless freedom fighter, while Government troops are uniformly presented as buffoonish, butt-kicking louts, so you can't help but love that.

Bruno Nicolai's score is full and moving, with the opening jaw-harp theme paying all the inevitable tributes (i.e., whistles, echo, chanting male voices) to Morricone's **The Good, the Bad and the Ugly**. A twangy crescendo of guitars each time announces Holy Ghost's arrival.

Like I said above, while it's short on plot, **HNWHG** is far from devoid of entertainment value, and SW fans should find plenty to like about it. [*With some input from Michael "Ferg" Ferguson.*]

Notes: Assistant director was Michele Massimo Tarantini.

Three Gun Showdown: Italian Fotobusta

Three Gun Showdown a.k.a. Sartana Does Not Forgive (Sartana non perdona, Italy/ Spain, 1968)

Plot Synopsis: (*ATTN: THIS PARAGRAPH CONTAINS SPOILERS!*) Sartana (George Martin), a bountyhunter, rides into the quiet border town of Canyon City, there to confront a wanted man. The outlaw attempts to buy his freedom in exchange for payment equal to the bounty on his head, and Sartana accepts; only to change his mind, then taking on all three outlaws in the gang. The leader had been present at the Los Alamos ranch the night Sartana's wife had been raped and murdered by a despicable outlaw named "Tall" Slim Kovacs (Jack Elam), along with his accomplice, Sharkey (Óscar Pellicer). Larry Kitchener (Gilbert Roland), a rival bountyhunter, is also in town to apprehend Slim for a $5000 reward.

184

When a sheriff's posse catches up with Slim, he is assisted in escaping by a bandit. In league with Slim, Mexican bandit chief José (Tomás Torres)—likewise worth five-grand in bounty—hijacks a stagecoach carrying gold, making prisoners of its passengers, then occupying the town with his gang. Sam, a poor Mexican peon ("Tony Norton"/Antonio Monselesan), has been forced to cooperate in a local bank robbery in order to earn money to return to Mexico. The sheriff is killed in an unfair duel with Slim after his gun has been secretly loaded with harmless blanks. Kitchener and Slim form an unsteady alliance, the former stringing the latter along with the intent of cashing him in for the bounty.

Upon his arrival, Kitchener to no avail warns Sartana not to interfere with his plans. When one of José's men attempts to rape one of the women from the stage, Sartana remembers the atrocity committed on his late wife, and intervenes. When Sartana is hung by his wrists in a barn with a crate of TNT for company, he is cut free by Sam, his ally. Sartana then takes care of José and Slim with some 'neutral' assistance from Kitchener. Paying Sam for his invaluable help, Sartana and Kitchener ride out of town side-by-side.

A quick-on-the-draw if unrelated *Sartana* ripoff (cashing-in on "Albert Cardiff"/Alberto Cardone's **Blood at Sundown** a.k.a. **$1,000 on the Black** [*1000 dollari sul nero,* Italy/West Germany, 1966]), this is a serviceable enough—and often damn

Upper picture: Mexican Poster
Lower picture: Spanish Pressbook.

185

good—programmer with plenty going for it, lensed at the Balcázars' studios in Barcelona. As was often the case with lower echelon spaghettis, the theme song is sung in English, but the singer's pronunciation is so off you can barely understand a word! That minor quibble aside, it's quite a memorable ditty. (Speaking of iffy English, a later glimpse at a wanted poster reveals that the lanky Elam character's professional nickname of "Tall" has been conspicuously misspelled "Call").

As **Three Gun Showdown** (a title I much prefer to the film's alternate **Sartana Does Not Forgive** one) opens, George Martin, looking suitably gristled and bristled, gazes into a chuckling mountain brook. Flowing water symbolically represents the passage of time as Martin's thoughts drift on back to the good ol' days when he was clean-shaven and wore an unbuttoned pastel pink shirt to show off his hairy chest while chucking brawlers through saloon windows. Martin's forced movements and broad grins during this flashback scene virtually reduce the action to parody, but this is as bad as the film ever gets, so stick with it. Prefiguring Leone's similar technique involving actor David Warbeck in **Duck, You Sucker** a.k.a. **A Fistful of Dynamite** (*Giù la testa*, Italy/Spain, 1971), Martin reminisces about romantic interludes with the love of his life, played by Donatella Turri in slow-motion (thematically analogous wistfully romantic flashback scenes had also been seen in "Sidney Lean"/Giovanni Fago's fabulous **Vengeance Is Mine** a.k.a. **$100,000 for a Killing** [*Per 100.000 dollari t'ammazzo*, Italy, 1967], co-starring Gianni Garko, Claudio Camaso and Fernando Sancho). When villainous Jack Elam's ugly puss infringes on his nostalgic reverie, Martin promptly snaps back to reality and the matter at hand once more. These initial eight minutes of **TGS** are all presented completely devoid of dialogue (a real cinch for the post-synchers!).

Three Gun Showdown; Filipino Newspaper ad

Once again, the value of money pales in comparison to the cathartic thrill of the kill. So strong is his hatred of the criminal element that Martin prefers to let a thousand bucks in paper cash flutter away on the breeze rather than permit his prey to escape. Although he's a bounty-hunter, remuneration comes second to Martin's personal quest for vengeance (a.k.a. justice); every bad guy he meets is emblematic of the killers of his woman. Most spaghetti antiheroes constantly played Russian Roulette with life, as if they ultimately valued their own even less than those of their enemies. Martin's character here is no exception, actually handing an outlaw a pistol before a duel to give him a fair fighting chance (dime-store psychologists might argue he does so in hopes of possibly expediting his own death, thus putting an end to his ongoing anguish). Contrary to his self-conscious presence in clunkers like Alfonso Balcázar's **Clint the Stranger** a.k.a. **Clint, The Nevadas' Loner** (*Clint el solitario*, Spain/Italy/West Germany, 1967), this time out Martin appears a lot more at ease, possibly due to his comfortably 'lived-in' appearance and the ego-boost potentially provided by the mere presence of his more prestigious supporting cast. The great Gilbert Roland could always be depended on to add some class to even a lowercase spaghetti western like **Three Gun Showdown** (it has the lowest profile of all his five genre outings, receiving no known theatrical / TV / videotape release in an English version [that we know of]). Billed no less than fourth under the three headliners hereon, "Tony Norton"/Antonio Monselesan plays peon under a *floppy* sombrero and profuse facial hair, and is almost unrecognizable. Looking diametrically different than he does here, the actor later put in memorably amusing cameos as sharp-dressed "Black Bart" types in such SW's as "E.B. Clucher"/Enzo Barboni's **Trinity Is Still My Name** (*Continuavano a chiamarlo Trinità*, Italy, 1971). Elsewhere in the cast, the ever-sultry Rosalba Neri, future leading lady of **The Great Treasure Hunt** (*Monta in sella!! Figlio di...*, Italy/Spain, 1972 [reviewed in this very ish]), bit-parts in the present film as a spirited captive stagecoach passenger in a halo-like white bonnet ("I don't need anyone to protect me!") who gets, uh, 'sexually objectified' by one of Slim/Elam's goons.

Name-brand American co-star Jack Elam was no stranger to cinematically-staged gun duels, having already been beaten to the draw in such classic westerns as John Sturges' shot-in-Hollywood classic **Gunfight at the O.K. Corral** (USA, 1957) and Sergio Leone's sprawling transatlantic SW epic **Once Upon a Time in the West** (*C'era una volta il* West, Italy/USA, 1968). With his all-black baddie duds, chameleon swivel-eyes, prickly pear mug and generally unhygienic appearance here, Elam is well-cast as Slim the degenerate. Employing cacophanous orchestration and crash-zooms of Elam's oblique-eyed pervert stare, Ms. Turri's violation—the primary catalyst of Martin her onscreen widower's rage for retribution—is not unnecessarily dwelled upon. In keeping with its revenge-seeded roots, inserts of her screaming face constantly remind Martin of his sole remaining objective in life. Plotwise (natch'), Three Gun Showdown owes all the usual debts to Corbucci's **Django** (Italy/Spain, 1966) and Leone's "Dollars" trilogy (especially **For a Few Dollars More** [*Per qualche dollaro in più*, Italy/Spain/West Germany, 1965]), and Martin—although not overly physically similar by any means—oddly somehow evokes Franco Nero in some shots (at least on the fuzzy old Spanish-dubbed US VHS tape of **TGS** [c/o

Videoways] I watched, anyway).

Elsewhere are the expected heavily-ritualized 'macho' western tableaux, as when
Slim and the sheriff face off, given one bullet each by Tomás Torres for the occasion. The click-click of empty chambers reverberates along the hushed street until
the sheriff shoots and misses. Slim's weapon then discharges and his opponent goes
down with a bullet-hole clean through the temples. When the preliminary showdown
between Martin and Roland happens, the former butts-out the latter's cigar in a glass
of whiskey, uses the soggy stub to draw a tiny tobacco-ash target on Roland's chest
right over his heart, then places the ruined remains of the cigar back into his rival's
mouth. In response, Roland pours his tainted drink into Martin's dinner plate, dips
the cigar in the food and uses it to paint mashed potato crosshairs between Martín's
eyes. Following this stoically-endured indignity, Martin dumps his spoiled grub onto
Roland's boots, then—in mid-spin—shoots Roland's pistol from its holster while
twirling his own gun with his forefinger! This whole scene is priceless, but without
the droll Roland's relaxed, unperplexed screen presence it might not have worked
half as well.

(*ATTN: SPOILER ALERT!*) The movie's title is at least two-thirds justified for
the finale, as Roland allots Martin and Elam one slug each. These latter then go to
it, clicking away until Elam's bullet hits Martin with no effect and he in turn fatally
plugs Elam.

While mopping-up the town with Torres' lawless horde, Martin shoots sticks of
powder alight and chucks 'em around like penny firecrackers on the Fourth of July.
A sequence with equestrian bandits being unhorsed via explosion is extremely
well-done; recalling a less-grisly retake of the doomed cavalry charge in Giulio
Questi's one-of-a-kind **Django Kill!** a.k.a. **If You Live, Shoot!** (*Se sei vivo spara,*
Italy/Spain, 1967). Clerical commentary is injected care of a bandit hanged from a
bellringer's rope in the church (see also "Anthony M. Dawson"/Antonio Margheriti's grim Gothic revenger **And God Said to Cain** [*E Dio disse a Caino...,* Italy/
West Germany, 1970], starring Klaus Kinski). But I've been intentionally saving the
best for last. Undoubtedly **Three Gun Showdown**'s greatest moment is an absolutely *incredible* shot when Martin picks-off a wounded assailant from an overhead
balcony after first being alerted to the man's presence by falling drops of his blood.
Then, in a single uninterrupted shot, the man's body flips over the hand-rail, performs a full lengthwise somersault and falls directly onto the camera, which peers
up from ground level below Martin's waist. Martin—one presumes, him being a
trained stuntman, that he refrained from resorting to a stand-in here—doesn't flinch
from his position more than an inch; even though the stuntman comes close enough
to actually brush past his hat-brim and jolt his pistol in passing! One ponders how
many takes this brief shot might have required: If they did it in one take (or even
more), both Martin and the stuntman who took the fall should be loudly applauded,
as potentials for mutual injury must have been high indeed. This remains one of our
all-time favorite Spaghetti Western stunts, ever... ¡*Muy increíble!*

188

While the film is elsewhere for the most part pretty standard (if definitely very solid indeed), this amazing shot plus Roland and Martin's volatile chemical interaction—as well as Elam's presence, of course—makes **Three Gun Showdown**, a sufficiently tough and uncompromising programmer, absolute essential viewing for diehard spaghetti fans. (Maybe if we're lucky an English-dubbed copy might surface some-day... especially in this new age of deluxe BD/DVD special editions. [Hint-hint...] Although there is a fullscreen Italian-language video rip of the film on YouTube [@ the URL *youtube.com/watch?v=XlN9UDqHBz0*] I downloaded and managed to find in-synch subtitles for, so it'll do me just fine till then!) [*With some input from Michael "Ferg" Ferguson.*]

Italian Poster: **Fasthand is Still My Name**

189

Fast-Hand Is Still My Name a.k.a. Fasthand (*Mi chiamavano Requiescat... ma avevano sbagliato / "My Name is Requiescat... But I Have Made a Mistake"*, Italy/Spain, 1973)

Plot Synopsis: (*ATTN: THIS PARAGRAPH AND THE NEXT CONTAIN SPOILERS!*) 1865. Even though the Civil War has recently ended, Union soldiers are forced to scour the countryside to mop-up stubborn pockets of resistance by Confederate renegades. One such band of looting raiders is led by Macedo (William Berger), who is pursued relentlessly by Captain Jeff Madison ("Alan Steel"/Sergio Ciani)'s four-man troop. While on patrol, Madison's men are ambushed by Macedo's greycoats and pinned-down, losing two of their number in the skirmish. In the meantime, Fort Mason has been overrun and occupied by the Rebels of Macedo, who blames Madison for the death of his brother, and murders the fort's commanding officer in cold blood. Arriving back at the stockade, Captain Madison suspects a trap, and the last remaining member of his command is killed. Chased on horseback by Macedo's men led by Sergeant Quincey (Francisco "Frank" Braña), Madison is overpowered. As payback for all of their men he has killed, the renegades murder every last one of Madison's captured Cavalry comrades. Madison is methodically humiliated, blindfolded, then Macedo shoots him in the gunhand before the gang abandons him—half-dead—and gallops off to rob a stagecoach, massacre some Northern settlers and burn down their home.

For over two years, Macedo's raiders terrorize the countryside uncontested, the reward offered for their capture gradually growing to $10,000. Pretending to deposit the payroll for the Union Pacific Railroad, Macedo and his thugs rob a bank, making off with the gold inside a hearse coach. Unexpectedly, Captain Madison—who had been rescued from the brink of death by kindly passing Indians—now a plain-clothes civilian, materializes like a ghost from the past to seek poetic justice for Macedo's wrongs. He intercepts the hearse and makes off with the loot, which is hidden inside a casket. Locked-up by a suspicious sheriff who catches him red-handed with the gold, Madison is sprung by Macedo's men, who are surprised to find him alive after their 'fond farewell' back at Fort Mason. The gang tortures him to reveal the location of the gold —now buried in a cemetery. Mary-Anne ("Karin Well"/Welma Truccolo), Macedo's lover, tricks Madison into escaping so that the gang can tail him to where the gold is hidden. Not fooled for a moment, Madison leads them on a runaround... right into his pre-set snare. In the deserted town of Blackstone Hill, Madison joins Swannah (Celine Bessy), the Indian girl responsible for nursing him back to life two years before, and whose family had been murdered by Macedo's band. When the renegades show up in search of his coffinful of gold sacks, Madison bumps them off with finely-orchestrated precision; until he and Macedo stand alone in the muddy high street of the ghost town, which is soon to have one more permanent inhabitant...

"Alan Steel"/Sergio Ciani as Capt. Jeff Madison says it all: "It's *REVENGE* I want!"

Made simultaneously by same director "Frank Bronston"/Mario Bianchi with **In the Name of the Father, of the Son and of the Colt** a.k.a. **The Masked Thief** (*In nome del Padre, del Figlio e della Colt*, Italy/Spain, 1971), if released the better part of two years later, here we have an economical but laudably serious oater that thankfully steers well clear of screwball post-*Trinity* shenanigans and maintains an unflinching pokerface throughout. Right down to its Motown-inspired theme song, Gianni Ferrio's piano jazz/blues and soul-sprinkled score often seems better suited to a Blaxploitation film of the same era, but somehow this cross-cultural juxtaposition works, adding an atypical mood to standard scenes like the nocturnal robbery of the bank.

Steely-thewed he-man Sergio Ciani, better known to sword-and-sandal fans as "Alan Steel", is well-cast as the rugged Cavalry captain, handling himself admirably during physically demanding sequences (a cinch considering he was a seasoned stuntman). When caught-up with by William Berger's revengeful Rebs, Steel must endure being tied between two stakes on his knees and forcefed a mouthful of live bullets; then, a circle of expectorating equestrian renegades make their displeasure clearer still by using him as a human cuspidor. This scene, with Steel inundated by gobbets of saliva from all sides, is almost as difficult to stomach as Franco Nero's systematic degradation and disfigurement in Corbucci's **Django** (Italy/Spain, 1966). In wavering, blood-red-saturated flashback, Steel is subsequently plagued by nightmares of personal indignities suffered at the gang's hands. Because Steel also lugs a coffin around with him and mumbles about being—for the time being only *figuratively*—dead, further Django comparisons are inevitable (although surprisingly enough Fast-Hand was apparently never released anywhere as a Django cash-in; not even in Germany, where more bogus "Django" titles were slapped on imported westerns—even many Hollywood ones—than anywhere else).

Playing the merciless Reb renegade gangleader Macedo, William Berger is more animated and gregarious than his usual taciturn loner characters, speaking with a Southern accent and forcing the Union garrison commander to chug-a-lug the entire contents of an inkwell before emptying his whole sixgun into him (the deep Union blue of the ink contrasts sharply with the vivid redness of the luckless Yankee major's blood). For another torture sequence, frequent genre heavy Frank Braña squeezes a gangmember's clothed scrotum and brands his unclothed abdomen with a red-hot iron bar for his botching of the gold delivery. Afterwards, Berger repeats his pet trick of unloading his .45 into this unfortunate underling. Braña repeats the 'hot rod' routine on Steel later, and in an amusing sight gag gets his omnipresent cigar punched flat right in his chops by the enraged Berger (it's such a funny moment, you won't be able to resist replaying it, possibly more than once!). Unruffled, Braña spits out the flattened stump of tobacco and glares back defiantly at him responsible for the affront. In an otherwise humourless film, this is as comedic as it ever gets. *FHISMN* relishes its sadism almost as much as Berger does. Extra subliminal kink is added in that actor's topless bed scene with his moll Welma Truccolo (alias "Karin Well"), who bears/bares a large burn scar—apparently the result of some earlier 'rough sex', possibly with Braña—between her breasts (a dubious detail also found in the incredible

Mexploitation 'pseudo-spaghetti' **Diabolical** [*El diabólico*, 1977, D: Giovanni Korporaal]). On the other hand, well aware that the muscleman cycle had long since worn its chariot wheels right down to the rims, Steel never once removes his own shirt, albeit occasionally leaving it unbuttoned to the navel (old habits are hard to shake). Because his gunhand had been crippled, Steel covers it with a black leather glove and uses his left hand to shoot a Winchester. At the conclusion, his quick appearances / disappearances and swooshing Zorro cloak endow Steel with an almost supernatural tint akin to Anthony Steffen's grim reaper gunman in Sergio Garrone's **The Stranger's Gundown** a.k.a. **Django the Bastard** (*Django il bastardo*, Italy, 1969). Shooting wildly at Steel—an hallucinatory apparition who at one point appears in the driver's seat of a hearse—Berger's mounting madness (sprung from greed and guilt) reaches its crescendo point.

Fast-Hand is overall much more presentable than the westerns made in this period by other ex-peplum strongmen, among them Brad Harris (e.g., "Robert Johnson"/ Roberto Mauri's sub-par if admittedly entertaining **Django... Adios** a.k.a. **Death Is Sweet from the Soldier of God** [*Seminò morte... lo chiamavano il castigo di Dio!*, Italy, 1972] and its two 'spinoff'—ehhh —'companion pieces', "Robert Morris"/ Roberto Mauri's **Wanted: Sabata** [Italy, 1970] and Roberto Bianchi Montero's **Durango Is Coming, Pay or Die** [*Arriva Durango... paga o muori*, Italy, 1971). As for *FHISMN*, violence is plentiful and sanguinary: Fernando Bilbao lets out an extended (*nine*-second!) scream of agony when pinioned by a falling beam in a barn. Another bandit bites the proverbial Big One when his midriff gets run-over by the horsedrawn hearse in a muddy high street. Braña is given a cold taste of Steel's namesake during a duel with farming implements, in which our hero pins the burly axe-wielding stuntman's throat to a post by pitchfork (hand-to-hand combat using specialized props was a Braña forte, and he repeated similar moves in who-knows-how-many other movies, not all of them westerns). Recognizing the telltale jingle-jangle of Berger's approaching boot spurs—hmmm, where have we seen that one before?!—Steel faces his nemesis uomo a *uomo, faccia a faccia*, if not necessarily *mano a mano*. The closing sequence set in the uninhabited town must have seemed like major déja vu to Berger; who had already played virtually identical sequences in both Mario Caiano's **The Man Who Cried for Revenge** a.k.a. **His Name Spells "Vendetta"** (*Il suo nome gridava vendetta*, Italy, 1968) and Sergio Garrone's **No Room To Die** a.k.a. **Hanging for Django** (*Una lunga fila di croci*, 1969). Berger's character here croaks with a degrading face-flop into a mud puddle.

Steel's latent Sartana-like properties (first hinted at by his squared-off drop-handlebar 'stache) rise to the fore when he reveals the ace in his hand, or rather up his sleeve: dropping Berger using a custom-rigged pistol attached to the wrist of his paralyzed right hand. . His ammunition is none other than the same two slugs which Macedo's men had forced him to swallow years earlier, evidently intent on killing via lead poisoning the slow way rather than via the usual high-speed injection method. Exactly *how* he went about salvaging these undigested bullets is mercifully not explained (One would imagine that a scene showing our hero rooting through his own excrement to 'recycle' these projectiles might well detract from his mystique somewhat!). When Celina Bessy as the doting Indian woman runs out and grasps his impotent gunhand, Steel pulls away from her and rides out of town, inferring that his manhood had been lost along with half his manual capacity. Whereas in American westerns the hero typically got the girl at the end, this alienated, melancholy (clinically depressive?) Italian antihero remains both antisocial and antisexual: the unavoidable by-products of a life devoted to murderous revenge. [*With some input from Michael "Ferg" Ferguson.*]

Notes: Credits for Spanish prints mistakenly deleted lead "Alan Steel", replacing the star's name with that of producer/assistant director "John Wyler"/Gianfranco Battistini! Master-at-arms was prolific SW stunt-grunt Gilberto Galimberti (alias "Gil Roland"). Certain French sources along the way have incorrectly listed "Frank Bronston" (a.k.a. Mario Bianchi) as a pseudonym for Frank Braña (which it usually wasn't, but… *¿Quien sabe?* ["Who knows?"]). Some shooting titles for **FHISMN**— namely "**They Call Me Requiescat**" and "**Kill and Play**"—blatantly (and belatedly) cashed-in on Carlo Lizzani's **Requiescant** a.k.a. **Kill and Pray** (Italy/Monaco/West Germany, 1967). In Québec, French Canada (August 1977), entitled *Requiem pour un tueur* / "*Requiem for a Killer*," Fast-Hand filled the bottom half of a double-bill with "George McRoots"/Giorgio Mariuzzo's **Apache Woman** (Italy, 1976). A rare trailer for the present film is included on Wild East Productions' old SW preview compilation DVD For a Few Previews More (USA, 2003).

"FAST HAND IS STILL MY NAME"

*All photos used in For A Few Reviews More! courtesy of Steve Fenton.. Except where noted.

Rare Greek VHS of **Fasthand is Still My Name**. MH collection.

Autographed photo of Robert Woods as Pecos Martinez in **My Name is Pecos.**
Photo courtesy of Michael Ferguson.

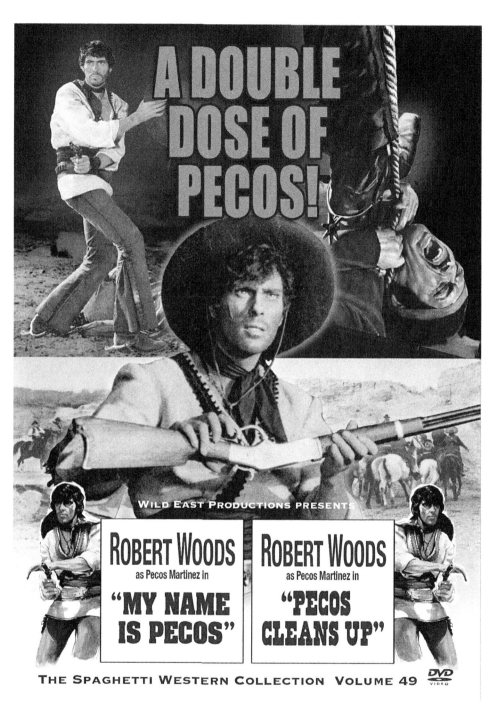

Wild East Productions release of a twofer of **My Name is Pecos** and **Pecos Cleans Up** on Blu-Ray.

Japanese Poster, **My Name is Pecos**

The Great Treasure Hunt: Serbian- Yugoslavian Poster

Upper: South Korean VHS Jacket for **The Great Treasure Hunt**
Bottom: Front and back Trans World Entertainment Vhs cover.

198

Friday, March 27, 2020: As I write this afterward, the world is being ravaged by the coronavirus. While myself and my family have yet to feel its wrath, it may only be a matter of time. My close friends I keep contact with... they also remain safe, but again... As I worked towards conclusion of this first volume of *The Spaghetti Western Digest,* I was not sure if in this current gloomy atmosphere if releasing the book would even be appropriate. I mean does a non-essential item such as a digest on Spaghetti Westerns even matter. And what about all the cash strapped folks out there not even able to purchase necessities. But a friend messaged me after I shared my apprehensions about releasing the book on social media and explained to me how the fans of the genre need something, anything to get their minds off the gloom and doom shroud covering all of us, the world over. I know speaking for myself, I have purchased very little non-essential items the last few weeks but the two non-essential items I did buy, were Spaghetti western related items. I have no clue what this virus has in store for me or my family and my friends, but I know one thing I am looking for things to get my mind off this current catastrophe and I am sure countless other are also. As you flip to this last page, I am hoping that for the time it took you to read this book, your mind was taken off the world's dire situation. All of us as a world have never been closer and we must all unite to defeat this virus and learn to slow down and value the moment and life in general.

After I had finished my second volume of *Spaghetti Westerns!* back in December of 2019, I was mulling over what my next move would be and after talking to a few of my friends I decided that a new publication was in order and so The Spaghetti Western Digest was born. And the people who agreed to help me fill this first volume were an A-Team of writers: Professor Van Roberts; the highly respected Dennis Capicik; Steve Fenton, the co-editor of the legendary *Monster Digest!* and Eugenio Ercolani, author of one of the greatest books ever on Italian popular cinema, *Darkening the Italian Screen.* The design wiz Tim Paxton designed the amazing cover, as he did for my two volumes of *Spaghetti Westerns!* Tom Betts as always was at the ready to help and agreed to open the book with a piece on his legendary zine *WAI.*

I have lots of people to thank for providing help and encouragement. First off, I must give special thanks to Tom Betts, Tim Paxton and Robert Woods, three amigos who are always willing to help a friend out. Thanks to Eric Mache for allowing me to use some of his vast Spaghetti western images in this digest and Ally Lamaj for sharing his spaghetti knowledge. Thanks to Phil Hardcastle as always, Rene Hogguer for helping to spread the word of my publications and John Crummett for always having a positive spin on things. Thanks to my brilliant amigos Javier Ramos and Eugenio Ercolani for the great interviews they provided and i am hoping to work with both in the future. Thanks to the great Chuck Cirino for answering my questions. As always thanks to Seb Haselbeck and Carl Black

Hopefully when issue two of *The Spaghetti Western Digest* arrives this summer-fall the virus will have died out and we can resume our normal lives. But regardless, don't give up Hope and... Safe and Happy Trails to You!

-Micheal Hauss

Printed in Great Britain
by Amazon